Carter County Tennessee

SINKING CREEK BAPTIST CHURCH RECORDS

1783–1905

WPA RECORDS

Heritage Books
2025

HERITAGE BOOKS
AN IMPRINT OF HERITAGE BOOKS, INC.

Books, CDs, and more—Worldwide

For our listing of thousands of titles see our website
at
www.HeritageBooks.com

A Facsimile Reprint
Published 2025 by
HERITAGE BOOKS, INC.
Publishing Division
5810 Ruatan Street
Berwyn Heights, MD 20740

1938

— Publisher's Notice —

In reprints such as this, it is often not possible to remove blemishes from the original. We feel the contents of this book warrant its reissue despite these blemishes and hope you will agree and read it with pleasure.

International Standard Book Number
Paperbound: 978-0-7884-8991-4

WPA RECORDS

The WPA Records are, for the most part, carbon copies of the original that was typed on onion skin paper during the Depression. Since these records were typed on poor machines by people who did not type well either and read by persons not always sure of the older handwritten material, the results are often less that perfect.

We have made every attempt to make as good a copy as can be made from these older papers. Sometimes there are water stains and burned edges around the paper.. This is the results of a fire at the home of one of the workers, Mrs. Penelope Allen, who was over most of the project.

The WPA Records are now very scattered between the State Archives, various Public and Private Libraries and other collections. Some day, there is a hope that all of these can be collected and stored in one place. In spite of their many mistakes and problems, these are still the most complete collection of Tennessee records found anywhere.

TENNESSEE

RECORDS OF CARTER COUNTY

MINUTES OF SINKING CREEK BAPTIST CHURCH VOL. I
1787 - 1791

COPYING HISTORICAL RECORDS PROJECT
Official Project No. 465-44-3-115

COPIED UNDER WORK'S PROGRESS ADMINISTRATION

MRS. JOHN TROTWOOD MOORE
STATE LIBRARIAN & ARCHIVIST, SPONSOR

MRS. ELIZABETH D. COPPEDGE
DIRECTOR OF WOMEN'S & PROFESSIONAL PROJECTS

MRS. PENELOPE JOHNSON ALLEN
STATE SUPERVISOR

MRS. MARGARET HELMS RICHARDSON
PROJECT SUPERVISOR

COPIED BY
MRS. VERA E. SHELL

TYPED BY
MISS EMMA M. BROYLES

NOVEMBER 1938

CARTER COUNTY

SINKING CREEK BAPTIST

CHURCH RECORD BOOK I
Jan. 13, 1787 thru August 13, 1791

INDEX

Note: Page numbers in this index refer to those of the original volume from which this copy was made. These numbers are carried in the body of the manuscript within parentheses, as (p 124).

SINKING CREEK BAPTIST CHURCH

RECORD BOOK I
Jan. 13, 1787 thru August 13, 1791

(p-1) A Register of the members with there n and Numbers as followeth--

	~~Wm Daniel and his wife Anne Daniel~~	-------------------------------	2
	Constituted upon the No of twelve	-------------------------------	
	Timothy Tracey and his wife Elender	-------------------------------	2
	Garet Reasoner and his wife Keziah R	-------------------------------	2
	~~Charles Reno~~ - David Jobe	-------------------------------	
	Meshek hail and his wife Catherene	-------------------------------	2
	~~Agnees Talbot~~ Elizabeth Tipton	-------------------------------	1
X	Saml Tipton John Reno	-------------------------------	2
X	Catharene Reno	-------------------------------	1
	Recd Joshua Kelley Wm Reno	-------------------------------	2
	Wm Daniel and his wife Anne	-------------------------------	2
	Patrick Cragin	-------------------------------	1
	ABegil Jobe	-------------------------------	1
			19
	James Chambers Recevd by Letter	-------------------------------	1
	Frances Tipton Receivd, by Letter	-------------------------------	1
	Elander Kite	-------------------------------	1
	Patty Winser	-------------------------------	1
	Nancey Chambers	-------------------------------	1
	Dorothy Hugdeburg	-------------------------------	1
	John Brown	-------------------------------	1
	Else Brown	-------------------------------	1
	~~Samal Praly~~ (Baly)	-------------------------------	~~1~~
	~~Mary Praly~~ (Baly)	-------------------------------	~~1~~
	Elenor Cooper - February 10th	-------------------------------	1
	Martho Vance	-------------------------------	1

(The original letter of Elenor Cooper, dated Oct 21, 1786; Found with)
(N. C. records. The entry on the Minutes must have been made February)
(10, 1787. (This note is by Mrs. Mary Hardin McCown))

(p-2) Wheare as a Church is Constituted externally Parties Entring into mutual a Grement in w maintain the Worship of God according to Gospel or and Refareing to the articals of their faith To Chu by their Delegates Constitutes them selves an association the Confession of their faith menifested to Each other

5 the Present Baptis Confescion of faith we a Dop as our Confession the Same which was a dopted a Philladelpha in the year 1742.

Dear Brethern we have had the Prevelege Seeing the association Plan and as Such wee have noth a Gainst the Plan but wee Conclude it is as hily necessary for to maintain and ceep up a Christian Corrispondance for Each Curch that Compoes an ass---- to a Dapt the Same measurs or Sistoms of Princ--- in Each Curch before they Can be Constituted in a R----------

association which eare a written Covenant and the Philladelpha Confescion of faith__________

Dear Brethern unless we find Such a People We Cannot Joine in Ascosiation with out Departing from the Rules that we have been Constituted upon and Rong our one Co-------nd Doct--- felliship where their is a ------- that ------- is a associa------

(p-3) onthly Meeting January the 13, 1787
------rding to Appointment Proseeds to Busness Unanimously a Grees to Send a Letter Bent Creek to the Sosiation their to Let them know -hat we will Sociate upon and what we will not

---

February the 10th 1787
At a Monthly meeting met to Gather according Apointment Proseeds to bisness---
March the 10th 1787 At a Monthly Meeting met to ---ther Acording to Appointment Proseeds to bisness----

-----ther Joshua Kelley and James Chambers Chosen by the Church Deligates to attend the Church at Chery Che in order to Remove the Bar that Seams to Bee betwen us

October 30th Day 1786 the Plan Plan of an association Holston River etc. etc. Wee Hold it nessaary to associate to Gather in Com------- in order to Give Council to the Respective Church Compoeses this association in order to Maintain our Christian felleship.

not as a Legishlative Body to impose Laws or Exercise any Superemacy Each Curch being an independent Body.

We eare -------------- hat of Churches --------------------------------

(p-4) nore Dear Brethern we would ferther Let -----ow that we would as Soon open our doors and take -n that deny our Princilles as to Joine association that Some of ~~them~~ the Churches has Received the Same Princibels and Some deny Receiving of them for we under Stand the association Last otober by ou r Delegates that their was Sum of the Churches had not came to the Rules that Sum among you Desire they Should Come to all tho their Deligates did not openly deny them measures that we belive ought to be Received in -rder that we Should waulk together as one People but t they Seed no need of Receiveing of them and ---at they Could Live as well with out them as they Cold with them-----

May the 12th 1787 At a Monthly meatin
Met together acordin to apintment proseads to bisnes.

quary. had John the Baptist the holy gost before he was born Anserd in the posidif he had

June the 9 1787
Met to gether acording to apintment proseads to bisness.

(p-5) At a Monthly meeting met to Gether to Appointment on the 11th of August 178-

Proseeds to Bisness as follows --------
acording to the Request of the ascotiaon we Desire to Answer their Request in Sending Delicates wich is ~~Josua~~ Joshua Kelley and James Chambers fo- attend the next assotiation in or to Remove those Deficulties.

At a ~~Church~~ Monthly Meeting September 8 1787 Met together according to apointment
Proseeds to Bissenness________

At a Monthly meeting met to Gether according to Apoint on the 13th of October 1787
Proseeds to Bisess as follows; _______

At a Monthly meeting met to Gether according to appointment on the 8th of December; 1787
Proseeds to Bisness as followeth_____
We the Church of Jesus Christ has heard the Cirkeller Letter from the association at Kindreks Creeks; being held 27, 28, 29 of Oct and Such we do Receive it as good.

(p-6) A Monthly Meeting met to gether according to apintment proseeds to bisness on the 13 of September 1788
the Church Chose Brother Tracy brother Job and Brother Brown to atend the association at the Northfork Brother Job to Rite the Church Letter
~~October~~
At a Monthly Meeting met to gether acording to apintment proseeds to bisness on the 11 of oCtober 1788
the Church Conclued the next monthly meeting in Corse to be a Common Meeting.

At a Monthly Meeting met to gether acoding to apintment prseeds to bisness on the 8 of November 1788 .

At a Monthly meeting met together acording to apointment Decmber the 13 1788: Proceeds to Bisness

At a Monthly Meeting met together according to appointment January the; 10th 1789 Proseeds to Bisness as foloeth Chosen by the Church Joshua Kelley James Chambers John Broon for to meet at Kindreck Meeting hous on the first Saturday in february for to meet the Dillicates of the other Churches for to hold Conferance according to the Confession of faith giving ---of artical

(p-7) At a Monthly Meeting met together Accor----- to appointment on the 7 Day of March 1789 Proseed to Bissness as foloweth______ Our Delicates Returned and hath made there Report to this Church in Regard of theBisness that they went to the Conference at Kindrick Creek and we all Unanimus a Gree with their Proseedance.

At a Monthly Meeting met together according to appointment on thd 11 of April 1789 Proseeds to Bisness as fowlows one member Received,_______

At a Monthly Meeting met together according to apointment on the 9 day of May 1789 - Proseeds to Bisness as foloweth - The Church looks upon Timothy Tracy and Kiziah Reasoner to be worthy of Excommunication for the Crime laid to their Charge viz for the sin of adultery.

3 At a Monthly Meeting met according to appointment Proseed to Bisness as

followeth June the 13: 1789 Brother John Brown and Samule Tipton Chosen by the Curch to Site Brother Reasoner to come to the the Church for to Remove their Greaveance Being under our Suspence.

(p-8) Monthly Meeting met together according apointment on the 11th of July 1789 Proseeds to Bisness as follows ______
The Church belives it to be right to Call a Church meeting upon any Just Caus

the delicate wich was sent ~~reports~~ was Brother John Brown and Samuel Tipton and reports that x Garet Reasonner Dus not in tend ~~+~~ to come

the Church Belives Garret Reasonner to have walked disorderly and doth Refuse to hear the Church we there fore doth Declare a Disfellow Ship with him

At a Monthly Meeting met together according to appointment on the 8th day of August, 1789
Proseeds to Bisness as follows it is the mind of this Church that any ~~man~~ man coming in the name of a Baptis and not Bringing ~~his~~ a Good a Thorrity from ~~from~~ his Church is not Purmitted to Preach in this Church

At a Monthly Meeting met together according to appointment on the 12 of September 1789 ____
Proseeds to Bisness as follows Brother James Chambers Request of this Church a Letter of Recommendation for to Travil with and it is granted
We have Chosen Brother Joshua P. Kelley and Mashek Hail and John Brown to attend the ascoation at the Buffwllow Ridg meeting hous

(p-9) At a Monthly Meeting met according to app------Proseeds to Bisness as follows October the 10th 178-

At a Monthly meeting met according to apoi------
Proseeds to bisness as follows November the 7 178-
Samuel Garland Censerd by the Church for giting Drunk and Swaring and geting angry ----
this Church declares that James Chambers never told the Church that he Sited Cisiah Resiner to meeting.

At a Monthly meeting met to Gether according to appointment proseeds to Bisness as follows December 10th 1789
This Church Prosseds to Samuel Garland Excommunication wich is for giting Grunk and Profain Swaring and wanting to fight.

At a Monthly meeting met to gether acording to apointment proseeds to bisness as follows Jeneary the: 9: 1790

At a monthly meeting met to Gether According to Appointment february the 13: 1790 Proseeds to Busness as follows

At a Monthly Meating met together Acording to apintment April: 10: 1790 proseeds to bisness as follows

---

May 8 1790 met together and prosceds to business This Church agrees not to send no delegate to that sociation over the mountain yet tel they know better what they vaciate upon (p-10) Church has Chosen Brother Joshua Kelley and Brother Chambers to go to the asociation at Big Creek at Murril meeting hous

June the 12 1790: At a Monthly meeting met according to appointment Proseeds to Busness as follows

~~Excommunication~~

Nething Brought before us

July the 01: 1790 At a Monthly Meeting met according appointment met to Gether and Proseeds Busneess as follows Charles Reno Requests a Coppy of his Excommunication and it is Granted to him and that is for obscenting him Self from the Church and for Refuseing to hear the Church

August 07 - 1790 met to gather and proseeds to Business this Church agrees to sends Brother James Chambers to set with the Church at the buffelow ridge to try to Remove our grevance

At a Monthly Meeting met together according to appointment proseeds to Busnees as follows on the 11th Day of September 1789

At a Monthly Meeting met together according to appointment proseeds to Busness as follows on the 9th of October 1790;

(p-11) Att a Monthly Meeting met according to appointment November the 13: 1790 Proseeds to Busness as followeh
Nothing Came before us ______

At a Monthly meeting met according to appointment December the 11th 1790

At a Monthly Meeting met according to appointment february the 12 1791 Proseeds to Busness as folows

At a Monthly Meeting met to Gether acording to apointment May the 7: 1791 Proseeds to Busness as follows this Church doth Chuse James Chambers for there preacher and allso there moderater

At a Monthly meeting met to Gether according to apointing the 11: June Proseeds to Busness as follows ______

July 9, 1791 met togather according to appointment this Church agrees to send Brother John Broon and James Chambers to attend the asociation at bent Creek meeting house the first saterday in August 1791

August the 13th 1791_____ Then met the Church on Sinken Creek and After Prayer proceeded to ________Business-1: motion made _ approvd to give Joel Cooper & Wm McDaniel 18/ to make a Doore & furnish the meeting house with seats.

E N D

TENNESSEE

RECORDS OF CARTER COUNTY

MINUTES OF SINKING CREEK BAPTIST CHURCH VOL. II (A)
1794 - 1803

COPYING HISTORICAL RECORDS PROJECT
Official Project No. 465-44-3-115

COPIED UNDER WORK'S PROGRESS ADMINISTRATION

MRS. JOHN TROTWOOD MOORE
STATE LIBRARIAN & ARCHIVIST, SPONSOR

MRS. ELIZABETH D. COPPEDGE
DIRECTOR OF WOMEN'S & PROFESSIONAL PROJECTS

MRS. PENELOPE JOHNSON ALLEN
STATE SUPERVISOR

MRS. MARGARET HELMS RICHARDSON
PROJECT SUPERVISOR

COPIED BY
MRS. VERA E. SHELL

TYPED BY
MISS MARGARET M. BROYLES

NOVEMBER 1938

CARTER COUNTY

SINKING CREEK BAPTIST CHURCH

CHURCH RECORD BOOK II (A)
April 13, 1794 thru Feb. 1803

INDEX

Note: Page Numbers in this index refer to those in the original volume.

CARTER COUNTY

SINKING CREEK BAPTIST CHURCH

RECORD BOOK II - (A)
April 13, 1794 Thru February 1803

JONATHAN MULKEY - PASTOR

Note: Page Numbers in this index refer to those in the original volume.

(p-1) Minutes of The Proceedings of the Church at Sinking Creek Since April 13th 1794

Under the care of the Revd Mr. Jonathan Mulkey

1795 April 18th The Church met at Sinking Creek JC JC JC

Church met according to apointing

First Church Book

DAVID GRATE

(p-2) April 13 at Church meeting at Sinking -------- agreed that the Dispute, or Difficulty B-------- John Reno & Joseph Tipton be Refered t- Isaac Denton Senr. Solomon Hendrix, Andrew Greer, William Watson & Edmund Williams on Tuesday the 15th of April at Sinking Creek meeting House and make Report to the next Church meeting JC

The above mentioned Persons met, & the Desputе Settled & Report has been made there on JC

Sunday April 13
William Haggard Recd under Recommendation & Samuel Tipton Recd by Letter - also that Letters of Dismission Issue to Hannah Hays ~~Sarah Mulkey~~

Letters have Issued accordingly -

May 11th Nancy Lacey & Nancy Clark Recd and Baptized at Sinking Creek Meeting House

June 15th a negroe woman named Jane Recd, under Recommendation at Sinking Creek Meeting House

(p-3) 1794
June 15 at Church Meeting at Sinking Creek, on Motion that Dorcas Anderson have notice by Thomas Hudibuck to attend Church Meeting on the Second Saturday in July at Sinking Creek meeting House JC. She did not attend

the mind of the Church at Sinking Creek July 12th that Thomas Hudiburg give Dorcas Anderson notice to attend Church meeting on the Second Saturday in Sept at Sinking Creek meeting hous

July 12 Read by the Revd Mr. Jonathan Mulkey, the Minutes of the association held at Cedar Creek on the fourth Saturday in May

Also a Letter from the Roan Oak District association Dated the ~~first~~ Saturday in May - 1- 1794 - motion made for Deacons to be considered on JC

Saturday 6th of Sept. Church met at Sinking Creek and after Divine Service Proceeded to Business when a charge was had & Laid in against Mary Odle & the Church Proceeded & Examined & (p-4) Inquired into the Charge, & She appeared Criminale, the Church therefore thought her worthy of Excommunication, & the Said Mary Odl has agree'd not to Blame this Church JC

Therefore we declare her Mary Odle, not to be of us neither are we to be charged with her conduct.

The Church agrees to Cite James Edin to Church meeting at Sinking Creek the Second Saturday in October, also that Brother William Davis & Edmund Williams do cite Brother Abs. Scott, to Church meeting, as above.

On motion made & Seconded, that a Church meeting be call'd & held at Sinking Creek meating House on the fourth Friday in Sept. in order to Chuse Church officers JC: JC: JC:

Friday the 26th day of September the Church met at Sinking Creek, & after Prayer have Directed Brother Daniel Stover to Cite Betsey Hilton to attend Church Meeting on the Second Saturday in October at Sinking Creek

(p-5) Are we to be charged with her conduct

On motion made & Seconded, the Church agree to wait on Brother Absolom Scott at his House on Wednesday the 21st of Janry 10 oclock, and that Brother Solomon Hendrix, Isaac Tayler, Thomas Hudiburg, Edmd Williams, Wm Davis & Jos Tipton be a Committee for the Purpose of Setling a Dispute Between Said Scott & William Watson & if not Finally Setled then to notify said Scott to attend next Church meeting JC

On Motion made & Seconded that the Proceeding & Recommendation of the Deacons be Read, the Same was Read accordingly, & concurd with which may be Conceiv'd of in the following words, to wit. December the 13th 1794 The Deacons for the Church of Christ at the Buffaloe Ridge met at the House of Joseph Crouch to wit. Zachariah McCubbin, Solomon Hendrix, John Cowen, Stephen Hicks.

To consult on matters for the welfare Peace, & good order of this Church, and first (p-6) Brought forward —

first on Motion made & Seconded, what is to be done with a member or members that neglect their Duty in not attending Church meeting JC

Ans: Deal with them as Transgressors; Unless they give Satisfaction

2d. What is to be done with a member or members when they do attend at Church meeting and ~~leave~~ leave their seats & Spend their time out of Doors & in Idleness. JC Deal with them as aforsd.

3d What is to be done with a member or members that doth agree to Provide, & help maintain their minister and then neglects & fails to do so JC
Deal with them as aforesaid - Then

4th we agree that it is necessary to Subscribe for the Support of our minister. and Further we

5th agree to Subscribe or make up a Fund for the Contingencys of this Church Annually by the Last day of March ~~Each year~~ (p-7)

6th On motion made & Seconded, it is agreed to Choose a Moderator for this Church, when the Revd Brother Jonathan Mulkey was unanimously Chosen JC.
The Church agree to meet at Abraham Cox's on Monday the 26th of Janry to Deliberate on Matters Relative to the Church JC

Janry 26th 1795 the Church met according to appointment, and prayer being made, Proceeded to Business

Then the Report of the Brethern who met at Brother Absolom Scotts on Wednesday the 21st of Janry to Settle a Dispute Between him & Brother Wm Watson was cald for, And the Brethern appointed to meet as aforesd. Report, that they met according t o order and that the Dispute Between Brother Absolom Scott & Brother Wm Watson, was amicably Setled to Mutual Satisfaction.

Janry 26 Brother John Carr moved for Letters of Dismission having a mind to Remove. and lea leave was obtaind, & the Clerk Directed to Issue the Same, When cal'd for

Febry 14th the Church met at Abraham Coxes on Sinking Creek & after prayer being made Proceeded to Business. Ordered that Letters be sent to the Revd John Newman in order to know Betsey Hiltons standing in the Church, and agreed that the contradiction Between Brother Jos Tipton & Betsey Hilton be Refer'd to next Church Meeting

(p-8) Saturday March 7th 1795 The Church met at Sinking Creek, and after Prayer being made the Church Proceeded to Business; When Brother William Boyd & Sister Rebecca Boyd, was Recd by Letter

Brother John Compton Recd by, Letter the Same Day.

The Same day Betsey Hilton was Declared to be out of Fellowship with us on Account of Certain Contradictions in her own Discourse

The Reference from Last meeting concerning Brother Tipton was brought Forward & Setled and not to be Revived any any more Except on new ground, & that in Gospel order

(Rest of page blank)

(p-9) Saturday April 18th 1795 The Church met at Sinking Creek, and after Prayer Being made, Proceeded to Business. When Brother William Hogg & Sister Naomy Hogg was Recd by Letter

April 18th

A Charge was brought forward against James Boring for Dancing at Sundry times & places — and he acknowledged the facts JC — And after Some Deliberation the said James Boring was, & is Suspended Communion with us.

Saturday May 9th 1795 The Church met at Sinking Creek Meeting House, & after Prayer being made Proceeded to Business, and first. The Charge against James Boring being Reasumed as he the sd. James did not attend Church meeting on the Second Sat. in May, the Church Proceeded against him as an offender, he having been Guilty of Danceing Since last Church meeting JC

Therefore we do declare him James Boring out of Fellowship with us nor to be of us; neither are we to be charged with his conduct JC

The same day Letter of Dismission Issued to Brother William Haggard

(p-10) Saturday 9th of May on Motion made & Seconded
The Church agrees that Sister Eleonar Cooper Sister Polley Humpries Brother Wm Medlock Brother Thos Maxwell & others who shall find Freedom to Act in a case of Martha Cox now Martha Whitson to meet where they may find it Convenient on the 17th day of May and make Report to the next Church Meeting

Saturday June ye 20th 1795
The Church met at Sinking Creek meeting house and after Prayer being made, Proceeded to Business when the Report of the Brethern appointed to Enquire into a case of Martha Coxe's now Whitson was Cald for - and they do Report & Say that She Martha Whitson did appear to be very Sorry for her past conduct, and Said that She wished the Church to forgive her if they Could & that She had a wish to Live & be with us JC

A Motion was made & Seconded for a member to attend at the association on Bent Creek on the first Friday in August next When Brother Solomon Hendrix was Elected for that Purpose JC JC

(p-11) The Same day a Motion was made & Seconded for a Communion Season at this meeting House on Sinking Creek, When the Second Sabbath in September was appointed JC: JC: Church meeting appointed at this Meeting House on the Second Saturday in July

Satur day 11th of July 1795 The Church met at Sinking Creek meeting House and after Prayer being made Proceeded to Business when Sister Anne Daniel was Recd by Letter JC

Sister Polley Haggard applyed for a Letter of Dismission ~~the Sa~~ which was granted, and Issued accordingly. JC

Church Meeting appointed at this meeting House on Saturday the

Saturday 12th of September Curch Met at Sinking Creek and after Sermon proseeds to Buisness first the minets of the asociation Letter Red and approvid 2 a Letter of dismission ordered for Bother Gilliam and his wife all So a Letter for Brother Bruks Smith and his wife 3 Brother ~~Hudeing~~ Bother Isaac denton and Bother Bogad appointed to Site Brother James Cooper to the next Church meeting.

(p-12) At a Church Meeting on Sinking Creek october the 17: 1795 after prayer proseeds to Busnees as followeth Brother Hudeburg Bogad and denton Has Sited James Cooper and he hath not appeared by Reason of Sum deficulty in the Way Lade over Till Next Curch meeting

October 1795: Brother Isaac Denton Tayler and William Davis David Job Goes by the Curches order for to Make an inquiry of Brother David pugh and Sister pugh what is the Reason of Brother Peter Miers Complaint the matter Debated and Settled Betwen them

January 9th 1796 At a Church Meeting on Sinking Creek after prayer being maid proseeds to busnees first a Charg Brought forred by Thomas Hudeburg against Brother John Cox and the said Cox Came forrad and Said that He was Worthy to be out of Socieit and their he Chooses to be Exclued and their fore we do this day ~~Excommunication~~ Excommunicate him the Said John Cox

(p-13) February 13th: 1796: Sarah Reno being Sited To Church Meeting the Caus Brought forred and proved and She was found Gilty of Fornication there fore We do give her up to Excommunication

Saturday March 12th 1796

the Church met at Sinking Creek prayer being maid the Church proseeds to Busness as foloweth Moshen first Meses Job being Sited to meeting and has not attened Theirfore Wee do Excommuncate him Neither Eare Wee to be chargeable with his futer Conduct

---

Prevecus to the Church Meeting in Aptil Brother Bowers having heard that Brother William Matlock Had been Several times at the Mason Lodge Labour'd for Satisfaction and did not Git Sadisfied but Rether the Contrary; At the Meeting in April the Mater became more publick, and was found to be moore Particularly Grievous to a Great Number of the members & after mutch altercation the matter was Refered to the Determination of a Committee Chosen for that purpose to Sit at Sinking Creek meeting hous

(p-14) The 2nd Saturday in May: Who met acording, and Report as follows 1st that it is Contrary to the Line of Christian duty, and 2nd Incompatible with the peace and Well being of the Church for any of its members to frequent at all free Masons Lodgs as the bulk of those men are of profain and Disorderly Lives, and that Evil Communication Corrupts Good Manners, the Church accorded With the Committee, and Wm Matlock Refused to be Lade under any Restriections by the Church or to Brak off absoluely his Corrispondnce With the free Mason Lodgs for Which he is Excommunicated

the Same day Brother Isaac Tayler not being Sadisfied with the Churches Dealing with William Matlock and doth Refuse to Give up to the Churchs Judgment and doth Continue His own Judment and theirfore Wee do Lay him under Suspence of this Church for the Sam

---

August 20: 1796) Curch met acording to apointment Proseeds to Busness as fowloeth a Bill of fauls Isaac Tayler charges the Curch with Injustice in the case of William Matlocks Excommunication alls with hard & ungospel dealings with him Self and So dissented from and Refuesed to Set with the Church for ~~wich~~ which he is Excommunicated

(p-15) Brother Thomas Hudeburg and Pellers (Petters) Miars apointed to Site Brother James Cooper to Next Church Meeting and the Matter Pospond to Next Curch Meeting

---

October 7:1796: The Curch met according to appointment Proseeds to Busness as foloweth James Cooper being Sited By by the Church and Refesed to hear the Church when She Calls and their fore Wee do Excommunicate him for the Same and theirfore Wee wish not to be Charged with his futer conduct.

January 14th The Church met acording to apointment prseeds to Busness as foloweth this Church doth Dismis Jane Barrow

January 18th: 1797 The Church met acording to apointment prseeds to Busness as foloweth this Church doth Excommunicate John Carr on Sartain Chargis Lade in by the Church at the fork of Little which is these 1st he is Gilty of persuadeing a Negro to Run a way from his Master By his own Confestion
2 he is Gilty of Pelfering trasfecing with Negros for Stolen property which is proved by a Number of Witnesses
3 he is Gilty of Drinking to Excess provid
4 he is Gilty of Swearing and Blasfeaming the name of God, proved; These are the Expers Words wich wee have acted uon in this matter

(p-16) June the 17th: 1797 the Church met according to appointment after Prayer being made prseeds to Busness as followeth Brother Solomon Hendrix is Chosen by this Church to attend the acosiation at Counses Creek Jefferson County on the Second fryday in August 1797 This Church doth appoint Church meeting on Fryday the 14 of July: 1797 and the Communin Season the Saboth followin

July 14: 1797
the Church met acording to apointment after prayer being maid proseds to Busness as followeth the Letter to the Sociation Being read and approved Isbel Chanc Received by Letter

August the 19th 1797 the Church met according to appointment after Prayer Proseeds to Busness as fowloeth ---- first the Letter from the assoction being Read and approved

October 12th 1797 the Church met according to apointment after Prayer Proseeds to Busnees Sister Phebe ~~Clark~~ Cox doth desire a letter of Dismistion and it is to be Issued.

(p-17) A Memd of Money Collected for the Contingency of the Church by Deacon Hendrix

~~Peter Nave~~ £ 0..1..3
~~David Grate~~ 0..1..6

Isaac Tayler 0..1..6
Thos Maxwell 0..1..3
Joel Cooper 0..1..6
John Poland 0..0..9
Jos Tipton 0..1..6
Jas Crouch 0..1..3
Leonard Bowers 0..0..9
Brooks Smith 0..1..6
Wm Boyd 0..1..6
David Job 0..1..6
Ann Radder 0..1..6
Jamima Ward 0..0..9
Sarah Davis 0..1..6
Eleanor Cooper 0..1..6
Eleanor Kite 0..1..6
(p-18) Pheobe Stover 0..0..7
Mills Ward 0..0..4 1/M
Andrew Green 0..2..3
Wm Pugh 0..0..9
Adam Rider 0..0..9
Edmd Williams 0..6..0 82

Thomas Mcfeld 0..1..6
John Poland 0..1..6
William Daniel 0..1..6
William Medlock 1..1½
~~0 0 0~~ 62

Solomon Hendrix 0..1..6
Inders Grear 0..3..0
Sister Ecton 0..0..9
Elizabeth Medlock 0..1..6
Pegg Stevens 0..1..6 35
Mary hendrix 0..0..9
Joseph Tipton 0..1..6
John Gillam 0..0..7½
Leonard Bowers 0..1..6
Thomas Hedeburg 0..0..7
18 10 d

(p-19) David Graet 0..0..9 1.18.9
Samuel Tipton 0..6..0
david Job 0..1..6
Ann Raders 0..1..6
Mary Humphris 0..0..9
William Borin 0..9..0
William Pugh 0..1..6
James Crouch 0..1- 3
John Compton 0- 0-9
Teter Nave 0- 0- 9
Joel Cowpers 0- 1- 3
Isaac Taylor 0- 1- 6
0-19-6 d

total sum 18-10
1.13..4

David Great paid 0..6..0

(p-20) At a Church Meeting Met acording to appointment December 16th 1797 Proseeds to Busness as foloweth Nothing Brought forred to be Record.

January y 20th 1798 at a Church Meeting met according to appointment Proseeds to Busnes as foloweth and nothing Record

february y 17th: 1798: At a Church meeting met according to appointment Proseeds to Busness as foloweth Nothing to be Recorded

March y 17th: 1798 Met according to appointment Proseeds to Busness as foloweth Nothing to be record

April ÿ 14th: 1798 met according to appointment Proseeds to Busness as foloweth Nothing to be Record

May y 19th: 1798 Met According to appointment Proseeds to Busness as foloweth and first

June 16th: 1798 The Church from a Sence of duty Excludes Joseph Tipton for his Railing frequently in Church meeting at Individuals also for unbecoming and unsavory discourse Saying that he Would Neither believe the Word nor Oath of some, and Lastly for Leaving the Church in an abrupt and angry maner Saying that he Would not Set or Live With the Church (p-21) Till Some alteration Should take place

July 14th: 1798 Met according to appointment after Prayer being maid proseeds to Busness as foloweth this day Wee doth Excommunicate Henry Stevens for that he hath not nor Will not hear the Church

August 18th: 1798 Met according to appointment after Prayer proseeds to Busness as foloweth Ann Crumpton hath obtained a Letter of Dismistion

September 15: 1798 The Church met according to apointment Proseeds to Dusness as foloweth
David Greats Bond is taking of

September 29: 1798 Sister Dorothy Hudeburg is to obtain a letter when Cauld for and it is Issueded

October 20: 1798——met acording to appointment proseeds to Busness as foloweth Sister Chance is Dismist by Letter

November the 17th: 1798 Met according to appointment Proseeds to Busness as foloweth Nothing Brought forred but a fast Proclamed

December the 15th 1798 Met according to appointment Proseeds to Busness as foloweth Nothing brought forward to be Recored

(p-22) January the 19th: 1799 the Curch met acording to appointment Proceeds to Busness as foloweth Nothing Brought forward to be Recorded

February 16th: 1799 The Church met according to appointment Proseeds to Busness as foloweth

Isaac Denton hath Requested a letter and his mother Ann Denton and it is Granted.

March 16th: the Church met according to appointment proseeds to Pusness as foloweth ~~Nothing brought forred to be Record~~ this Church doth order that Sister Dorothy Hudeburg Shall have a letter and it is Granted

April 20: 1799 the Church met according to appointment Proseeds to Busness as foloweth this Church doth Excommunicate Nancy Young for Certain Chargis wich is dancing and and disobaing the Churchs Call When Sent for

May 18: 1799: the Curch met acording to appointment Proseeds to Busness as foloweth Nothing to be Recorded

June 15: 1799 the Church met according to appointment Proseeds to Busness as foloweth first Sister Martha Whitson is to have a Letter of Dismistion and it is to be sent

(p-23) July 20: 1799 Met according to appointment Proseeds to Busness is foloweth 1 Brother Maxwell Chosen to attend the Asociation at Bent Creek the 9: of August 1799 also Phany Little is to have a leter of Dismistion and it is to be Sent to hir

August 16th: 1799 met according to appointment and Chose a Committee to Consider Whether Thomas Hudeburg Should have a Letter or not and they joinly a Gree that he Should; and the Clark ordred to Write it and Send the Same to the Said Hudeburg and also the Minets of the Acosiation being Read and approvid

November 16th: 1799: the Church met according to appointment Proseeds to Business as foloweth first this Church doth Exclude John Gillam from under its care for be having Exceeding bad 2 Elizabeth Gillam is to have a letter of Dismistion

decem 14:1799 Met according to appointment proseeds to Busness as foloeth this Church doth Exclude Elizabeth Madlock from under heir care for that she ~~that~~ hath been found with Child, and Sister Rachel Harrel is to have a Letter of dismistion

January 19:1800 Met according to appointment proseeds to Busness as foloweth Nothing brougt forred

february 15: 1800 Met acording to appointment Proseeds to Busness as foloweth Nothing brought forred

(p-24) March 15th: 1800 Met according to appointment Proseeds to Busness as foloweth this Church dismist Brother William Daniel from the offis of Deacon and another to be appointed

April 19:1800 Church met according to appointment Proseeds to Busness as foloweth Jonathan Buck and Zeruiah Buck Received by Letter and Brother Jonathan Buck Elected Deacon

May 17:1800 Church met according to appointment Proseeds to Busness as foloweth this Church doth Exclude Milly Forde from under hir watch care for having Borne a Child un lawfull be gotten Martha Whitson Received by Letter and also Brother Aaron Cunningham to have a letter Sent to him

June:14: 1800 the Church met according to appointment proseeds to Busness as foloweth first this Church Sends Brother Hendrix and Brother Maxwell to Cite

Brother Zebelon Smith to next Meeting and Wife this Church hath chosen a Communion Seson to be the third Sunday in August and the fryday before to be the fast day

(p-25) July 19th: 1800 the Church at Sinking Creek met according to appointment Proseeds to Busness as foloweth 1st Brother Joseph Tipton is Restord to fellowship a Gain - 2 this day Zebelon Smith is declared to be out of felowship for as mutch as he has been Gilty of fiting and intends to fite again

August: 15: 1800: Met according to appointment proseeds to Busness as folows 1, Brother Absolom Scott caus cauled and Laid over

October 18: 1800 Met according to appointment Proseeds to Busness as foloweth Brother Scott came forward and Give Sadisfaction to this Church and is Restord to his Seate again - James Crouch and wife hath obtained Letters of dismistion

November 15: 1800 Nothing Brought forward

December 20: 1800 Nothing Brought forward

Know Meeting in January

(Rest of page Blank)

Loose Record

June 20: 1801 Met according to appointment proseeds to Busness as foloweth st--th Communion Seson to come mence the 3 Sabboth in Septemsber and also Brother Solomon Hendrix to go to the Sociation at the Buffolow Ridg being the 2 friday of August 3 Abraham Odell is Received by Letter

July: 18: 1801 Met according to appointment Proseeds to Busness st. Rechard Kite takeing in to membership by Experance

(p-26) March 18: 1797

	£	S	d
David Job	0	1	3
Solomon Hendrix	0	1	6
Joel Cooper	0	0	11 3
Zeb Smith	0	1	6
Adam Hider	0	0	6
Lenard Bowers	0	1	6
Joseph Tipton	0	1	6
Samuel Tipton	0	1	6
Phillomon Lacey	0	1	6
Thom Macfearld	0	1	6
Thom Rideburg	0	0	9
William Boyd	0	1	6
James Crouch	0	1	6
John Cumton	0	1	6
William Daniel	0	1	6
Elender Coper	0	1	6
Andrew Greer	0	3	0
Phebe Mcfawl	0	0	9
Pnele Stover (Phebe)	0	0	9
Milley Worde	0	0	9
Polley Linkhorn	0	1	6
Elizb Exton	0	1	6
	1	9	4

	£ $ d
Tetter Nave	0 1 6
John Gilliam	0 1 6
Brux Smith	0 1 6

(p-27)

~~Brux Smith and wife~~
July 14th. 1798
Henry Stevens Exc
April 20: 1799 Nancy Young

1799 John Gillam Exc
1799 Elizabeth Matlock Exc

May 17: 1800
Milley Word Exc

Rachel Hartel Letter
Rec by Exp Wm Yates
1796 Rec by Exp Rachil Pugh Oct: 7:

July 14th Isbel Chanc
1797

August 16: 1799 Thomas Hudeburg
Dismist

99 Elizabeth Gillam Dis --
99 Rachel Harrel Dis --

January 9, 1796
John Cox - Exco:
12 March Moses Jobb - Exco:
14 May Wm Matlock - Exco:
february
3, 1796 Sarah Reno Exco:

apg. Isaac Taylor Exc: 1796
—et James Cooper Exc: 1796
John Carr Exc: 1797
Joseph Tipton Excommunicated

January 14: 1797
Jane Barrow Dismist
October 14 1797 Phebe Cox Dis (erased)

September 29, 1798 dorothy Hudeb-----
dismist

October 20: 1798 Isble Chance d

October 20: 1798 Brux Smith wife
dismist

August 18: 1798 Ann Cumpton dismist

Janary 19: 1799 Isaac Denton
Ann Denton dismist

(p-28) December 13th The Deacons meet at Joseph Crouch To Wit- Zac McCubbin Sollomon Hendriks John Cowen Stiven Hicks To consult matters for The peace and well far of this Church - first What Shall be done this with a member or meme That Neglect Thir duty in atending Church meeting - Deale with them as a Transgressor unless They give Satisfaction - 2 What Shall be done with a member or members When Thay Do attend at Church meeting To Leave thir Seats and spend thir Time in Idleness out of Dore Ans Deale with them as a for Said
3 What Shall be done with a member or members That doath agree to Help thir minister and Then will not. Deal with them as a for said

5 We a gree To Subscribe for the Subporte of our Minister - 6 We gree To Chouse a moderater the benefit of This Church 7 We a gree once a year To Throw in once a year mites in to fund for to ~~ra~~ use of the Church

(p-29) March 20: 1802 Met according to appointment proseeds to Busness as foloweth David Job is to Cite Brother davis to next meeting Brother Bowers is appointed by the Church to attend Cobb Creek Church as a Delegate this Church doth Exclud David Great for Slandering

Adam Rader came ----------- and a ~~mumt~~ Refusing to give the Sadisfaction that this Curch Required of him

June 19: 1802 Met according to Appointment proseeds to Busness as foloweth 1st Boher hendrix chosen to go to the ascosiation and Brother Samuel Tipton to attend all so ----- has chosen Brother Hendrix Tipton deal with Brother davis at the Sociation and them that they will cawl for

Mary Dopson Received by Lettar

July 17- 1802 met according to appointment proseeds to Busness as foloweth it the Communion Seson to come mence the third friday in September

September 17 1802. met according to to Busness as followeth David Job is the meeting hous at Bent Creek as a William David caus Lade over till

(p-30) Met according to appointment October 16th 1802 proseeds to Busness as foloweth 1st Robert Casseday Received by Expearance Elizabeth Casseday by Experance

October the 20: 1802 the Church met according to appoint Proseeds to busness as foloweth st

February the 19th 1803
The Church met according to apointment after proseeded to Busness as follows First Brother Daniel Stover appointed Clerk by the unanimous voice of this Church adjourned till meeting in Course at Brother Buck

E N D

TENNESSEE

RECORDS OF CARTER COUNTY

MINTUES OF SINKING CREEK BAPTIST CHURCH VOL. II (B)
1797 - 1800

COPYING HISTORICAL RECORDS PROJECT
Official Project No. 465-44-3-115

COPIED UNDER WORK'S PROGRESS ADMINISTRATION

MRS. JOHN TROTWOOD MOORE
STATE LIBRARIAN & ARCHIVIST, SPONSOR

MRS. ELIZABETH D. COPPEDGE
DIRECTOR OF WOMEN'S & PROFESSIONAL PROJECTS

MRS. PENELOPE JOHNSON ALLEN
STATE SUPERVISOR

MRS. MARGARET HELMS RICHARDSON
PROJECT SUPERVISOR

COPIED BY
MRS. VERA E. SHELL

TYPED BY
MISS EMMA M. BROYLES

NOVEMBER 1938

CARTER COUNTY

SINKING CREEK BAPTIST

CHURCH RECORD BOOK II(B)
June 1797 thru Nov. 15, 1800

INDEX

Note: Page numbers in this index refer to those of the original volume from which this copy was made. These numbers are carried in the body of the manuscript within parentheses, as (p 124).

K

L

M

N

P

S

T

W

Y

CARTER COUNTY

SINKING CREEK BAPTIST CHURCH

RECORD BOOK II (B)
June-1797 Thru Nov. 15, 1800

(p-1)

David Job		1	0	0
Solomon Hendrix		1	0	0
William daniel		0	10	0
William Boind		1	0	0
Thomas Maxfeld		0	10	0
William davis	paid	0	6	0
David Pugh		0	10	0
William Hogg		0	10	0
Elizabeth Ecton	paid	0	1	6
Patrick Cragan		0	6	0
David Great		0	6	0
John Cumpton		0	8	0
Tetter Knave	paid	0	12	
Nancey Worland		0	10	0
Mary Lindhorn		0	12	0
Joel Cooper		0	12	0
Joseph Tipton		1	0	0
Samuel Tipton		0	10	0

Superscription for
March 16: 1799

William Pugh	0	1	6

March 16: 1800

William Pugh	0	1	6
Solomon Hendrix	0	1	6
Joel Cooper	0	1	6
David Job	0	1	6
William Boyd	0	1	6
William Daniel	0	1	6
Peter Nave	0	0	9
Andrew Greer	0	3	0
Samuel Tipton	0	1	6
John Poland	0	1	6
Thos Maxwell	0	1	6
David Great	0	0	9
Philemon Lacey	0	1	6
Joseph Tipton	0	1	6
Mary Humphris		1	3
Elizabeth Ecton	1	0	9
Andrew Greer		3	0
Daniel Stover		1	6
William Boren		0	9
David Great		1	6
Lenard Bowers		1	[illegible]
Mancey Watson		1	0
David Pugh		0	1

(p-2) December 20: 1800 The Church met according to appointment Proseeds to Busness as foloweth ---

(p-3)
June (TORN OUT)
appoint
to Business
Hendrix is Cho
Sociation at Coun
on the Second friday in
This Church agrees to hold Chur
on friday the 14 of July: 1797 an Communean Seasen the Sunday after

July the 14 1797 the Church met according to appointment after prayer proseeds to Business as fowloeth the Letter to the association being Read and approved - Isbel Cheanc Received by Letter Brother Davis cume forred and Ecknowledged his folt and is Lade over tell next meeting in Corse

August the 19th 1797 the Church met acording to appointment after prayer Being maid proseeds to Busness as followeth - 1 the Letter frome the asxociation being Read and approved 2 Brother Davis is Released from the Bonds of this Church

(p-4)

torn out rch meeting
ording to apoint
ds to Busness as
ch Chose Brother
ey and Solomon Hendrix
am Daniels and Joseph Crouch and
uch to attend upon Settlen a debate
en David Great and Rachel Whitson
the friday before our next meeting
in corse, and Brother James Crouch to Let him
Nnow when and Wheir 2 Samuel Tipton Lenard Bowers is to Site Brother Greer to next Church Meeting

Met according to appointment the 14th of October 1797 Proseeds to Busness as followeth this Churchs Choice is that Brother Solomon hendrix and William Hogg and David Job to attend at a Sartain Day to attend fas of meers said for his Land and other property to be the 25 of October

Sister Phebe Cox does desire a letter of Dismistion and it is to be Issued this church Send Brother Thomas Maxwell to Site Brother Greer to Next Church meeting.

(p-5) at a
December (TORN OUT)
first

January 20:
According to apointme eeds to Busness as ~~Feuls~~ foloweth and Nothing
Record Dav
1 First David
At a Church Meeting met acording to appointment on the 17: Day of february 1798 proseeds to Busness as fowleth first this Churchs Choice to Send Broher John Balis and Bother Cooper and Brother Lacey to go and Laber with Sister Hendrix and to Site hir to next meeting.
Bother Bowers is to Site Bothe Cox to next meeting and allso Brothe James Crouch to Cite Brother Stover to next meting

(p-6) (TORN OUT) ing to
as foloweth
ens cite tation
ting in Corse
April 14 met according to appointment proseeds to Busness as fowloeth first this Church Sends Brother Samuel Tipton and Philleman Lacey to Go to Brother Grer and Laber with him in Regard of Leting his Darter going to the Dansing School and the Report to be maid to next meeting
this Church Send Brother William daniel and James Crouch to Cite a Brother Stevens to next Church meeting
3 This Church hath chosen Brother William Boid and Joel Cooper and David Job to try to find the dammage Brother Hudeburg hath Sustand by Howel Ivy Sute in Law which bother Joseph Tipton is to Stand Good for that; he is to stand between the said Hudeburg and all dammag.

May the 19: 1798 Met according to appointment Proseeds to Busness as foloeth First Brother Greer matter Brought forred and Laid over till the after Part of the day.

(p-7) Brother Stevens matter Brought forred and Laid over till Next Church meeting
This Church doth Lay Brother Joseph Tipton under ~~conser~~ Censher for his dis-order ~~in as match as he Left the Church in a hasty manner and for Talking un a-becoming member This Church Sends to Brother Greer to Site Him to Next Church Meting~~

This Church Sends Brother John Poland and Teter Nave to Cite Brother Grear to next Meeting

June y 16: 1798 Met acording to appoint Proseeds to Busness as foloweth First Brother Grer Caus Brought forred and According to the Report of the Mesengers this Church Lays it over till Next Meeting in Corse

This Church doth Excommunication Joseph Tipton for his ill Conduck and in as much he woold not hear the Church

The Church Chuses Brother Mulkey and Brother Denton to Cite Brother Great to next Meeting

(p-8) July 14 1798 met acording to apointment proseeds to Busness as foloweth first David Great is Suspended from the preveldge of this Church This Churchs Choice is that William Boid and Solomon Hendrix and David Job to try to Settle a matter betwen Sister Worly and Brother Maxwell to attend at Mr Worldlys being 25 of July
Secondly this Church doth Excommunicate Henry Stevens for not hear of the church

August 18th 1798 Met acording to appointment Proseeds to Busness as foloweth 1 David Greats Matter Brought forred and debated and this Churchs Choice to Send William Daniel and David Job to go to Cheerke Meeten with a petion to that church Ann Cumton hath obtained a Letter of Dismistion

Saturday 15th of September 1798 the Curch met according to appointment Proseeds to Busness as foloweth first Bother Bales Chosen Moderrator the asca. Letter being Read and approved David Greats bonds is taken off

A Cald Curch Meeting to be held the 29 of September at Sinking Creek

(p-9) Solomon Long Saml Dento Samend Capt — Abraham Job his, Abraham Job his, Abraham
At a Cauld Church Meeting

Septembe 29 1798 met according appointment Proseeds to Busness as foloweth first Joseph Crouch Chosen Mcderator Sister dolly hudeburg is to have a letter when cald for

October 20th: 1798 Met according to appointment Proseeds to Busness as foloweth Sister Chance is to obtain a Letter of desmistion

November the 17: 1798 met according to appointment after prayer Proseeds to Busness as foloweth the Church Proseeds to Proclaim a fast the forth Satturday in November.

TORN) er the 15 1798 met according to appoint
OUT) Busness as foloweth first this
) church cite Brother Watson to next
) and Samuel Tipton to cite Nancy Young

(p-10) January the 19th 1799 the curch met according to appointment Proseeds to Busness as foloweth Brother Watsons matter Brought forred and got through This Church Sends Samuel Tipton and John Gillam to cite Sister Young to next meeting
A Request Laid in to this Church by Brother Watson in be half of Brother Hudeburg to know whether this Church Could Send him a Letter or not, Lade over tell next meeting.

february the 16: 1799 the Church met according to appointment Proseeds to Busness as foloweth first Brother Joseph Crouch Chosen Moderater Brother Isaac denton is to have a Letter and it is Isshu
this Churchs Choice Samuel Tipton to cite Sister Young to next meeting.
the Church Lays over the Sending a Letter to Borther Hedeburg tell next fall

March the 16 1799 The Church met ac (torn out)
to appoint Proseeds to Busness a first Brother Balis Chosen (torn out)
church doth Send a Letter (torn out)
n w (torn out)

(p-11) This Church doth order that Sister Hogg Shall have a Letter allso a letter to be Send to Sister Phany Borin to to Know why Shee went away with out a letter
this ~~Send~~ Church Sends Brother William Baonean and David Job to cite Sister Little and Sister Stevens to next meeting ~~and a Letter to be Sent to Sister Martha Sex to know why she went away without a Letter~~

April the 20: 1799 Met according to appointment Proseds to Busness as foloweth first this Church Sends Brother James Crouch to Cite Absolom Scot to Next Meeting 2 this Church doth Exclude Nancy Young from this Church for her danceing and Disobaing the Churches Call when Sent for

18th: May Met acording to appointment 1799 Nothing

June the 15th: 1799 Met according to appoint and prosds to Busness as foloweth first Sister Martha Whitson is to have a letter of Dismistion

July 20th 1799 Met according to appointment Proseeds to Busness as foloweth first: Brother Maxwell Chosen to attend the acotiaon at Bent Creek on the 9 of August 1799
allso fanny Borin to have a Letter of dismition

November 16, 1799

(p-12) Met together according to appointment Proseeds to Busness as foloweth first this Church doth This day up to excommunication John Gillam for his Bad Condck in as much as he has Give out Such Sinful Langwag 2 Elizabeth Gillam is to have a Letter of Dismstion 3 Brother Boid and Sister Rebcah his wife and close to go cite Sister Elizabeth Matlock to next meeting 4 this Church Sends Samuel Tipton and Lennard Bowers to Cite Brother Greer to next meeting 5 this

Church Sends Brother James Crouch to cite Brother Watson to next meeting.

Met according to appointment December 14: 1799 first this church doth Exclude Sister Elizabeth Matlock from our felloship Brother Watson Citetation Lade over tell Next Meeting.

Rachel harrel is to have a letter

Brother Watson Deceased

January 19:1800 Met acording to appointment Proseeds to Busness as foloweth 1

February 15th:1800 Met according to appointment Proseeds to Busness as foloweth

15: 1800 March Met according to appointment proseeds to busness as foloweth first the Church Dismist William Daniel from the offis of Dacon and a Nother to be appointed

19: Apriel 1800 Church met according to appointment and proceeded to busness and first (p-13) Jonathan Buck and Zaciriah Buck received by letter 2nd brother Buck Elected as Deacon 3rd A Subscription for brother Miers last adjourned till meeting in course

June 14: 1800 Met according to appointment Proseeds to Busness as foloweth first this Church Sends Brother Hendrix and Brother Maxwell to Cite Brother Zebelon Smith to next meeting and wife allso
this church hath Chosen a Communion Seson to bee the the the third Sunday in August and ~~the fast day fed~~ the friday be fore to be the day ~~before~~ of fasting

July 19th: 1800 Met according to appointment proseeds to Busness as foloweth 1st Brother Joseph Tipton is Restord to felowship again
this day Zebulon Smith is declard out of felowship for as much he has been fiting and intending to fite again

August 16 1800 Met according to appointment proseeds to busness as foloweth Brother Scot matter Laid over till next meeting

October: 18: 1800 Met according to appointment Proseeds to as foloweth Brother Scot has come forred and give Sadisfaction to this Church and is Restord to his Seat A Gain.

(p-14) Comand you
Brother hood
these promise
David Job Brother
Jonathan Mulkey we or either of us Do promise to pay
Abraham Job Abraham Job

Abraham Job

Bill of faults. Isaac Taylor charge the Church with Injustice in the case of Wm Matlocks Excommunication also with hard ungospel dealings with him self and so dissented from and refused to Set with the Church for which he is Excommunicated.

This Church hath granted James Crouch an wife a Letter of desmistion

November 15: 1800 the Church met according to appointment and Proseeds to busness as foloweth.
st

E N D

TENNESSEE

RECORDS OF CARTER COUNTY

PAPERS RELATING TO SINKING CREEK CHURCH
1783- 1875

COPYING HISTORICAL RECORDS PROJECT
Official Project No. 465-44-3-115

COPIED UNDER WORK'S PROGRESS ADMINISTRATION

MRS. JOHN TROTWOOD MOORE
STATE LIBRARIAN & ARCHIVIST, SPONSOR

MRS. ELIZABETH D. COPPEDGE
DIRECTOR OF WOMEN'S & PROFESSIONAL PROJECTS

MRS. PENELOPE JOHNSON ALLEN
STATE SUPERVISOR

MRS. MARGARET HELMS RICHARDSON
PROJECT SUPERVISOR

COPIED & TYPED BY
MRS. CARRIE B. STUART

SEPTEMBER 1938

CARTER COUNTY

PAPERS RELATING TO SINKING CREEK CHURCH 1783 - 1875

INDEX

Note: Page numbers in this index refer to the typed pages.

TENNESSEE

RECORDS OF CARTER COUNTY

PAPERS RELATING TO SINKING CREEK CHURCH
1785 - 1876

(Taken from old papers relating to Sinking Creek Church, now in the possession of Fred F. Hinkle, of Carter County, Tennessee.)

Copied By Carrie B. Stuart, Morristown, Tenn. August 1938.

July ye 5th 1785 Washington County
Watauga Hereby Constituted the Church of Christ on holding Believers Baptism Original Sin Effectual Calling the preseverance of the Grace of God in the Saints &c with the confession of faith printed in filladelphia in 1773 as the most Consistant with our prinsabels of aney we have seen Being Assembled to worship God and Considering of you to Gather with us who intend to Associate in Virginia at the Regular Association and Being Acquainted with some matters held By Some of you which we cant have fellowship we have thought fit to request you to appoint Some Day that we may meet togather to Confer aboute those things that if posable there may be no Devisions Between us when we come there, to appeach each other with for how can we think of holding our peace at sutch a time to suffer our brethren to be imposed on and so we oblig'd afterwards to hold Communion with sutch as we cant hold in fellowship, and not be Consconce condemd for so doing,- we have no more to say at this time But pray your complyance with our petition which we have sent by Br..Timothy Tracey-

Wm..Reno-Clark
in Behalf of the Church

The Minutes of the association Met at big Creek at Murrells Meeting house first Saturday in June 1790
Letters from Seventeen Churches in union were read Thos. Murrell chosen Moderator and Francis Hamilton Clerk- adjourned till monday morning 8 O-clock

Met accoding to adjournment--------the total number of Members 537 in fellowship---

Received by baptism 67 by Latter 34 Dismiss'd 11 Excom,t. 6

In Consequence of some Difficulties Subsisting between the Churches on Little pigeon River Wm. Murphy Isaac Barton Wm. Lovell & Jonathan Mulkey and Tidence Lane was chose as helps by Sd Churches to Look into their Standing

2 Query by holston Church. What Can be done for Excommunication Who's Churches are Dissolved or render'd incapable of acting
ans,d 1st when Excommunicated give them a State of their Charg in writing
2nd the Church which they offer, is to Enquire whether the Church be incapable of acting &c and if it be not then to proceed as tho we had Excom. them ourselves--

3rd Query from Glade Hollow Church Shall a Deacon after Violating the Righteous Law of God and being Censur'd by the Church--Be again Restor'd to his Deaconship- ansd. Yes if the qualifications agreable to the Word of God be found in such person--

(Papers Relating to Sinking Creek Church- P. 2.)

4th Query whether it would not be necessary that some able Ministers Should visit the Churches, ans,d yes and in order thereto we advise that Ministers visit the Churches as much as their power and in order there to we advise that the Churches in General Composing this association Consider their Duties towards their Ministers--
5th Motion to the Committee By Bro. Lane whether Ordination to the Ministry Distinct from the pastoral Charge is agreable to Scripture or not & Referr,d

Bro Wm Murphy and Isaac barton Chosen Delegates to the Virginia association, to sit on the North fork of Roanoak the first Saturday in october 1790 Bro Wm Murphy to a Letter to S,d association containg our association plan to be Inspected by Tidence Lane Wm Lovell and Thos Murrell as a Committee, and a Coppy to be retain,d in their hands-

Adjourn,d till the fourth Saturday in october 1790 at the upper war ford of french broad River Meeting house.

(A Portion of a Report of Association November 1791)

6 forks of Pigeon	Wm. Reno Spencer Clack --Stockton Henry Haggard	15	6	2	.	2	.	100
7 B. E. fork Pigeon	James Matthews Joph.Layman Abram Stover Richrd Shields	5	1	.	.	.	1	40
8 Upper F Broad	Saml Pharis John Netherton	1	.	.	.	.	.	57
9 Stock Creek	John Parker John Thurman James King	.	.	.	.	.	.	28
10 Buff Ridge	Jonathan Mulkey Anthony Epperson & Joph.Tipton	2	1	8	.	1	.	47
11 Cove Creek	Wm Wall Chas Robertson & Methias Wall	.	1	5	.	.	.	36
12 Holston River	Wm Murphy george Eavens & Elisha Dodson	.	.	.	1	.	.	57
13 N fork H	Jno Frost Thos Frost Isaac Newland	1	.	.	.	.	.	100
14 Watauga	Wm Daniel & Joel Cooper	.	.	4	.	.	.	15
15 Glade Bottom	Thomas Mansford	.	3	.	.	.	.	33
16 Cherokee	John Bayles & Samuel Bayles	1	1	7	.	.	.	59

2 Isaac Barton Moderator Francis Hamilton Clk
3 Wm Murphy, Jonathan Mulkey, Wm Reno Thos Mansford Benjamin gist & Isaac Barton a Select Committee to arange the Business to be attended to on Monday--
4 after Divine Service, Adjourned till monday morning, 8 Oclock

Minutes of the Holston association of Baptist held at Lick Creek meeting House the second Friday in August 1802.

Friday August 13th 1802--

1 After worship proceeded to business and chose Thomas Murrell Moderator and Philip Haile Cleark--
2 Brother Jonathan Mulkey delivered the introductory sermon from Acts 20th & 28"

(Paper Relating to Sinking Creek Church- P. 3.)

3 Letters from 37 churches were read and the following acct taken

	Churches	Ministers & Messengers						
1	Buffalo Creek	John Hall John Conley John Parker	10	5	11	.	2	50
2	Beaver Creek	John Bayles Francis Hamilton	3	1	4	.	.	25
3	Popler Creek	West Walker	2	5	1	.	1	23
4	Mockason	James Burton Jno Buster	49	1	1	2	.	74
5	Big Creek	Thos Murrell Johnson Hutton	10	1	46	2	.	74
6	Sulfr Spring	Geo. Roberts John Kenltingworth	1	.	1	.	.	26
7	Big Pigeon	Joshua Kelley Abraham McCoy Aron Cunningham	50	15	.	.	.	135
8	French Broad	Robt Gentry Duke Kimbro Jas. Witt	2	4	2	2	.	36
9	Boyd Creek	Wm Johnson Jno. Ammonett Jas. Randolph	15	2	.	.	.	49
10	Black Water	Danl Flannery Evans Wm Wallin	.	.	.	.	.	69
11	Flat Creek	Rich'd Newport Geo..Holmark	7	6	1	.	.	30
12	Newfound Creek	Thos Snelson Jno. Grantham Dan'l Ponder	20	8	.	.	.	39
13	Glade Spring	Robt. Hammon David Whiteman	2	.	.	.	.	28
14	Cole Creek	John Weldon Robert Armstrong	.	.	.	.	.	28
15	N Fork Holston	Geo Linour John Zion	38	1	28	.	1	45
16	Lick Valley	Elijah Doley Jas. Cunningham	21	3	0	0	0	30
17	Holston River	Wm Evans Geo Evans	9	5	5	.	1	33
18	Buckhorn Valley	Jno Jamison Jos Sinclear	9	6	2	2	.	27
19	Powels Valley	Wm Jons James Rentfro	113	13	11	.	.	126
20	Cobs Creek	John Smith	.	.	1	4	.	79
21	Fork Pigeon	Rich'd Wood Thos Hill Henry Haggard Abra.Stover Spences Clack	15	15	36	2	1	149
22	Cherokee	Wm Calvert Saml Baylis	77	3	0	0	1	127
23	Lick Creek	Saml Smith Saml Baker Jno Crosby P. Haile	9	8	2	1	0	52
24	Hicory Creek	Isaac Brock Wm Helms	0	0	0	2	0	16
25	Big Valley	Wm Thompson Jno. Bradberry	11	4	48	1	0	51
26	Long Island	Wm Nash Michl Ronald Ezekial Ronald	19	4	7	1	0	44
27	Dumplin Cr.	Stephen Collin Jno.Cole	16	2	3	0	1	35
28	Glade Hollow	Jno Jesse & Wm Owens	142	8	6	6	1	355

(Papers Relating to Sinking Creek Church-P. 4.)

29 Beaver Ridge	Aquillow Low Jas Scott	0	0	12	0	2	26
30 Big Spring	Jesse Dodson Wm Stroud	105	25	0	0	0	160
31 Buflow Ridge	Jono Mulkey Nathl Shipley Anthony Epperson Jas brous Sam Tipton	61	6	1	0	0	265
32 Gap Creek	Wm Randolph Giles Perman	12	17	2	1	0	51
33 Richland	Robt Fristo Benjamin Murrell	1	2	3	0	1	31
34 Bent Creek	Jas. Roddie Caleb Witt	0	3	3	0	1	26
35 Tompsons Sett.	Ruebn Wheler Jas. Fulkison	0	0	0	0	0	74
36 Davises Cr.	Jño. Box	0	3	4	0	1	28

A correspondent letter from Pate's Creek association Peter Wood their Delegate, ditto from Green River ass,n John Mulkey & John Murphy their Delegates--

2 Peter Woods & Richard Wood & John Murphy togeather with the Moderator & Cleark a committee to arrange to be attended too tomorrow

3 Appointed Brethren Francis Hamilton to rite a Corresponding letter to Pates Creek association Abraham McCoy to answer that from Green River Ditto Spencer Clack to write a Corresponding letter to New River association also--Brother Wm Nash to write to the Strawberry association

4 Glade Spring Church Boyds Creek Do..Rich Valley Ditto Newfound creek Buncombe County Cole Creek Sulpher spring Powells Valley Tompsons Settlement all appoyed for and obtained admission into our Union

5 This association conclude the former praitice of Inviting persons to aseat in this association not Delegated by their respective Churches may be continued with the Excpions of the priveledge of the Deligates of any church that do object against the persons at this time

6 With Respect to the Deficulties Subsisting between Beaver ridge & Chesnut Ridge Churches This association acquieses in the work of the Committees of Inquest and appoint Brethn..Jesse Dodson Wm Jones Richd Newport to wait on chesnut ridge church and use their utmost indeavours in order to reconcile her to the advice of the association which is their publick gifts discest from ministerial labours while the association committee wait on them---

7 Queary from Richland Creek & Hicory creek churches may a member of another Society be admitted to communion with any of our sister churches being in Judgment of charity renew,d by grace answ,d in the negative

8 Queary from dumplin creek & powels River is it consistent with the word of God to receave persons into their membership that has parted with their husband or wife & is living with another while the first is liveing answ'd not consistent with the word of god

9 Remonstrance from lick Creek Bent creek fork of pigeon & Beaver Ridge concerning the deacons wife answ'd agreed to leave the respective churches to their discression

10 in answer to the request of gap creek Church respecting an inquest into the Standing of bent creek church we advise that the respective churches composing the union each send such of their members & as many as will most conduce to bring Sd Bent creek to a right Standing according to the gospel on the first Wednesday in October

(Papers Relating to Sinking Creek Church- P. 5.)

11 Queary from big valley church- is the laying on of hands on baptist members a gospel ordinance Queary from ditto Is the dedication of Infants a gospel ordiance or no ansd not a Gospel ordinance
12. Respecting the case of the head of Flat creek Church the association agrees to send a committee consisting of 4 members viz. Richd Wood Henry Haggard Thos Hill Duke Kimbrough to meet at their next church meeting in order to give her such advice as they think most conducive to their consolation.
13. the Request from Bent creek Church Respecting the ordanation of Bro Caleb Witt not granted
14. with Regard to the line concluded upon last association, respecting the division of the association we agree to alter it so as to start from Houstons Powels Valley to Martain Creek from thence to the flat gap on Clinch mountain from thence to Stubblefields Ferry from thence to the mouth of Nolachuckey thence to Englishes mountain
15 we agree that the next association known by the name of holston be at Rich Valley meeting House abraham's Creek the second friday in August 1803 and that Bro. Barton preach the Introductory sermon & in case of falour Bro. Jonathan Mulkey supply
16. agreed to compensate Bro. Wm Johnson with 10 Dollars for past services and that the next assn. know by the name of Tennesse asso be at the big spring meeting house the fourth saturday in august 1803 and that Brother Richard Wood preach the introductory sermon and in case of Falour Bro. Jno Hall Supply
17 apporperated to the Cleark for his services 3 dollars

Saturday-24th of Sept 1802 church met at the Bufflow Ridge after devine Servis proceded to Bisness first the minits of the assn Red 2nd Minutes & 3 a dore opned for Exp Jones Mebane Wm Bayel Ellender -----Elizabeth Mebane & 4 Nancy Martin is excluded from membership so She is no more of us neither are we to be Charged with hir conduct------

Minets of a Committee of inquest held at Big Creek Meeting hous the first Wednesday in october-1802-Chosen Richard Wood Mo,d & frances hambelton Cl,ke
2 pursuant to the advice of the association having made deligant inquiry in to the Standing of bent Creek Church do find that their distressed Condition Seemes measurable to have taking rise in Consequnc of a Charge by tidance Lane against Brother Barton on a Count of Centement which Centement wee do Conceive to Consist in a misunderstanding and on mature Consideration Wee do Unanimously think said Centiment not to affect the general Union So therefore it is our advice to the Church to Release Br, Barton from the Bonds Wee do Conceive him to be under in Consequence of S,d Charge; and use Such Measures with Br, Lane as She Conceives to be agreeable to Gosple order

By order of the Committee
Richard Wood Mod,r
frances hamilton-Clk--

April the 14th 1832 We the Baptist Church of Christ at Sinking Creek now in session to the union meting of the 3 division to be held at Buffalow Ridge meting house to begin the Friday before the 3d Sebath in may-

Sendeth Christain Salutations vary diear Brethren we humbly petion you to Consider our situation and give us the next union meting to be held at Sinking Creek the friday before the 3 Sabath in October next and we have Chosen our beloved Brethren Solomon Kendrix David Pugh and Peter Kuhn to bear our petition and set with you in counsil and may the grat hed of the Church be with you and direct all your Conseltation that it ad to Zions glory and the good of his people brothren pray for us
farwell

---oOo---

Carter county Tennessee May 11th 1833

The union Meeting of the fourth division of the Holsten Baptist association now convened at the Stony creek Meeting house according to apointment, to the Union Meeting of the third division to be held at Sinking creek meeting house carter county commencing friday before the third Sabath in october next and following days----

Very dear brethren in the Lord we rejoice that the time has roll,d round for our anual union meeting and that we are spared to meet at the time & place But have to lament our want of Zeal in so good a cause but we feel thankfull to God that we meet some of our brethren who we trust are willing to unite with us. We received your correspondence by the hand of your messenger Bro R Bayles whom we Gladly receive as a token of your brotherly love and esteem altho we anticipated there would have been a great many more of our brethren to unite with us that it would be more like a union indeed dear brethren we wish that the correspondence may still be kept up between us and for that purpose we have chosen our beloved brethren Bery White J. Carter and Valentine Bowers to bear this our correspondence to you and we hope you will receive them as the token of our fellowship with, and pray the Great head of the church that he would crown our meetings with the best of consequences that Glory may redown to his name Brethren pray for us and the prosperity of Zion universally, farewell, our next uninan meeting is to be held at the holsten meeting house Sullivan Co..commencing friday before the 3d Sabath in May 1834

---oOo---

Sullivan County Tennessee October the 11th 1833

The Church at Muddy to the Union meeting to be holden at Sinking Creek Meeting house Carters County we petition the Brethren that our next Union meeting be with us and that It be on the Second Sunday in October next begining the friday before Signed by order of the Church
John Spurgin Clerk protem

---oOo---

As the professors of Christianity are so Divided in their principle And practice that they cannot commune togather; we believe it Necessary to Covenant and agree and reduce to writing a short scatch of our principles: also those Social and relative Duties Injoind..on us As church members: which we believe was practiced of old times amongst The people of God as may appear from the following pages of Scripture Viz, Joshua 24 Chap 25 verse 2nd Kings 23d Chapter 2 & 3 verses Nehemiah 9th Chap 38 vers Jeremiah 50th Chap 5 vers.,2 Chronicles 15th Chap & 12 vers and Similar passages and passing by the several sects of Pedobaptist and antopedobaptist with whome we cannot agree such as the Seven Day baptist the no Sabbeth baptist and those that dip 3 times in baptism with all of whom we think it not expedient to Commune that Due order may be maintained in the house of God And Dispute may be avoided so as that we Do not shut out of our Friendship by Esteem those christians who only differ from us in contra essentials but as a Distinct Society Embody ourselves under the following-Rules regulations and articles vvvvvvvvvvvvvvvv

First We believe in one only true and living God Father Son and Holy Ghost and that these three are one God Equal in poer and Glory

2nd. we believe in his Soverignty in us and over us and that he has a right to Command and Dispose of us according to his purpose and that it is our duty to Submit to and obay him in all things--

Third We believe the holy Scriptures in the old and new testament to be the only Safe and Infalible Revelation of his will made known to men and as such an Infalible Rule for faith and practice) Fourth we believe it is the office of the holy Spirit to open and apply the Scripture or the Missteres there in Containd for the Right Understanding of his will as reveal.d in his word) 5th we believe that We are by Nature Children of wrath and that we are Inable to Recover our Selves from that State of Misery 6th we believe that help is only laid in Jesus Christ the only Begotten Gift of God for that Purpose to Save all those who through grace Come to the father By him and our hope of acdeptance with God is only through The Imputed Righteousness of Christ aprehended and Received By Faith alone 7th from the Commands and Examples of Christ We hold with believers baptism by Immersion and the laying on of hands on Baptised Believers the election of Free grace by the predestination of God in Christ Jesus Effectual Calling by the holy Ghost progressive Sanctification through Gods Grace and truth the final perseverance of The Saints in Grace and holiness the Resurrection of the Body after Death life Everlasting to the Righteous Eternal Judgement and Death to the wicked 8th as Church members We do promis to bear with Each others weakness and Infirmities with much tenderness not to Discover them To any out of the Community where it may be avoided Nor in the Community but by Gospel order as in Math 18th Chap 15th 16th & 17th verses and other Scriptures of like Import---9th..we promis to watch over Each other in love and in the Spirit of meekness Guarding against all jesting lightness and Foolish talking which is not Convenient or any other thing--That Doth not becom the followers of the lamb Seeking Each others good in pertilar and the advancement of the Visable Kindom of Christ universally not forsaking the assembling of our Selves togather But Duly to fill up our places at our respective Meetings Especially our Church meetings Except we are providentially Hindred and the Reason to be Rendered at the next Church Meeting if call,d for Provoking to love and to good works & 10th we believe it our Duty to use Reasonable industry for a temporal Sustanance and to be liberal in our Communication for the worship of God and The furtherance and Support of the Gospel of Christ) and For the full declaration of Sentiments we Refer to the Word of God which is able to make us wise unto Salvation 1834 &c

Finis

David Pugh Clerk
Protem

May the 23rd 1834

(Papers Relating to Sinking Creek Church-P. 8.)

Confession of Faith adopted by the Association at Philadelphia in the year 1742 and lately reprinted by their order which we heartily receive as comprehending the Articles of our Faith, and believing it to be agreeable to the Gosepel of Christ, recommending it to the careful perusal of one another and our Families and all our Friends. But 2nd and in particular manner we profess to believe these following very great and most important Doctrines as being essentially necessary to Salvation Viz. That the Holy Scriptures of the old and new Testaments are the word of God and our only certain and infallible Rule of Faith and Obedience containing everything needful to know, to believe or do in the Service of God, and being able to be wise unto Salvation through faith which is in Christ Jesus by which we expect to be Judged in the last day, and to which our opinions & practices ought at present and always to be conformed and therefore all Christians who can read ought to Search them daily praying to God for the light of his holy Spirit, without which none can Effectually understand them. 2d There is but one the only living and true God Almighty Creator preserver and Disposer of all things visible and in whom we live move and have our being and to whom alone Divine Worship and adoration is to be rendered and ascribed both in this and Eternity, both by men and angels, as being most worthy of it and that will not give his Glory to another nor his Praises to Idols having been strictly forbidden us to worship or adore any but himself 3d That there are three persons in the Godhead the Father the son and the Holy Ghost the same in Substance Power and Eternity and therefore not to be divided in his Essence tho distinguished by Several peculiar Properties and personal relations 4th That our Lord Jesus Christ the second person in the Godhead--- ---------- (Part missing) Sanctified in a measure and so kept by Power of God unto Salvation That they are never Suffered finally to Apostattize, or fall away finally to Perdition; and such only shall obtain Eternal Happiness or enter into the Kingdom of Heaven as are thus wrought upon Converted and Changed in time, as the Holy Scriptures plainly Dictate. 6th That Christ will return from Heaven where he now reigns in Glory to Judge Men and Angels at the end of this World, that by his Power he will raise the Dead, both the just and unjust, that all that are in their graves shall hear his voice and shall come forth, that he will Receive the Righteous and reject the wicked forever, & 2nd we also engage as aforesaid to conform to the following Rules of Disciple as well as to all others Warranted by the Word of God. 1st Not to forsake the assembling ourselves together but Constantly attend out appointed Meetings as far as the Lord shall Enable us, whether for the immediate Worship of God or for to order Business relating to our Church affairs, whether on the Sabbath or on the week days not neglecting any of them but upon necessary occasions and for good reasons to be given to the Church at our next meeting. 2d To bear each one his part according to his abilities in Defraying such Expences absolutely necessary for maintaining the worship of God in decency and order becomeing the Christian name seeing he strictly enjoins it on us in his Holy Word. 3d Not to devulge the infirmities of one another or to tell them to such as are not of our communion (or) by any means when it can lawfully be avoided 4th Not to remove our Residence or abode to any distant part without informing the Church and advising with our Brethren 5th Not willingly to live in the neglect of any known duty to our God, our Country, our Neighbor, our Brethren (or) ourselves, but to Endeavor to walk in all the ordinances and commandments of the Lord, Blameless, 6th to bear Reprooff and to reprove each other in case of Visible

(Papers Relating to Sinking Creek Church P. 9.)

Faults in Christian Charity and Brotherly Love as ordered by Christ in the Gospel

---oOo---

August 1843

State of Tennessee)
Washington County) the Baptist Church of Christ at Sinkin Creek to the ministers and messengers Composeing the holston Baptis assocition to be held at Mcfeatre bent in haukins County Tennesee commenceing the second Friday in August and folling days sendeth Christinan saluetation we gladly imbrace this oppenty of coraisponding with you by letter and deligates for which purpus we send our breathren Henry Knarse Wm hatcher and Jas White to represent us and set with you in Council as to our faith and order we hold the tennants of the united Baptist and Continus in the apolstels doctren and in fellow Ship haveing peace among ourselves yet we have some cause to complain that we are in a cold state in Relegin at present brethern pray for us that the Lord would bless us with a glorious revivel

---oOo---

To the Baptist Church of Christ on Sinking Creek in Caster County Greeting------
Whereas a Settlement took place between Thos Hudeburk and me last faul concerning a bond of 100 £ left in Cap,t Nevilles hands at Fort pit which bond S,d hudeburk lifted and received the contents thereof, together with the interest, or at least has used such measures as to prevent me from any recourse to recover what since the settlement I find In justice I ought to have-and as I have ever considered the Church of Christ under the influence of a principle of justice and Equity by virtue of the union subsisting between Christ and the Church I refer the matter to your consideration hoping you will as your people as it is your duty take the matter under your consideration--and to enable you rightly to judg of the matter I have sent the papers up for your help in case you take the matter in hand the sum I apprehend coming to me is rather above than under 200 dolars which is too great a sum for orphans (whose right now is laid before you to consider of -----, But and if you are willing to keep in your bosom such as would in violation of the laws of justice distress the fatherless and the widow and such as would shew their attachment to the God of this world by the unjustly engrossing to themselves the mammon thereof then I refer you to the coming day where it shall be made appear to angels and men by the great dispencer of imparcial justice that I have been wrongst by one whom you nurse up in the bosom of the church But God would direct you in your duty and grant you all Grace is the prayer of yours &c

Catharine Reno

July 21st 1798

---OoO---

January the 17th 1838

To all whom it may concern this is to certify that I had a conversation with Mrs. Jenkins relative to a report which said that Joshua Adams had drank to excess at their house, to the best of my recollection. I asked her what cause she had to think that Br Adams was drunk, her answer was that he stargered against the door cheek as he come into the house at night. She said nothing, concerning his drinkinng after he come to the house at night. I asked Brother Kyte (whom I understood was there through the day,) if he saw anything like intoxication about him, to which question he answered in the negative

John D. Early

Wee the under subscribers all do say that we went to Mrs. Ginkins and we asked hear about the re(p)ort conserning fathers drinking to which She saide i never saide so for inether Saw him drink any in the day nor at knight and if he was drunk Shee did knot no it

Mary ann pery   rachel cuper

I Do Sertify that I was with Joshua Adams on the day when it was said that he had drink to mutch But I do Sertify that I was with him through the run of the day and I saw nothing of the kind So help me God

Granville Kite

---oOo---

State of Kantucky cumberland county

April 10th 1848 Dear father bayless i want you if you Please to take my case in to consideration And lay it Before the church a prare for releif.. the clerk of the Church to wit brother humphreys sais the church Doe most hartily recommend me as being in good fellowship and standing in your church ifeal very thankful to you brethren and sisters for your kindness towards me..but the way brotheren and sisters the letter is wrote i doe not like and can not lay it in to a church..my reasons why may ast for in the first place the letter contains my letter and my husbands acusation secondly i cannot see where in my husband lied or defrauded henry King as brotherean said in his few lines to us. these is my reasons for not wanting to lay in this letter brothren i thank God that not with standing i am pore in this world i feal that if this house of clay ware desolved l have a house eternal in the heavens..brothren i hope you will nont consider me as i Cannot give in this letter in disorder to send you back this letter and brothren And sisters consider this matter sisters take the matte(r) to yourselves consider this matter i leave it for your consideration.. hoping you will send me another letter without my husband's acusation couched in hit..we are poore but have always benne or tried to be onest but had we benn able to pay our debts when we left tennessee i presume we would both have benn yet in the church but poverty is no disgrace Dear brethren and sisters we feal to love the lord as good as we ever did and are not tierd of the service of god and want you to pray for us..not with standingii bowman have benn excluded And if i have done wrong i know that god has forgive me and i hope the brothren and sisters will i know i want to doe write if i can i want to be onest and if i ever get able to pay king i will pay him what i ow him and if i have defrauded him out of anything i will replace it i owed him for a small brown mare which he was to take in irning of waggons for and i ast him again and again for the work 3 or 4 years i was At him for the work and he never fetched it some 12 months before we started out heari notified him verbily before brother barbery to fetch on his work for i told him i was going to kantucy. i told him a few days before we started i was going to kantucy and beged him to take my note and i would pay him as soon as i could but he would not doe it but waited till i started and followed me with an oficer and took all we had nearly to travel on left us with 62 and a ½ cents and would have taken our all if it for the situation my wife was in..and the bad name he wold a have got by hit but we had a few bills and 62½ cents in money and the lord on our side and bless god we got hear safe and sound in spite of henry king bro. Smith peters we can doe a great deal better hear i write this to let you know what i came hear for not to get away from what i owed but to get to a market where we could get something to pay our Dets so brothern y see my aconolidgement its before you i am poor in this world but cannot help it when we come heare the clerk of this church persuadid us to goe and give our hands to the church that the church might watch over us till we got a letter from you..we enclose the letter you sent us in this sheat..Direct your letter to Monrowe bane post office Cumberland county kantucy

Stephen and Alpha Bowman

(Letter of Dismissal)

State of Tennessee Carter County Jan. 15th 1848
We the Baptist Church of christ at Sinking Creek being convinced together and application being made for a leter for Brother Steven Bowman & Sister Alphy Bowman and owing to charges brought against him for faulshood & Defraud excluded him from the fellowship of the Church but do most hartily recommend sister alphy bowman as being in good standing with us and Dismissed from us when united with any other church of the same faith and order done by order of the Church

Jesse Humphreys Church Cleark

(A letter of seven years previous)

State of Tennessee Sullivan County Sept. 18th 1841
The Baptist Church of Christ at Holston holding the doctrine of Election through grace final perseverance of the Saints in grace close communion &c greeting
Whereas Brother Stephen Bowman hath petitioned for a letter of dismission and granted this is to certify that he is in full fellowship with us & regularly desmiss,d from us when joined to another church of the same faith and order done by order of the church
Signed in behalf of the clerk

Joshua Edwards
Clerk Pro tem

---oOo---

Resolution)
Resolved that each male member belonging to this Church, (who is not actually an object of charity;) pay annually into the Treasure of the same, according as the Lord prospers him, and that we make it the duty of the Deacons of this Church, to write down each name and annex thereto the amount thought by them to be a liberal Contribution for each; and that the said list be prepaired by them and read at our next Cession.

Resolution offerd by parson Ed Silver but Refused By the Church.

---oOo---

(Papers Relating to Sinking Creek Church-P. 12)

August the 15th 1849

the Reason why I Right these few lines to you is because I have sinned and dun Rong & therefore I am ashamed to see you my Brothern I do confess like David of old when Nathan went to him I have sinned & dun rong I do honestly and with Shame Confess it sorrey am I that I did rong I dont want to do rong nor to do Eavil I have no desire nor propensity my Brothern to do rong nether to do Eavil all tho I Confess that I have Dun rong I am ashamed of being guiltey of Doing of this rong I jest say this my Bothern to let you understand me that I Dont intend of Doing of rong if I Can avoyed it it is not my wish nor desire to do eavel and on the Account of my Doing of this rong I Dont know whether I Could sattisfy aney man what was the Cause I have no harm at aney person as I no of in the world one thing more I Dont want to be a heathen man to non nor a Republican to the Church Members I jest submit to the voyce of my brothern I am willing to Confess and to for sake as fair as I no how and if that wont do nor give you Sattisfaction I cant go no ferther I am your well wisher untill Death

Richd Jefferson to my Brothern at
Sinken Creek

August the 15th 1849

---oOo---

May the 16th 1851

In complyance to a request of the Church at Sinking Creek through her messenger J. H. Hyder)

I certify that Mary never acknowledged to the stealing the cotton nor have I any certain evidens that she took the cotton. The circumstances about the time the cotton was missing were sutch that they induced me to believe that Mary had taken it. She lived about the house is one circumstance that caused suspicion to rest on Mary I never believed Mary to be dishonest before nor since In concution I do not know whether she took the cotton or not, She replaced the Cotton to keep down any more fuss about it but always said she did not steel the Cotton it was not the taken of the Cotton that had Marey Brought to the Church for I told Abraham Tipton about the Cotten some two years ago and why did they not have hur then Brought Before the Church then at that time if thar ware so much hurt at hur about it the truath is if Marey Neaver of toald what Abraham Tipton wife toald hur about Runing off the Negroes and selling them thare Neaver would Been aney stur about the cotten But when Marey toald James J. Tipton that Patcy toald hur that the negroes would Be Run of and soald and that marey oald Mistress wanted hur to Come up to thare hous that the oald woman Could Deliver hur up to Abraham for James would not Give them up to Abraham and if thay would Come up to Abraham house the oald Wooman Could Deliver them up to Abraham hur atterna in fact and Indead Marey Dun like oald Zackias did when he said Sare if I have wronged aney man-----

Joanna Tipton

---oOo---

There has been nothing between me and Mary scince Nov was a year agoand when the cotton was in circulation J. Johnson hisself invited Mary to the communion tabble and They have' now brought that up for spite because they are made with the whites onc,s as for me and Mary we are now in perfect friedship I have nothing agianst her at present I hope that God here will be a guide to both of you

Joanna Tipton

(Papers Relating to Sinking Creek Church-P. 13)

the difficulty betwein myself and Mary was Settled Satisfactory one year ago and if it is brought up now it will be just through prejudice

Joanna Tipton

---oOo---

E Ten Carter County Sinking Creek Church
bit by a wolf and waid in a balance Church Dealers I was not dissatisfyed your three turn outs last church meeting and now I do Sincerely desire for you to give me and my daughter Eliza Hannah the same escap John S.. can do as the blind man did he can Speak for himself Sinking Creek Church has got on a sandy foundation and it was Onse built upon a rock built by Father Mulkey but it is like Jurusalem scercely one Stone left upon another if it could cry O Jerusalem Jerusalem So I drop this from my feeble hand to let it be nown that we dont care about membership no longer their so you may now my desire so bould faces is out and the shoe is worn out a new one own and Set at Liberty so we give you our resignation & strain at a nat and Swallow a camel—

Eliza Humphreys

---oOo---

Query Bettey Sims did Samuel McGey offer anything unsivel to you answer Yes
Query did he Gain his Pint With Shame and Confution he did
Query by What means by his Senseal Love to me and the promis of Marrag
Query did he advese you to make Way with it he advised me to take something to Prevent it

---oOo---

(On other side of query was written the following)
to John Denton forty weight of fethers and your Bald horse and that John Denton Should git me a plow and that you should Send the horses by the 15 of April

---oOo---

We the Gospel Church of Jesus Christ on sinking creek Being Constituted a Cordain to Gospel Order upon the confession of faith adopted by the Baptist association met at philadelphia September 25 1742 and hath signed Covenant.which Confession we own as Containing the doctrin of our faith and practice and what you want to know more

Inquire of our deligates
Joshua kelly James Chambers
Garret Reasoner John Brown

---oOo---

(The following was written by Fred F. Hinkle in regard to the within letter)

In two instances only, does it appear that any person in these parts, was actucally imprisoned on account of religion, although they suffered much abuse and persecution from outrageous mobs and malicious individuals. The one, it seems, was a licensed exhorter, and was arrested for exhorting at a licensed meeting house. The magistrate sent him to jail where he was kept until court; but the court upon knowing the circumstances discharged him.

(Papers Relating to Sinking Creek Church-P. 14)

"Shenandoah County Virginia
Septr 6th 1783

This is to Certify that Samuel Tipton, a member of the Baptist Church on Shenandoah has continued in full fellow ship untill now- and conducted himself as an ordarly member of Society- but being under obligation of moving, from our part of the country, we therefore dismiss him from under our care- leaving him at liberty to join with any other orderly Baptist Church--

Signed for and in behalf of the
Church By)
) James Ireland Modr
) Jeremiah McKay Clerk "

The other was James Ireland, who was imprisoned in Culpepper jail, and in other respects treated very ill. At the time of his imprisonment, Mr. Ireland was a Separate Baptist, but he afterwards joined the regulars. The reason why the Regulars were not so much persecuted as was the Separatist, was that they had, at an early date, applied to the General Court, and obtained licenses for particular places of preaching, under the toleration law of England; but few of their enemies knew the extent of these licenses; most supposing, that they were by them, authorized to preach any where in the county.

----Benedict's History of Baptists
Page 33

---oOo---

CHURCH LETTERS

This Baptist Church of Christ at Little limestone concuring with the Confession of faith adopted at philadelphia Certify that John Brown is a member in fellowship with us and Dismist from us when joynd to any Church of the same faith and order Sind By order of the Church
Second Saturday in Septr 1785

John Bayles C

---oOo---

The Church of Jesus Christ on Sinking Creek In North Carolina Washington County holding Believers Baptism by Immersion and the Doctorn of orriginal Sin by the fall of man and Gods Electing Love in Christ Jesus and afectual Calling and a final Presavearance of the Saints and of Etarnal Judgment To any Church of the same Faith and order Sendeth Greeting

Know ye that our beloved Sister Agnes Tolbot and at the same time A member In full Fellowship with us: and as Such we Recommend her to you to watch over her in the Lord and when She is Received by you She is hereby Dismissed from us Given by the Unanimous Consent of the whole church--
at a Meeting held on Sinking Creek the 10th day of September in the year of our Lord one thousand and Seven hundred and eighty five

Joshua Kelly) Past

David Job Clk.

Timothy Tracey) El,d.
Meshek Hail) Da,k

(Agnes Tolbot was the wife of Matthew Talbot II who was one of the first preachers of the Baptists in Tennessee (see Benedict, Goodspeed, Sunlight and Shadows by Bell, Judge Williams in "The Baptists of Tennessee."

She was married to Matthew Talbot about the year 1774. The Talbotts moved to the Watauga Settlements from Bedford County, Va. Aside from preaching, Matthew Talbot was engaged in stock-raising, and owned about 1500 acres of land, at the mouth of Gap Creek.

Ramsey's Annals of Tennessee contain many references concerning the Talbot family.

---oOo---

These are to Certifie that Frances Tipton is a member of Baptist Church on Cherokee Creek in Washington County in State Franklin. Concuring with the Confession of faith adopted by the Baptist-association at Philadelphia and as She is Removed from us we Recommend her to any other Church of the Same faith and order where She Shall be more Convenient to which when She is joind is dismiss,d from our watch Care She is and we hope shall Remain in our fellowship not to use the non Scriptural Ingramatical and obsolete term full fellowship

by order of Church
Wm Murphy C. C.
1785

---oOo---

The Church of Jesus Christ Meeting at Sinking Creek, holding believers baptism, Particularly Eternal Election, unconditional Justification by the Righteousness of Jesus Christ and the final Perseverance of the Saints in grace, to any other Church of the same faith and Gospel order with us

Sendeth Greeting.-----

Whereas our beloved Sister Dorothy Hudeburg is about to remove her residence from us to Some other part of the Earth where the Lord in his providence may Cast her lot:- These therefore are to Certify that She is a Member in full Union and Communion with us, and of a blameless life and Conversation for ought we know, and as such we recommend her to you to watch over her in the lord, and when She is receiv,d by you She is wholly Dismissed from us.

We Commend you and her to god and the word of his grace which is able to keep you from falling Amen.---

Signed by order of our Church

Septm 2nd 1785 David Phillips Minister

---oOo---

The Baptist Church on Georges Hills in Maryland Holding Believers Baptism By Emersion only, Laying on of Hands Eternal Unconditional Election Final Perseverance &c To any Church of the same faith and order, sindeth Christean salutation,

Know ye that our Sister Elenor Cooper is at this time A Member of our Church in full fellowship, and as such we recommend Hir to you to watch over Hir in the Lord, and when she is Received By you she is Hereby dismissed from us, october the 2nd 1786-

signed by order of the Church

Moses Ayers Cl,k

---oOo---

At a church meeting held at Browns Meeting house South Country Line in Caswell County. Under the pastoral care of Bro Joseph Davis our Sister Isabel

(Papers Relating to Sinking Creek Church-P. 16)

Crane being about to Remove from us we Recommend her as an orderly member of our faith and order and as such Dismis her from our watch care when join,d to another Church of our order Sign,d by the Clarke by order of the Church

Clifton Allen, Cl.

March 9th 1794-

---oOo---

From the Church of Christ Greeting deare brethren we Recomend unto you our well beloved Sister Catey Kelley who has been a worthy member In our Church theirfore we give her up as A member In full fellowship and when Received by you then dismised from Us Catauby Church prefessers of the Baptist faith and order Signed in behalf of the Whole Church--

To any Sister Church that Sister Caty's Lot Should be cast by the hand of Providence that is most Convenient to her December the 2nd 1797) signed by
)

Samuel Phillips
Absolom Smith
George Greenway C

---oOo---

November 3 Day 1798

The Baptist Church of Chirst at Mill Creek, Shenandoah County Virginia Do Dismiss our Beloved Sister Mary Barns an ordirly member in full Fellowship and when joined to Another Church of the Same Faith and order is no longer under our Care Signed by order of the church in behalf of the same.

Jesse Wood, Clk.

---oOo---

Baptist Church of Christ South River Shenndoah County State of virginia holding the principels of Sound doctrine contain'd in our Confession of faith, to any Sister Church of the Same faith and order, whereas our beloved Sister Mary Dopson hath inform'd us that She is about to Remove out of the bounds of this Church and hath made Application for a letter of Dismition, these are to Certify that the Said Sister is an orderly member in full fellowship with us, and that She is dismess'd -from under our Care when Join'd to any Sister Church of the Same faith and order---

october 20th 1799 by order of the church

Jeremiak McKay C.l.k.

---oOo---

Carter County est tennesse we the Baptist Church of jesus christ on the head of Kanes creek meeting house holding the doctrine of election, the persevareence of all sants Believer in Baptism by Immertion the Resurerection of those Bodes and eturnal judgement do heare by Certify that our beloved sister febey Baron is an orderly member to joine another Church of the same faith and order and when join,d to another then Dismised from us Signed in behalf of the Church

June 25th 1831 Wm Widby C C

---oOo---

(Papers Relating to Sinking Creek Church- P. 17)

Sullivan County) The Church of Christ Mudy creak holding the doctrine of
Tennessee-----) election final perserverance of the Saints in Grace believers Baptism by Immersion &c do dismiss our beloved Sister Elizabeth Kuhn as an orderly Member and in good Standing with us in our church when joined to any other of the same faith and order done by order of the Church

10th Sept..1831 Amoz James C. L. K.

---oOo---

Virginia Montgomery County
We the members of medow Creek Church Holding to the Doctrin of the united Baptist Do hereby Dismiss our Beloved Brother John D Carty a member with us In full fellowship- & one who has Bee Legally ordained to the minesteril office- & has walked worthy of the vocation wherewith Called; & when joined to another Church of the same faith & order Is no Longer under our Care-------

Signed By order & In Behalf of the Church
October 3- 1831

Hiram Howard CLK

---oOo---

State of no Carolina)
Yancy County) Bethlehem Church of the United Baptist order setting at Green Mountain M House November 14 1836 in conference do certify that our sister Dorcas Owens was in full fellowship with when she left here last spring & we still hear that She is in order we therefore say by these lines that She is Regularly Dissmiss'd from us

done by order of the whole church day above named

S T E Morgan
Clk protem

---oOo---

State of No Carolina)
Yancy County) Bethlehem Church of the United Baptist order (of F broad Association) conven,d at Green M, House this 14th November 1836 do certify that Micajah Owens was in full fellowship with us when he left here last April & we think & believe from the best account that we have from him that he remains so & we say by these lines he is now Dismiss,d from us done in behalf of the whole Church day above named

S T E Morgan
Clk protem

---oOo---

Owen County Ky Sept. 10 1837

The Baptist Church of Christ Poplar Grove holding and believing as follows 1st that there is one true living God the Father Son and Holy Ghost these three are one God 2d The Old and New Testament are the infallible rule of our faith and practice 3rd The total depravity of man 4th The doctrine of Election by Grace 5 The imputed righteousness of Christ alone 6th The final perserverance of the saints in grace 7th The reserrection of the dead and final Judgement both of the just and unjust this is to certify that our beloved Brot Isaac Crouch and Sister Dulceny Crouch his wife is in full fellowship with us and is dis-

missed from us when joined to any other Church of our Faith and order
Signed by order of the Church the third Saturday in Aug 1837
Howard Early Clerk
Jos. Crouch Mod

---oOo---

State of North Carolina Wilkes County.
The Baptist Church of Christ New Salem, in session Saturday preceding 1st sabbath in June 1837. Our faith. Salvation by Grace. Final perseverance of the Saints in grace. Believers the only subjects of Baptism. The mode Immersion. &c

To any sister Church of like faith Greeting:

Whereas Sister Mary Morgan petition,d us for a letter of dismission, being removed from us, We recommend her as a member of this constitution and in full communion with us. And when joined to you, then dismiss,d from us

By Church Order
G. P. Smith, M,d

Attest. Wm. D Beck C. C.

---oOo---

Ten. Blount county Dec'r. 28th 1839

We, the Six-Mile: Baptist church of christ Do Hereby certify that our much Beloved Brother David T. Wright, is a member in full fellowship with us and we Dismiss him from us when Joind to any other church of the Same faith and order. Done in church conferance at Six-Mile this 28 of Dec. 1839

Signed by order of the church
Jeremiah Hammontree Ch Clk..

---oOo---

Tennessee Blount County
Nov. the 28th, 1840.

Dear Brother Ensor, Your lines petitioning for Dismission from us at Six-Mile Church, was read this Day in our hearing. And we do therefore agree to comply with your requests and Send you a letter of Dismission.

Six-Mile Church

State of Tennessee Blount County.
Nov. 28th 1840

We, the Six-Mile, Baptist Church of Christ Do hereby cirtify that our beloved Brother, Madison T. Ensor is a Member of good Standing, & in full fellowship with us; And we Dismiss him from us when Join'd to any other church of the Same faith and order.

Signed by order of the Six-Mile Church
Jeremiah Hammontree, C,l,k.

---oOo---

The State of Alabama Pickens County
we the baptis church of Christ at Pilgrums Rest do here by certefy that our beloved Sister Polly Jackson is a member in full fellowship with us and is dismissed from us when joined to any other Church os the Same faith and order

this done in Church Conferance and by order of the Church this the 2 day of January 1841 Stephen P. Doss Cl. C

(Papers Relating to Sinking Creek Church P. 19)

State of North Carolina)
Ashe County)

We the Baptist Church of Christ at Cane Creek holding the doctrine of Election the final perseverance of the saints and believers Baptism by emersion &c, now in conferance- Whereas our beloved sister Deborah Johnson hath applyed for a Letter of dismission We do hereby certify that she is in full fellowship with us and will be dismissed from us when joined to any other church of the same faith and order this done by order of the church this 16th October 1847

Dudley Learthing, C. C-

---oOo---

N..C.. Caldwell Co..)
May Session 1848)

The baptist Church of Christ At Dover whereas our beloved Sister Nancy Reed hath petitioned us for a letter of dismission we therefore recommend her a member In full fellowship with us and dismist from us When Joind to any other Sister Church of the same Faith and order this done by order of the Church And signed by

H.. Holsclaw C..C..

---oOo---

State of Tennessee)
Green County)

The Baptist Church of Christ at Concord now in Session do hearby Certify that our Beloved Brother Wm.. C.. Newel is in full fellowship with us and is and ordained minister and is Dismissed from us when joined to any other church of the same faith and order Done by order of the Church September the 1849
15th

Jos.. C.. Murray
Clerk

---oOo---

Sullivan Co- Tenne-) Double Spring
Sat- Apr- 20th 1850

We the united Baptist church of Christ at Double spring do hereby certify that our beloved Sister Martha Jane Lisenbey is a member in good standing and full fellow ship with us and as such we dismiss her from us. When joined to another Church of the same faith and Practice) Ordered by the church in conference

Jas.. M. C. Lisenbey) Clerk

---oOo---

State of Tennessee)
Sullivan County)

We the Baptist Church at Holston Dismiss Elizabeth Ann Combs in full fellowship With us when Joined to any other Church of the Same faith and Order done by order of the Church this 15th day of January 1853

Reuben Hick
C. Clk

---oOo---

Georgia Catoosa County) We the Baptist Church of Christ at Ebonezar do hereby certify that our Colored Brother & Sister William and Melvina Job are in full fellowship with us and are hereby dismissed from this church when joined to another of the Same faith and order

Done in conference July 18th 1'57

Robert Williams Clk Prot.

---oOo---

State of Tennessee
Johnson CO

We the baptist church of christ at Sugar grove now in cession & application being mad fur a Letter of dismission fur James H Duncan we therefore dismiss him in Full fellowship with us Legally ordained when Joined To any other church of the saime Fath an orde

Done by order of The Church this 2 day of August 1873

C. P. Clawson Mod
Jacob. F. Dugger C H C

---oOo---

State of North Carolina Buncombe County
We the Baptist Church of Christ at Ebenezer now setting in conferance to my dear beloved brother and sister Jacob and Cassa Gilbert in full fellowship with us-------------

---oOo---

the
June 5 Day 1875
Johnson County Tenn

Sugar Grove Church

This is to certify that Mary E. Bunten & Neoma. E. Vines is in good Staden & in full fellow Ship with us an when joind to Any other chur of the same faith and order then dismissed from us done by order the church

W. B. Dugger MOD Jacob F. Dugger
Clk

---oOo---

ENIGMA

there was a thing in days of old of which I make a wonder
it had in it a living soul which after god did hunger
it never sin,d in all its life it was so well behaved
this thing obeyed God though it was no profeser
it was given as a rod to punish a transgresser
(later was added)
When Jonah disobeyed God put him in Jail
And three days Jonah stayed in the belly of the whale
The one who didthose lines record
Has long sinc e gone to his reward-
So his enigma I have solved
After many years have revolved

This April 10th 1898
A. M. D.

---oOo---

DEPARTED.

The departed! the departed
They visit us in dreams,
And they glide above our memories
Like Shadows over streams!
But where the cheerful lights of home
In Constant lustre burn
The departed the departed
Can never more return

The good the brave the beautiful
How dreamless is their sleep
When rolls the dirge like music
Of the ocean tossing deep
Or when the hurrying night winds
Pale winter's robes have spread
Above their narrow palaces
On the cities of the dead

I look around and feel the awe
Of one who walks alone
Among the wrecks of former days
In mournful ruins strowed
I start to hear the stirring sounds
Among the aspen trees
For the voice of the departed
Is borne upon the breeze

TENNESSEE

RECORDS OF CARTER COUNTY

SKETCH OF SINKING CREEK BAPTIST CHURCH

COPYING HISTORICAL RECORDS PROJECT
Official Project No. 465-44-3-115

COPIED UNDER WORK'S PROGRESS ADMINISTRATION

MRS. JOHN TROTWOOD MOORE
STATE LIBRARIAN & ARCHIVIST, SPONSOR

MRS. ELIZABETH D. COPPEDGE
DIRECTOR OF WOMEN'S & PROFESSIONAL PROJECTS

MRS. PENELOPE JOHNSON ALLEN
STATE SUPERVISOR

MRS. MARGARET HELMS RICHARDSON
PROJECT SUPERVISOR

TYPED BY
MRS. CARRIE B. STUART

SEPTEMBER 1938

---oOo---

S K E T C H

OF

SINKING CREEK BAPTIST CHURCH

BY

FRED F. HINKLE, CHURCH HISTORIAN

---oOo---

CARTER COUNTY

SKETCH OF SINKING CREEK BAPTIST CHURCH

INDEX

T

W

TENNESSEE

SKETCH OF SINKING CREEK BAPTIST CHURCH
BY
FRED F. HINKLE, CHURCH HISTORIAN

NOTE: Mr. Hinkle serves as historian of the church and has assembled a fine collection of material relating to Sinking Creek.

Sinking Creek Baptist Church is located on the highway between Elizabethton and Johnson City, Tennessee.

Copied by Mrs. Carrie B. Stuart, Morristown, Tennessee
September, 1938.

History is a narrative of past events; a relation of facts respecting civil, political, religion, etc., insofar as the fallibility of human testimony will allow.

To be of any real value the writer of history must have reached a stage where the highest value is placed on accuracy. He should be conscientious in research, exact in records, and impartial in judgment.

That Baptist beginnings in Tennessee are obscure, will be admitted by all students of her history. That obscurity prevails, is largely due to carelessness on the part of her historians and the lack of effort to obtain reliable data.

It is lamentably true, however, regardless of how scrupulously careful one may be, errors do creep in--errors which are apparent on a moment's reflection, even to those who commit them. They occur without the least intent to warp the subject, as for instance, a statement recently made that Jacob and Abram Tipton were killed in the French and Indian War instead of the Indian Wars, and that Abram Tipton was killed in the Cherokee War instead of Joshua Tipton, who was killed on the Little Pigeon River in what is now Sevier County.

It is interesting to note that a writer of an article recently appearing in the "Johnson City Press", entitled, "Local Church History Inaccurate" is at fault in the same offense of which he complains. He writes:

"If Matthew Talbot founded Sinking Creek Church, it was about 1780 or after, since he did not appear in the Watauga country prior to the formation of Buffalo Ridge church so far as can be traced in the records." Matthew Talbot was in the Watauga settlement many years before 1780, a fact well known to the writer.

Upon laying the corner-stone of the Buffalo Ridge Memorial Church, the principal address of the occasion was delivered by Judge S. C. Williams. Speaking of Tidence Lane, Jonathan Mulkey and others, he said:

"It must not be understood from what has been said here that Tidence Lane was the first Baptist preacher in the Tennessee country...the honor of priority must go to Mulkey, or another whose claims have so far been unregarded by historians of Tennessee Baptists--Matthew Talbot. There is mention of Benedict as one of the earliest Baptist ministers, but he does not undertake to give the exact date of the appearance in the west of Mulkey or Talbot. So far, we are left to ascertian from other sources, or speculate as to the respective dates. Ramsey names Talbot as an early settler on the Watauga an the Watauga in 1775, and stops there."

(Baptists of Tenn. p-15)

Of the coming to the west of Matthew Talbot and other early settlers, Ramsey, in his Annals of Tennessee, says:

"Mr. Andrew Greer was an Indian Trader and at a very early period came with Julius Dugger to the west. They are believed to be the first men who settled south of the Virginia line...After them came the Robertsons, John Carter, Michael Hyder, the Seviers, Dunjains, McNabbs, Matthew Talbot, the Hortons, McLinns and Simeion Bundy....Soon after the arrival of the immigrants named above, came the Beans, the Cobbs, the Webbs, and subsequently the Tiptons and Taylors. (p-140, Annals of Tenn.)

Matthew Talbot received a deed for lands from "Black" Charles Robertson, Trustee of the Watauga settlers for lands granted by the Cherokees in the treaty at Sycamore Shoals, March 21, 1775. The patent for this land was signed in May of that year. This farm was located at the mouth of Gap Creek and contained several hundred acres. It was not far distant from Sinking Creek Church. "Fort Watauga was located on the lands owned by Matthew Talbot, an old settler". (Annals of Tenn. p-140) On July 21, 1776 it withstood an assault when attacked by Indians under the command of Old Abraham. (See Ramsey p-157; Haywood p-65). In 1776 Baptist McNabb built the first mill on Buffalo Creek, and about the same time Matthew Talbot built another on Gap Creek (Ramsey, p-142). It was at this mill the troops rested on their first days hike to give battle at King's Mountain.

"Priority cannot be taken from Buffalo Ridge Church, as is amply demonstrated in Rev. S. W. Tindell's book, "The Baptists of Tennessee." In this book, which gives an account of the organization of Buffalo Ridge Church, the authorities, place the date variously from 1778 to 1787. Ramsey gives the date 1779..the year that Tidence Lane became the first regular pastor in Tennessee. Goodspeed, in his History of Tennessee, says: "In 1783 Cherokee Baptist Church was organized..four years later Buffalo Ridge was constituted". David Benedict who visited this country in 1810, collecting material for his History of Baptists, places the date 1780, and in his later edition, 1787. Judge Williams gives 1778 as the more prabable date, assigning as a reason that the Lane family were on Boone's Creek in that year.

Whether based on tradition or written testimony, it is a fact fairly well established that Buffalo Ridge Church was established some time between 1778 and 1787. It was organized by Tidence Lane and a group of New Light Baptists from Sandy Creek in North Carolina. After a very fruitful and prosperous period, lasting for more than a century and a quarter, the work lagged and finally stopped. In 1916 the Church was dropped from the rolls of the Association. "For nearly ten years, except for an occasional funeral, the doors never swung open, no signs of life, while moss covered stones at the head of graves by day and night, kept up their silent vigil." (Baptists of Tenn. p-52)

A community having formed at Gray's station, located some two or three miles from the old church building, the Baptists decided to form a church, a meeting called looking to that end, the old church abandoned and a new organization perfected. They took the name of Buffalo Ridge Memorial church. At the organization of the Sunday School, not an officer or teacher was a member of the Buffalo Ridge Church. (Bapt. of Tenn. p-53)

"The idea that there were two Baptist Churches in Tennessee collected sometime after 1765 and broken up by the Indian wars of 1774 is quite preposterous". Notwithstanding, however, there was at least one church on Tennessee soil as early as 1774 whether Benidict confuses Tennessee with southwest Virginia or not.

A church was organized and a "Meeting House" erected in Sullivan County, Tennessee, prior to March 21, 1774. At that time, that portion of Tennessee was thought to be in Virginia. Lands settled, were located and surveyed by Floyd, Doach, Preston and Smith of Fincastle county, Virginia. These first lands surveyed are a matter of record in that county. On March 21, 1774, Anthony Bledsoe received title for 740 acres of land located at "Meeting House" on Branch Waters of Holston River. "It was on the Ft. Chisel Road to Long Island" (Summer's Hist. Southwest Va.) "Anthony Bledsoe lived in 1769 at Ft. Chisel. He moved a short time later with his brother Isaac and the Shelbys, further west into what is now Sullivan County, Tenn. His station was not far from Long Island. (Annals of Tenn. p-190). Road overseers appointed in Fincastle County, in 1776, were: John Carmack, from Beaver Creek to Bledsoe's: David Steele, from Bledsoe's to Meeting House; John Adair from Meeting House to Amos Eatons.

In view of the foregoing, it is within reason to believe Benedict was correct with regard to the tradition of two earlier churches.

That the Meeting House above mentioned was of the Baptist order, is of course, an admitted assumption, in the light of present investigation. But such of those who were Presbyterians living in that neighborhood in the fall of 1773, were members of the Sinking Springs Presbyterian Church near Wolf Hills, or what is now known as Abingdon, Virginia. They joined with the Ebbing Springs Congregation in a petition requesting the Rev. Charles Cummings to assume pastorship of those two churches in that year.

Pioneer churches, then, as now, were located near the center of population, keeping always in step with the settlers as they advanced on the frontier. The center of population at that time was within striking distance of Sinking Creek church. Nearby, at the home of Charles Robertson, the courts were held, as they were also at the home of Matthew Talbot. One of the earliest elections held was at the home of John Reno, a member of this church, who moved to where Robertson formerly lived. The first mills were but a few miles away, and Sycamore Shoals, just over the hill, was the scene of the Indian treaty in 1775, and the rendevous for the soldiers who gathered to form the army that fought the King's Mountain battle.

Matthew Talbot is believed to have been the founder of Sinking Creek Church. The first four ministers in this church were Talbot, Jonathan Mulkey, Joshua Kelley and James Chambers.

As other Baptist churches were formed in the new world, a misunderstanding arose on doctrinal points, particularly between the New Light Baptists and the Regulars. Buffalo Ridge church was of the New Light order and Sinking Creek were "Regular" Baptists. That the question was "hot" is indicated thruout the first minutes of Sinking Creek Church. In 1790, we read: "This church agrees to send Brother James Chambers to set with Buffalo Ridge for to try to remove our grevance".

Jonathan Mulkey was ordained to the ministry in 1775 or 1776. He was in Carter's Valley in 1775" (Ramsey's Annals of Tenn. p-144). Tradition current in 1843 credit Mulkey with being one of the founders of this church. He was pastor from 1794 to 1826--just a few minutes before he died.

Joshua Kelley was pastor in 1785. His name is signed to a letter of dismission to Agnes Talbot in that year. David Job was clerk, Timothy Tracy Elder and Mesheck Hail, Deacon. An interesting side-light is connected with this letter. Some one has made a penciled notation on the back of it, "The oldest letter we find". Some one else has written under it --in ink, apparently recently, "Not Correct, S. W. T.", as if that could possibly alter the facts.

Kelley lived on Blavins Branch, about three miles above Elizabethton, and was a neighbor of the Greers. He removed to Jefferson County about the year 1790, and was long active in religious and civil affairs. He was appointed Justice of the Peace by Governor Blount, but declined to serve.

That Baptists were few and weak in the Watauga country, is an unwarranted assumption. Many families whose names are familiar in early Tennessee history, are to be found on the roster of Sinking Creek members. They furnish a portion of the men who fought at Point Pleasant, in the Indian campaigns, and at King's Mountain.

Of the list of patentees receiving title for lands acquired at the Sycamore Shoals treaty, among those who were the very earliest settlers of the west, the Greers, Talbots, Lincolns, McNabbs, Bogards, Dentons, Fletchers and Hyders, were members of this church.

When the inhabitants of the Watauga in 1776 prayed the government of North Carolina to annex the district, in addition to the above, are many other names found in the records of this old church.

At a later date, many other prominent names are listed--names of men and families who played an important part in the development of this state. There are included--William Davis, Edmund Williams, Isaac Taylor, William Boyd, John Brown, John Hammer, the Pughs, Tiptons, Loves and many others. Thomas Love was church clerk at the time of his death.

Judge S. C. Williams, in his interesting address at the Buffalo Ridge Memorial Church, gave as a reason for placing the prior date of 1778 for the founding of Buffalo Ridge Church, the fact that members of the Lane family were on Boone's Creek in that year. Is it not also within reason, under the same premises, to believe that Sinking Creek Baptists were organized into a church? That they did not do so immediately, is a reflection on their integrity, and not in keeping with the tenets of their faith.

The only desire of present day members of Sinking Creek, is, that due credit may be given these brave pioneers, who helped blaze the trail into the Western Wilderness, and their religious activities rescued from oblivion. To abandon the house of our fathers, change the name of her constitution, her members remove themselves to Elizabethton or Johnson City for sake of convenience, not only would lose this church her claim to perpetuity, but cast a shadow upon the men and women who made our place possible.

A
REGISTER OF MEMBERS OF SINKING CREEK BAPTIST CHURCH
FROM
1785 to 1866

Compiled by Fred F. Hinkle

The names found in this Chapter are taken from the Minutes of the earliest date up to and including the reorganization of the Church following the Civil War period. They do not represent, however, a complete list of all the members of the Church. Unfortunately, the clerks failed to enter the names of the candidates when joining either by letter or experience, and the names contained in this list are, in a great number of cases, found at the time of leaving the church, or when their names come up in the usual routine of business. They represent a fair list of the members of Sinking Creek Church.

This list has not been checked, and is subject to change.

A REGISTER OF THE MEMBERS OF SINKING CREEK CHURCH.

Book I--to 1791

Tracy, Timothy
Tracy, Elendor
Reasoner, Garrett
Reasoner, Keziah
Reno, Charles
Jobe, David
Hail, Mesheck
Hail, Catherine
Talbot, Agnes
Tipton, Elizabeth
Tipton, Samuel
Reno, Catherine
Kelley, Joshua
Reno, William
Daniels, William
Daniels, Anne
Cragin, Patrick
Jobe, Abegil
Chambers, James
Tipton, Francis
Kite, Elander
Winson, Polly
Chambers, Nancy
Hudelburg, Dorothy
Brown, John
Brown, Elzee
Praley, Samuel
Praly, Mary
Cooper, Elenor
Vance, Martha
Reno, John
Duncan, John
Garland, Samuel
Cooper, Joel
McDowell, William

Book II (a) 1794 to 1803

1794

Tipton, Joseph
Denton, Isaac, Sr.
Hendrix, Solomon
Greer, Andrew
Watson, William
Williams, Edmund
Haggard, William
Tipton, Samuel
Hays, Hannah
Mulkey, Sarah
Lacy, Nancy
Clark, Nany
Jane (of color)
Anderson, Dorcas
Hudelburg, Thomas (Min.)
Odle, Mary
Edens, James
Davis, Williams

1795

Carr, John
Boyd, William
Boyd, Rebecca
Compton, John
Hogg, William
Hogg, Nancy
Boring, James
Humphreys, Polly
Medlock, William
Maxwell, Thomas
Whitson, Martha Cox
Daniels, Anne
Haggard, Polly
Gillian, (?)
Smith, Brooks
Smith, Mrs. Brooks
Bogard, (?)
Cooper, James

1796

Cox, John
Reno, Sarah
Jobe, Moses
Bowers, (?)
Matlock, Wm.
Barrow, Jane

1797

Chane, Isabel
Cox, Phoebe

(Reg. of Members of Sinking Creek Baptist Church p-2)

Scott, Abe
Stover, Daniel
Hilton, Betsy
Taylot, Isaac
Pugh, David
Pugh, Mrs. David
Miers, Peter

(A memo of money collected in 1797 for the contingencies of the church by Deacon Hendrix.) :

Nave, Peter
Greate, David
Taylor, Isaac
Maxwell, Thomas
Cooper, Joel
Poland, John
Tipton, Joseph
Williams, Edmund
Daniel, Williams
....ders Greer
Stevens, Pegg
Gillam, John
Raider, Ann
Pugh, Wm.
Crouch, James
Crouch, James
Smith, Brooks
Raider, Ann
Davis, Sarah
Kite, Elenor
Ward, Mili
Pugh, William
McFeld, Thomas
Medlock, William
Ecton, Sister
Hendrix, Mary
Bowers, Leonard
Tipton, Samuel
Humphreys, Mary
Compton, John
Bowers, Leonard
Boyd, William
Ward, Jamima
Cooper, Elenor
Stover, Phoebe
Greer, Andrew
Hider, Adam
Poland, John
Hendrix, Solomon
Mattock, Elizabeth
Tipton, Joseph
Hudelburg, Thomas
Jobe, David
Boren, William
Taylor, Isaac

(Register of Members Continued)

1798
Stevens, Henry
1799
Denton, Isaac (Jr.?)
Denton, Anne
Young, Nancy
Little, Phany
Gillian, Elizabeth

1800
Buck, Jonathan
Buck, Zuriah
Smith, Zebulon
Lacy, Phelemon
McFoule, Phoebe
Stover, Penele
Linkhorn, Polly
Ecton, Elizabeth
Cunningham, Aaron
Scott, Absolum
Cassady, Robert
Cassada, Elizabeth
Seviers, Henry
Yates, Wm.
Pugh, Rachel

Book II (b)

1797
Crouch, Joseph
Whitson, Rachel
Balis (ess), John
Worley, Sister
Booners, Wm.
Little, Sister
Stevens, Sister

(Subscription for March 16, 1799):
William Pugh
David Job
Peter Nave
John Poland
Solomon Hendrix
William Boyd
Andrew Greer
Thomas Maxwell
Joel Cooper
William Daniel
Samuel Tipton
David Greate

(Reg. of Members of Sinking Creek Baptist Church p-3)

Philemon Lacy
Elizabeth Ecton
William Bowen
Nancy Whitson
Joseph Tipton
Andrew Greer
David Greate
David Pugh
Mary Humphreys
Daniel Stover
Leonard Bowers

(List of Subscriptions found on last page)

David Job
Wm. Boyd
David Pugh
Patrick Cragin
Peter Nave
Joel Cooper
Solomon Hendrix
Thomas Maxwell
William Hogg
David Greate
Nancy, Worland
Joseph Tipton
William Daniels
William Davis
Elizabeth Ecton
John Compton
Mary Linkhorn
Samuel Tipton

(The following names are found in the general index for Book IV, beginning 1803:)
"The names of the members of the Sinking Creek Church, to-wit:"

Boren, Sarah
Solomon Hendrix
Mary Hendrix
Mary Humphreys
Susannah Humphreys
Isabella Hendry
Peter Kuhn
Robert Cassady
Mrs. Robert Cassady
Anne Raifer
Sister Burres
Sarah Boren
Sis Virgeon (?) Parker
David Pugh
Mrs. David Pugh
Casaig (?) Bowman
Elendar Wright
Mary Bogart
Margaret McNabb
Elijah Buck
Rahcel Whitson
Sis. V..tence Hunt
John Dunlap
Sis. John Dunlap
Ruth Rockhold
Mary Rockhold
Orpha Dopson
Mary Barnes
Alexander Waters
Mrs. Alexander Waters
Margaret Stevens
Joseph Cobb
Joshua Edwards
Mrs. Joshua Edwards
Sister Irvin
Elizabeth Lyons
John Nave
Elizabeth Pierce
Elizabeth Pierce
John Polin
Elizabeth Bowman
Catherine Smallin
Mary Lincoln
Abram Nave
Mrs. Abram Nave
Leonard Bowers
Mrs. Leonard Bowers
Daniel Stover
Mrs. Daniel Stover
George Lacy
Nancy Lacy
Samuel Tipton
Joseph Renfro
Mrs. Joseph Renfro
Joel Cooper
Mrs. Joel Cooper
Richard Karr
Sister Kite
Ludie Taylor
Margaret Musgrove
John Hampton
Mrs. John Hampton
Mary Dopson
Sister Boyd
Abram Odle
Mrs. Abram Odle
Jonathan Buck
Mrs. Jonathan Buck
James Edens
Mrs. James Edens
Seley Landowner
Sister Hammock
Elender McNabb
Robert Cassady
Mrs. Robert Cassady
Rebekah Little
Katherine Kelly
Elizabeth Kuhn
Susannah Young
John Lincol'n Caesar
Tipton's Bob
Hunt's James
Polly Ivy
Henry Nave
Mrs. Henry Nave
James Peters
Mrs. James Peters
Jonathan Lippe
Mrs. Jonathan Lipps
Lydia Lewis
Leah Fletcher
Mary Lincoln
Clemma Love
Thomas Evans

(Reg. of Members of Sinking Creek Baptist Church p-4)

Taken from Minute Book IV

1803

Elijah Crouch
Woods, Thomas
Pugh, William
Myers, Bro.
Bogard, Henry
Watson, Hannah
Young, Nancy
Odle, Mary
Greer, Bro.
Linville, Thomas
Linville, Jamima
Parker, John
Parker, Margaret
Reeves, Mary
Hammer, Margaret
Lovelace, Sister
Pierce, Elizabeth
Daniels, Elizabeth
Buck, Thomas
Houston, Benjamin
Redmon, Susannah

1807

Humphreys, Hannah
Willot, Polly
Kuhn, Margaret
Ginger, Chaney
Patterson, Martha
Carriger, Elizabeth
Smith, Sarah

1808

Hampton, Nancy

1809

Buck, Elijah
Polin, Polly
Kite, Bro.
Pugh, Susanah
Sanford, Robert
Sanford, Polly
Kelly, Thenchen
Denton, Martha

1810

Humphreys, Martha
Hiter, William
Hendrix, Cora
Kelley, Polly
Kelley, Caty
Irwin, Lydie
Embree, Elizabeth
Erwin, William
Pugh, Elizabeth

1803

Burres, Mary
Miller, Jacob
Brumit, Samuel
Bogard, Elizabeth
Boyd, Wm.
Marrock, Mrs. Margaret
Crager, Patrick
Bailess, Margaret

1804

Watson, Sis. Wm.
Hyder, Hannah
Hyder, Easter
Bailes, Daniel
Cassady, Elizabeth
Kuhn, Peter
Lacy, Philemon
Lacy, Mrs. Phelemon
Wright, John
Lincoln, Thomas
Lincoln, Mrs. Thos.
Rockhold, Polly
Jamima (of color)
Phares, Gideon
Dunlap, John
Dunlap, Caty
Buck, Cleopa
Black Bob (of color)
Edens, James
Black Anthony (of Color)

1813

McCray, Bro.
Black Hannah (of color)
Lacy, George
Kuhn, Elizabeth
Harris, Caty

1814

Tilson, Polly

1815

Bowman, Keziak
Viney, Stacy
Bogart, Margaret
Black Winn (of color)

1816

Renfro, Bro.
Renfro, Sis.

Lansdown, Luily
Brumit, Samuel

1817

Hamrick, Sis

1804

Hammer, Jacob
Woods, Polly
Maxwell, Thos.

1805

Woods, Rosey
Smith, Sis. Sidney
Smith, Sarah
Gresham, Sis. Aley

1806

Gray, Sarah
Threesmith, Edward
Woods, Charles
Threesmith, Elizabeth
Hammer, John

1821

Peters, James
Powers, Abigail
Evans, Thomas
Musgrove, Margaret
Hampton, John
Hampton, Mrs. John
Nave, Sarah
Nave, Elizabeth
Nave, Margaret
Buckles, Anna
Nave, Rebekah
Berry, Nancy
Carriger, Lavica
Cobb, Jacob
Cole, Seley
Hathaway, Elizabeth
Musgrove, Samuel
Evens, Clarisa
Gentry, Sarah
McFall, Susannah
Hunt, Tiner

1822

Cobb, Rebekah
Edwrads, Joshua
Edwards, Mrs. John
Carty, John
Simerly, Wilmoth

1823

Love, Bro. Saler
Miller, Nancy
Beeley, Sarah

1824

Brian, Nancy
Kuhn, Elizabeth
Barker, Gean

(Reg. of Members of Sinking Creek Baptist Church p-5)

Tipton, Elizabeth
Milsaps, Jesse
Disney, Elizabeth
1811
Wright, Polly
Wright, Henry
Wright, Elender
Bowman, Polly
Wilds, Clemmie
Buck, Barbara
Buck, Zuriah
Hannah (of color)
Bogard, Polly
Parkinson, Leah
Jeneer Humphreys
Grimsley, Wm.
Willet, Polly
Hunt, Martina
Gibson, Orpha
1812
Wright, John
Peters, Millie
1828
Hatcher, Agnes
1829
Ross, Charity
Allen, Franky
Mays, Rachel
Love, Thomas D.
Hampton, Mary
Stevens, Rebekah
Matheson, Hannah
Kuhn, Elizabeth
1830
Wright, John
Cooper, Margaret
Hatcher, Orpha
Hatcher, Asneth
1831
Cassady, John
Cassady, Elizabeth
Hatcher, Sarah
1832
Boren, Phoebe
(Note: Bayless, Pastor)
Hart, Leonard
Nave, Sarah
Threesmith, Margaret
Perry, Thomas
Perry, Mary
Broyles, John
Broyles, Eliza

1818
McCorkle, Polly
1819
McNabb, Polly
Lipps, Jonathan
Lipps, Mrs. Jonathan
Holtsclaw, Mark
Hart, Phoebe
Hart, Polly
Dougherty, Easter
1820
Nave, Henry
Nave, Mrs. Henry
Evens, Thomas
Ivy, Polly
Cobb, Joseph
Mottern, Alexander
Evens, Elender
Bowers, Valentine
Mottern, Geney
1835
Pugh, Wm.
Cooper, Joel
Wright, David
Wright, Sarah
Cassady, James
Wheeler, Elizabeth
Kuhn, Mahaly
Cassady, Franklin
Cassady, John, Jr.
Vaune, Rachel
Wilson, (?)
Sweeny, John
Broiles, (?)
Tipton, Mary
Sweeney, Susanah
Hatcher, Wm.
Tipton, Samuel
Hatcher, George T.
Hatcher, Thomas
Hatcher, John
Ensor, Madison
Hopper, Wm.
Hopper, Anne
1836
Hyder, J. Hampton
Buckner, Daniel
Buckner, Polly
Cassady, Nancy
Price, Rachel
Barnes, Catherine
1837

Hendrix, Edward
Whitson, Sarah
Perkins, Susanah
Hammer, Rebekah
Jones, James
Parker, Joseph
Miller, James
Buck, Nancy
Renfro, Fanny
1825
Tipton, Fanny
McNabb, Henry
McNabb, Edward
1827
Walther, Bisba
Owens, Elizabeth
Hammit, Sister
Thompson, Orpha
Dunlap, Sarah
Smalling, Catherine

Hyder, Jonathan
Crouch, Delcina
Hatcher, Rheuben
1842
Peoples, Asuriah
Peoples, Eliza
Barnes, Mary
Bowman, Stephen
Hatcher, Agnes
Mitchell, Sarah
Rowe, Rachel
Moore, Mary
White, William
White, Nancy
Cassady, Rebecca
Young, Rebecca
Smith, Mary
1843
Smalling, Rachel
Lyons, Sis. E. D.
1844
Duncan, Jesse D.
Swanner, Joshua
Swanner, John A.
Swanner, Mary
Matin, Mahaley
Matin, Wm.
Matin, Washington
Jefferson, Henry
Kuhn, Andrew
Kuhn, John

(Reg. of Members of Sinking Creek Baptist Church p-6)

Broyles, Sina
Perry, Nancy
Pugh, Wm.
Perry, William
1833
Nave, Tennessee
Gilbert, Isaac
Gilbert, Casey
Ellis, Charlotte
Wheeler, Wm.
Ensor, Hannah
Peoples, James
Hampton, Thomas
Hampton, Annie
Ford, Nancy
Hilton, Elizabeth
Hatcher, Elizabeth
1834
Adams, Joshua
Adams, Tabitha
Broiles, Matthew
Broiles, Annie
Carr, Richard
Hale, Temperance
Carty, John

Hampton, Mary Eliza
Owens, Macaja
Owens, Dorcas
Morgan, Mary
White, James
Nave, Susanah
Britt, Tina
1838
Nave, Henry
Nave, Mary
Hampton, Wm.
1839
Nave, Susan
Hammer, Orpha
Martin, Jamima
Lyons, Mason R.
1840
Kite, Granville
Wright, David T.
Tipton, Anthony
1841
Meyton, Nancy
Jackson, Mary
Nave, Valentine
White, Anna

McFall, Joel
McFall, D. J.
McFall, Maryanne
Cross, Susanah
Baleys, John
Jobe, Abraham
Matin, Elizabeth
Cres, Jackson
Lowdymilk, Elizabeth
1845
Nave, Wm.
Hart, Mary
Taylor, Wm. (of color)
Matin, John
Carethers, Nancy
Carr, Richard
Carr, Mrs. Richard
Hampton, Susanah
Hampton, Anna A.
Hampton, Fannie C.
Scalf, Rebecca
Carter, Thomas
Carter, Mary
Sweenie, Eli

August the 19th 1865

The Baptist Church at Sinking Creek meet after worship meet for business 1st agreed to make a new record of the members of the church,

William Pugh joined 1833
William Wheeler 1833
Duncan, Jesse 1844
Catherine Barnes 1836
A. Carr 1843
Nancy Jefferson 1834
Sarah Carr 1845
Will Jobe (of color) 1846
Nancy Hicks 1846
Richard Jefferson 1847
Marier Humphreys (oc) 1847
Mary Wolf 1850
Rebecca Murray 1852
Susanah Taylor 1850
Martha Barnes 1848
Mary Lyle 1850
James Taylor 1850
John Wolf 1852
Mary Saylor 1852
Nanerva Pugh 1852
James People 1852
John Humphreys 1855
Lucinda Hicks 1856

Archibald Caldwell joined 1859
Sarah Pugh 1859
Margaret Wolf 1859
Maryann Taylor 1859
Rachel Rowe 1860
Hannah Cooper 1854
Rachel Pugh 1854
Jane Adams 1854
Martha Jane Linville 1850
Perney Wolf 1849
Charlotte Duffield (of co) 1840
Richard Stanley 1866
Edmund Philips (of col) 1866
Landon Duffield 1866
Clema Jane Taylor 1866
Columbus Shipley 1866
Jesse Humphreys 1866
Eliza Humphreys 1866
Henry Price 1866
Wm. Taylor 1866
Marget Taylor 1866
Martha Orins 1866
Martha Jane Loudy 1866

(Reg. of Members of Sinking Creek Baptist Church p-7)

Tennessee Adams	1856	Elizabeth Wyatt	1856
Elizabeth Car	1859	Susan Carolyn Carr	1859
Martha Jane Carr	1859	John Bayless	1857
George W. Carr	1866		

Chronological History of Sinking Creek Church.

1774 or 1775 - Organized probably by Mathew Talbot and John Chastain.
1776 - Disbanded because of Indian Wars
1777 or 1778 - Reorganized by Talbot, Mulkey and Joshua Kelley
1783- Talbot moves to Georgia.
1783 - Joshua Kelley, Pastor
1783 - New building erected
1783 - Tiptons move to Tennessee.
1876 - Holston Association organized; Sinking Creek declines invitation to join
1791 - Mrs. McDowel scalped by Indians
1794 - Jonathan Mulkey, pastor
1796 - Adopt resolution against Secret Societies
1816 - Solomon Hendrix and Joseph Renfro represent Sinking Creek in Missionary meeting
1820 - Stony Creek Church Constituted.
1826 - Adherents of the 'Arian, Socinian, or Unitarian'doctrine excluded from Church.
1826 - Death of Jonathan Mulkey
1832 - Death of Thomas D. Love
1836 - Daniel Buckner joins Church, J. H. Hyder Converted.
1831 - Peter Kuhn ordained.
1842 - J. H. Hyder ordained.
1853 - Adopted resolution opposing sale of Intoxicating Liquors.
1861 to 1865 - Civil War period; Hyder Pastor
1864 - Rees Bayles died.
1923 - Reorganized by James Stout; Church remodeled.
1930 - Organized permanent Sunday School
1932 - Organized B. Y. P. U.
1935 - Organized W. M. S.
1935 - Pioneer's Homecoming Celebration.

---oOo---

Pastors of Sinking Creek Baptist Church.

Mathew Talbot	J. Hampton Hyder	Rees Bayless
Joshua Kelley	A. J. F. Hyder	William C. Newell
James Chambers	J. H. Duncan	James B. Stone
Jonathan Mulkey	Thomas H. Crouch	E. Spurgeon
James Edens	E. P. White	Irwin Lewis
E. H. Hicks	Wm. Braswell	S. W. Tindell
S. L. Buchanon	R. F. Stout	George Countryman
T. F. Roberts	James Stout	Robert Black
M. P. Upchurch	J. Craig	Erby Hodge
		Arthur Roberts

The pioneers who settled on Watanga River in 1766 to 1886 were men of sterling worth, and well fitted to become the fathers of a glorious state. They possessed courgae, patience, and above all, practical common sense. They worked hard and lived plain. They faced peril and hardship without flinching, and if threatened with the loss of liberty or rights, they arose with firm intensity o f purpose to defend these against encroachment.

Hardly had they finished the arduous task of clearing the soil and building their homes, when the need was felt for a sort of government that would restrain the evil Courses, and establish justice and authority between men. In 1772 they met at the Watanga Old Fields, formed a written Constitution, and adopted the Articles of Association, the first ever chosen by a community of American-born freemen on the continent of North America.

It is claimed by various historians that these men were unregenerate, ignorant, impoverished, irreligeous, and that no organization could be found in America with sufficient missionary zeal and power to penetrate the wilderness and proclaim the gospel in the New World. Unwarranted assertions, every one of them.

The impelling forces that turned the face of the colonist westward to seek his home in the dangerous wildreness, had religion for its chief incentive - the dislike for the servile supporters of the King, and an increasing desire for liberty and democracy - the conflict between the King's soldiers and the Regulators in North Carolina - and the outbreak of religious persecutions in Virginia.

In 1774, the center of population was at Sycamore Shoals. Another settlement extended from Wolf Hills in Virginia. Religion then, as now kept in step with the settlers as they advanced on the frontier.

Two churches were built - one at Sinking Creek near Sycamore Shoals, the other in Sullivan County near Bledsoe's Fort. Due to the Indian Wars of 1775-6, they were, for a little while, disbanded, to be revived when peace was again restored to the settlers.

---oOo---

TENNESSEE

RECORDS OF CARTER COUNTY

MINUTES OF SINKING CREEK BAPTIST CHURCH VOL. III
1803 - 1879

COPYING HISTORICAL RECORDS PROJECT
Official Project No. 465-44-3-115

COPIED UNDER WORK'S PROGRESS ADMINISTRATION

MRS. JOHN TROTWOOD MOORE
STATE LIBRARIAN & ARCHIVIST, SPONSOR

MRS. ELIZABETH D. COPPEDGE
DIRECTOR OF WOMEN'S & PROFESSIONAL PROJECTS

MRS. PENELOPE JOHNSON ALLEN
STATE SUPERVISOR

MRS. MARGARET HELMS RICHARDSON
PROJECT SUPERVISOR

COPIED BY
MRS. VERA E. SHELL

TYPED BY
MRS. CARRIE B. STUART

FEBRUARY 22, 1939

CARTER COUNTY

MINUTES OF SINKING CREEK BAPTIST CHURCH VOL. III
1803-1879

INDEX

Note: Page numbers in this index refer to those of the original volume from which this copy was made. These numbers are carried in the body of the manuscript within parenthesis, as (P. 124)

C

R

ERRATA

These names were omitted in copying index.

MINUTES OF SINKING CREEK BAPTIST CHURCH
VOLUME III

Feb. 19th 1803 - 1879

As the professors of Christianity are so divided in their Principle and practice that they cannot commune Together: We believe it necessary to Covenant and a-Gree and reduce to writing a short scatch of our principle: Also those Socials and relative duties Injoin[d] on us as Church members: which we believe was practiced of old times: Amongst the people of God as may appear from the following passages of Scriptures Viz &--- Joshua 24 chap 25 Vers- 2[d] Kings 23[d] chap 2 & 3 verses- Nehemiah 9th Cap. 38 vers Jeremiah 50th Chap 5 vers 2 Chronicles 15th Chapt & 12 vers and other Similar passages-

- And Passing by the Several Sects of Pedobaptist and antopedobaptist with whome we cannot a gree such as the Seven day baptist the no Sabbath baptist and those that Dip 3 times in baptism with all of whom we think it not Expedient to Commune that due order may be maintained in the house of God..and Disputes may be avoide[d] yet So as that we do not shut out of our friendship by Esteem those Christians who only Differ from us in Contract assention But as a Distinct Society Embody ourselves under the following rules regulations and articles JC. JC. JC.

1[rst] We believe in one only true and living God Father Son and holy Ghost and that these three are one God Equal in power and glory-

2nd We believe in his Soveriegnty in us and over us & that he has a right to Command & Dispose of (p II) us according to his purpose & that it is our Duty to Submit to and obey him in all things 3rd We believe the holy Scriptures in the old and New Testament to be the only Safe and infalible Revelation of his will made known to men and as such and an Infallible rule for faith and practice 4th We believe it is the office of the holy Spirit to open and apply the Scriptures ot the Mysteries Therein containd for the right understanding of his will as revealed in his word)

5th We believe that we are by Nature Children of Wrath and that we are utterly Inable to recover our Selves from that fate of misery and 6th we believe that help is only laid in Jesus Christ the only begetting Gift of the father for that purpise To save all those who through grace come to the father by him and our hope of acceptance with God is only through the Imputed righteousness of Christ apprehended and receiv[d] by faith alone

7th from the Commands and Examples of Christ we hold with beleivers baptisms by Immerssion and the Laying on of hands on baptised Beleivers Perticularly the Election of free Grace by the predestination of God in Christ Jesus Effectual Calling by the holy Ghost progressive Sanctification throug Gods Grace and truth the final preservance of the Saints in Grace and holiness the resurrection of the body after Death life Everlasting to the Righteous Eternal Judgment and Death to the wicked &c &c 8th As Church members we do Promis to bear with Each others weakness (p III) And Infirmities with much tenderness not to Discover them to any out of the community where it may be avoided nor in the Community but by Gospel order as in Matt 18th Chap 15th & 17th verses and other Scriptures of like Import

9th We promis to watch over each other in love and in the Spirit of meekness Guarding against all Jesting lightness or foolish Talking which is not convenient or any other thing that doth not become the followers of the lamb- Seeking each others good in perticular- and the advancement of the Visible Kingdom of Christ universally Not forsaking the assembling of ourselves to-gather But duly to fill up our places at our respective meetings Especially our Church meetings. Except we areprovidentialy Hindred and the reason to be rendered at the next Church Meeting Provoking to love and to Good works JC. 10th We believe it our duty to use reasonable Industry For a Temporal Sustanance and to be liberal in our Communication for the worship of God and the furtherance and support of the Gospel of Christ--and for a more full decleration of our Sentiments: we refer to the Baptist Confession of faith adopted by the Philidelphia association in the year of our Lord 1742 &c &c

Finis Daniel Stover C CK

November the 22d 1807 JC.-

(p IV) (Blank)

(p V) A Presedent for Licence to Preach.

To all whom it may Concern

This is to certify that Bearer Blank is a regular Member in our Communion and has been Call,d into the work of the Ministry So far as to preach the Gospel and Exercise his Talent in teaching When God in his Providence may call him

Done by order of the Church at Blank Meeting House in Blank County and State Blank 1

JONATHAN MULKEY
DANIEL STOVER
G C K

State of Tenn. Steate of

(p VI) A presedent for dismissing mem

A presedent of a Letter of Dismission

The Church of Christ at Sinking Creek Carter County State of Tennessee: Holding Beleivers Baptism By Immersion the doctrians of Eternal and perticular Elections through the predestination of Christ Jesus from all Eternity with all the articles of the Baptist Confession of faith adapted by the philidelphia assc. &c

To any other sister Church of the faith and order. Greeting &c.

Whereas our beloved Blank hath this day made application for a letter of dismission thin may therefore Certify to you that He or She is a member in full union with us and and when Join,d to any other Sister Church of the Same Faith and order Dismisst from us.

Done by order of the) DANIEL STOVER
Church this day of 1823) C CLERK

(p VII) Names of the Members of The Sinking Creek Church To Witt- &c-

Solomon Hendrix 1
& wife
Mary Hendrix 2
Mary Humphries 3
Susannah Humphries-Decesd November 1821 4
Jabareller Hendry Dismisst p 5
Peter Kuhn 6
Robert Casady & wife 8

(Rest of page cut off)

(p X) Blank at top, Bottom cut off

(P. 1) February the 9th 1803

The Church met at Elijah Crouches according to appointment and after worship proceeded To Business as follows 1^rst^ Brother Daniel Stover appointed Clark by the unanimous voice of the Church adjour^d^ till meeting in Course at Broth Bucks &c-

March the 19th 1803

The Church met at Jonathan Bucks according to appointment and after worship proceeded to Business as Follows 1^rst^ Receiv^d^ Thomas Wood under the watch care of this Church by recommendation 2nd Brth Jonathan Buck came forward and acknowledged that he had done Contrary to Church Decipplen for preaching the Gospel without obtaining lave of the this church he now begs leaves of the Church to preach the Gospel which was granted him by the unanimous voice of the Church
Adjourn^d^ till meeting in Course at Sinking Creek

April the 16th 1803

The Church met according to appointment and after Worship proceeded to busness as follows 1^rst^ On motion that Brth Wm. Phugh Cite Brother Mires to next Church meeting 2nd Received Margret Bogart by Experience adjour,d till meeting in Course at Sinking Creek

(P. 2) May the 14th 1803

The Church met at Sinking Creek meeting house according to appointment after worship proceeded to Business as Follows &c. 1^rst^ the Reference from Last meeting & Brought forward concerning Broth Mires he has not attended according to Citation the matter is prospon^d^ Broth Pugh contimue the Churches messenger to Cite Bro^th^ Mires to next meeting.
A door open,^d^ for the Reception of members Receiv^d^ 4 By Experience to wit.. Henry Bogart Senr Hannah Watson Nancy Young & Mary Odle adjour,^d^ till meeting in Course at Sinking Creek

June the 14th 1803

The Church met acording to appointment after worship Proseeded to Business as follows &c the reference from Last meeting attended too Brother Mires has a Second time neglected to attend under this consideration The Church thinks him worthy of Cencure untill a further Hearing we therefore appoint Br^{n} Greer and Wm. Pugh to labour with him and to Cite him to next meeting 2^{d} A door open,d for the reception of Members
Reciev,^{d} Thomas Linville & Jemima his wife by Letter
Adjour^{d} till meeting in Course at Sinking Creek &c &c ---

(P. 3) JULY the 16TH 1803

The Church met at Sinking Creek acording to appointment and after worship proceeded to Business as Follows 1^{rst} the Reference from last meenting Call^{d} for concerning Bro. Mires he has not attended the Church to give Satisfaction for the Charge Laid against him as he has been Chagerd for getting drunk and Selling a parcel of land a Second time We therefore think our duty to Exclude him from fellowship no more to be of us neither are we to be charged with his futer Conduct 2d On Motion that their be a Delegate Chosen to attend our next association Chosen to wit Solomon Hendrix
Adjour^{d} till meeting in Course at Sinking Creek

AUGUST the 20th 1803

The Church met at Sinking Creek meeting House according to adjournment after worship proceeded to Business as follows 1^{rst} A door open^{d} for the Reception of members Reced^{d} 5 by Experience to wit.. John Parker Margret Parker Mary Reeves Mary Burres Jacob Miller adjour^{d} till meeting in Course at Sinking Creek &c &c

(P. 4) The Church met at Sinking Creek meeting house according to adjournment after worship proceeded To Business as follows 1^{rst} A Door open^{d} for the Reception of Receiv^{d} two By Experience to wit. Samuel Brummitt Elisabeth Bogard Second on Motion made & is agreed that Wm. Pugh be appointed To Cite Brother Wm. Boyd to next Church meeting 3^{d} on motion it is agreed that B^{r} Solomon Hendrix Be appointed to Cite B^{r} Joseph Tipton To our next meeting in Course Adjour^{d} till next meeting in course &c &c

NOVEMBER the 19th 1803

The Church met according to adjournment after worship proceeded to Business as follows &c
1^{rst} The matter relative to Brother Boyd Call^{d} for and Postpond 2 the matter relative to Brother tipton cal^{d} forward and postpond 3 on Motton is agreed that Brother Bowers Be appointed to go and see Brother Greer concering his Delay about the meeting House
adjourd till meeting in Course

(P. 5) DECEMBER the 17th 1803

The Church met at B^{r} Hendrix after worship proceeded to Business as follows 1st Brother Boyd being Cited to come forward to next Church meeting came forward and gave Satisfaction for his misconduct-
2nd Brother Tipton having been previously Suspended for his misconduct was restord on his giving Satisfaction Lastly adjourd till meeting in course to be held at Jesse Whitson--
(Note written in later) Refference made by Henry M Saylor in the year 1903)

January the 14th 1804

The Church met at Jesse Whitson after worship proceeded to Business as follows 1rst Br Wm Pugh Br Wm Boyd & Br Abram Bogard appointed to Superinted the Covering of the meeting Hous 2 adjourd till meeting in Course at Br Sollomon Hendrix

February the 18th 1804-

The Church met at Br Hendrix acording to adjournment after Worship proceeded Business as follows 1st Sister Margret Matlock applyed for letter of Dismission and Issued acordingly 2 adjoud till meeting in cours at Sinking Creek meeting House

(P. 6) March the 17th 1804

The Church at Sinking Creek meeting hous aco to adjournment after worship proceeded to Bu-- as follows 1st Brother patrick Cragen applyd For letter of Dismission which was granted and Issued accordingly 2d adjourd till meeting in Course at Sinking Creek &c --

April the 14 1804

The Church met according to apointment after worship proceeded to business as follows Nothing to be recorded
Adjourd till meeting Course

May the 19th 1804

The Church met at Sinking Creek meeting hous according to adjournment after Worship Proceeds to Business as follows 1st the Church Covenant being Read and approv,d of 2 on motion and Seconded the Communion Season to Commenc on the third friday in August on Motion Made and Seconded that Broth Jonathan Buck and Br Wm. Pugh be appointed by the Church to Labour with Br Absolom Scott and Mary Burres and make report at the next Church meeting adjourd till meeting in Course at Sinking Creek

(P. 7) June the 16th 1804

The Church at Sinking Creek meeting house according to adjournment after Worship Proceeded to Business as follows 1rst The reference from last meeting being Cald for Concerning Bro. Scott & Sister Burres The report of the Brethren Says which is Said to be Settled 2d on motion that their be a member appointed as a Deligate to the association at Cherokee the 2 Friday in August next Jonathan Buck the Churches Choice for the purpose & 3d Margret Bailes movd for a Dismision which was granted by the unanimous voice of the Church adjourd till meeting in course at Sink Creek

July the 14th 1804

The Church met at Sinking Creek according to appointment after Worship proceeded to Business as Follows 1rs Nothing to be recorded adjourd till meeting in Cours

August the 17th 1804

The Church met at Sinking Creek meeting hous according to adjournment after worship Proceeded to Business as follows the minutes of the association read and approv,d Adjour[d] till the Ensueing day
(P. 8) The Church met According to adjournment and after Sermon proceeded to Business as follows 1[rst] Brother Odle brought a Charge against Sister Acton In consiquence of her taken an oath the Church think it her Duty to Cite Sister Acton to the next Church meeting
Bro W[m] Pugh & David Pugh the Churches Messengers A Difficulty between B[r] A. Scott and Sister N. Wattson Brought forward the Church think Duty to Send members as a Committee to try to gain Satisfaction appoint to wit Leonard Bowers Joseph Tipton John Parker & Solomon Hendrix and to make report to the next Church meeting 3[d] on motion it is agreed that Bro Solomon Hendrix Be appointed to attend the committee at the Mockesson Gapp adjoun[d] till meeting in Course

September the 15th 1804

The Church met at Sinking Creek according to appointment after worship proceeded to Business as follow The matter relative to Sister Acton brought forward and upon Examination She being found guilty of the Charge Laid against her By B[r] Odle in Consequence of her taken an oath which we Look upon her not to be Clear in
We therefore Declare her the Said Sister Acton to be no more of us Neither are we to be Charged with her futer Conduct (P. 9) the matter relative to Brother Scott and Sister Wattson brought forward and the report of the Brethern says the have gaind Satisfaction & A Door open[d] for the reception of members recev[d] one by Experience to wit..Hannah Hyder adjour[d] till meeting in course

October the 20th 1804

The Church at Sinking Creek according to adjournment after worship proceeded to Business as follows: 1[rst] Sister Ann Dannels requested a Letter of Dismission on acount of her removal which was granted and Issued accordingly
2[d] Information being Rec[d] by this Church that Sister Jemima Young has Commun[d] with the presbeterian Brethern and Said Conduct being Contray to our order the Church appointe Brethren W[m] Pugh Rob[t] Cassaday to visit her and cite her to next Church meeting
3[d] a door open[d] for the Reception of Members Rec[d] to wit) Leah Linvill by Experience
4th Brother Adam Hyder & Easter his wife Request Letters of Dismission from this Church on acount of their removal which was granted..and Issued accordingly adjour[d]

November the 17th 1804

The Church at Sinking Creek and after worship proceeded to Business as follows ---Brethren appointed to Cit Jemima ---- Do report and say that said
(P. 10) Jemima Confesseth the She did Commune as Before Stated but does not repent of her Conduct on which account She is Declar[d] out of Fellowship with us Neither are we to be Charged with her futer Conduct 2 Door open[d] for the reception of members Rec[d] by Experience one to wit Jacob hammer and Baptisd the following Day.

December the 15th 1804

The Church met at Sinking Creek and after Worship proceeded to Business as

follows W[m] Boyd came and Inform[d] this Church that He was Drunk and was offering to fight He Desir[d] this Church to Exclud him we thinking his Crime to be worthy of Excommunication we therefore Declare the Said Boyd to be out of fellowship with us neither are we to be Charged with his futer Conduct
2[d] Report Says that Sister Polly D Woods is in pregnant state Brethren appointed to Cite her to next meeting to wit)
John Parker &
Robert Casada
3[d] on motion it is agreed that their be Brethren appointed as a Committee to Settle a Despute between Daniel Bailes & Elisabeth Casaday Chose to wit) Joseph Tipton Leonard Bowers Jacob Hammer Jonathan Buck Solomon Hendrix Abraham Bogart Joel Cooper Who are to make report at the next Church meeting adjourn[d]

(P. 11) January the 19th 1805

The Church met at Sinking Creek meeting House according to appointment after worship proceeds To Business as follows &c the reference Cal[d] for from last meeting Concerning Polly Woods she has not attended acording to Citation but the report of the Brethron Says She has Confest herself Guilty of the Charge We Therefore Declare her out of Fellowship with us Neither are we to be Charged with her futer Conduct.
2[d] the Report of Brethren that were Chosen to Settle the greivens between Daniel Bailes and Elisabeth Cashaday Says the have Settled the Despute
3[d] adjourn[d] till meeting in Course.

February the 16th 1805

The Church met at Sinking Creek according to appoint after Worship proceeded To Business as follows 1[rst] a matter of Difficulty Between Joseph Tipton & Thomas Maxwell Brought Before the Church and Motion made and Seconded that B[r] Leonard Bowers Solomon Hendrix & John Polin Labour with them and make report at the meeting 2[d] Motion made and Seconded that Sister Nancy Worley Be Cited to next meeting B[r] Leonard Bowers the Churches messenger adjourn[d] till meeting Course

(P. 12) April the 20th 1805

The Church met acording to appointment after Divine Service proded to Business as follows first the matter relative To Brother Tipton & Maxwell Brought forward the report of the Brethren say the have Settled it 2[d] the matter relative to Sister Nancy Worley prosepond till next Church meeting adjourn[d]

May the 18th 1805

The Church met at Sinking Creek meeting house according to appointment after worship proceeded to Business as follows firs to matter Relative to Sister Nancy Worly Cal[d] for Not Settled But Continued till Next meeting adjourd

June the 15th 1805

The Church meet according to appointment after worship proceeded to Business as follows the mater relative to Sister Nancy Worley Brought forward Viz:- Leaving her family in a Disorderly manner which we think Contrary to

Good order Espesially more for present ill Conduct in giving the Church offence in her dealing with her where in She has ripend herself for Excommunication We Declare Her the Said Nancy Worley to be nor more of us nor are we to be Charged with her futer Conduct (P. 13) 2 on motion that thefe be a Deligate appoint[d] to attend our next association Chosen to wit: Abraham Odle adjourn[d]

August the 17th 1805

The Church met at Sinking Creek acording to appointment after Sermon proceded to Business first the minutes of the association red & approved 2 Brother Thomas Maxwell & his wife apply[d] for Letters of Dismission & granted and order[d] the Clark to Issue the Same 3[d] Bro tipton Censur,d for publick Disorder adjourn[d] &c

September the 14th 1805

The Church met acording to appointment after Worship Proceeded to Business as follows 1[rst] Bro tipton came forward and requested the reason that the Church had Censurd him the Church answer was for publick Disorder He then got much Displeased with the Churches proceedence accuses the Church with unjust Dealings with hin and went out in a very great rage the Church then in a unanimous Concent Excludes him from fellowship nor are we to be Charged with his future Conduct 2 Charge brought before the Church agains Rosey Wood using some very abrupt Language She being Dealt with in a gospel order her reply was that if she had it to do again she would repeat the same the Church think her Worthy of Exclusion Declare her the said Rosey Wood out of fellowship with us neither are we to be Charged with her future Conduct (P. 14) 3[d] on Motion made and Seconded that B[r] Brummet and Brother Wood be cited to next Church meeting on a count of certain difficulty Between them John Parker and Robert Casaday the Churches Messenger adjourn[d] &

October the 19th 1805

The Church met according to appointment after Worship proceeded to Business as follows The matter relative to Bro Brummet and Bro Wood Brought forward Brother Wood found in the rong and will not be Concicted the Church think him worthy of censure from Church privaledges till further conviction 2 Sister hannah Hyder a Sister Mary hammar apply[d] for letters of Dismission which was granted and Issued accordingly adjournd

November the 16th 1805

The Church met at Sinking Creek meting house according to appointment after worship proceeded to Business as follows 1[rst] &c the relative to Brother Wood brought forward and for his neglecting to her the Church he is Excluded from fellowship By the unanimous voice of the Church
2[d] the Church has rec,d information and has Been Sufficiently othenticated that thomas Maxwell is Guilty of Slander in a way of Disorder for which he is Excluded from fellowship with this Church adjourn[d]

(P. 15) December the 14th 1805 1805

The Church met according to appointment after Worship proceeded to Business as follows &c (on Motion made and Seconded that the Delinquents Be Sited to Church meeting Bro Absolom Scott to be cited Samuel Brummet the Churches messenger Sister Lissey Smith and Sarah Smith be cited to Next meeting Solomon Hendrix the Churches messenger Sister Aley Grissem be cited to next Church meeting Joel Cooper the Churges Messenger adjournd &c

January the 18th 1806

The Church met according to appointment after Worship proceeded to Business as follows 1rst the reference cald for Br Scott being cited has not attend it is therefore Continued till next Meeting in Cours.
adjourned &c ------

February the 15th 1806

The Church met acording to appointment after worship proceded to Business as follows The matter relative to Brother Scott Cald for He has a Second time refusd to attend the Churches Citation he conduct has ripend him for Exclusion yet by the request of one member only Suspend him from Church privaledges till next meeting and continue his citation John Parker Samuel Brumit the Churches messengers this day Mary Hammer returnd her letter of Dismision which She Recd or to her the 19th 1805 adjournd &c &c

(P. 16) March the 15th 1806--

The Church met acording to adjournment after Worship proceeded to Business as follows &c the matter relative to Bro Scott Cald for Bro who Came forward and gave the Church mutual Satisfaction and is restored to a Seat adjourd ----

April the 15th 1806

The Church met acording to appointment after Worship proceeded to Business as follows &c &c
a doow opend for the Reception of members 2 Receivd by Letter to wit Sarah Gray & Elisabeth Pearc Adjourd &c -----

May the 17 1806

The Church met acording to appointment after Worship proceeded to Business as follows &c A Door opend for the Reception of members Receid one by letter)to wit(Edward Threewitt Appliation made to the Church by Bro Greer of a matter of Grievence between him and Sister Pugh is agreed by the Church to Chose members as a Committee to Settle the Desput Chose Solomon Hendrix Ab Bogart Jacob Hamer Ab Odle John Parker to meet at Sister pugh,s on Jun 6 and tö make Report at the next Church meeting adjourd till &c--

(P. 17) June the 14 1806

The Church met acording to appointment after Worship proceeded to Business as Follows &c--------
The matter relative to Broth- Greer and Sister Pugh Cald for the report of the Committee Say it is Settled to mutual Satisfaction 2d Brother Charles Woods is restord to a Seat and Requests Dismission which was granted 4th appointed Bro Samuel Tipton as a Deligat to attend the association adjournd-

July the 19 1806

The Church met acording to appointment and after worship proceeded to Business as follows 1rst A Door opend for the reception of members. Recd By letter Elisabeth Threewitt 2 By Expereinc (to wit) John Hammer Margrit Hammer his wife adjourd &c------

August the 16th 1806

The Church met acording to appointment after worship proceded to Business as follows 1rst Broth John Parker Wm Pugh appointed to attend an Inquest at Gapp Creek in Septeber allso appointed Bro Jonathan Buck Leonard Bowers to attend the Inquest at Mcfeterses Bend on October 3d as a Committee the Church Reced Information By report that Hannah Wattson is in a pregnant State we appoint Brethren Solomon Hendrix Jeol Cooper to Cite her to next Church meeting.

(P. 18) October the 17th 1806

The Church met at Sinking Creek according to appointment after worship proceeded to Business the Matter relative to Sister Hannah Wattson Cald for the report of Brethren Say that She obsconded herself from them and has refusd to obey the calls of the Church Her Charge Has been Sufficiently authicenticated & under this Circumstance we declare her out of Fellowship with us Neither are we to be Charged with Her futer Conduct Brth Jonathan Buck made application to the Church For Written Licence to preach the Gospel which was granted by a unanimous voice & adjurd

November the 15 1806

The Church met and after worship proceeded to Business as follows 1 Door opend for Reception of members Recv,d one by Experience (to wit) John Nave and at his request to be Baptisd at Isaac Lincoln 5th Sabbath in this month for the Conveniency of his family &c adjourd At a Cald meeting last Saturday in November Sister Iovelace & Elisabeth Pearce Recevd by Experience Baptisd Elisabeth perce & John Nave the Insueing Day

(P. 19) December the 20th 1806

The Church met acording to appointment after worship proceeded to Business as follows 1rst Elisabeth Daniels aplyd for & obtaind a letter of Dismission 2 appointed Brth Stover and Br Bowers to cite Thomas Buck to next Church meeting adjournd &c-----

January the 17th 1807-

The Church met and after worship proceeded to Business as follows the matter relative To Brother Thomas Buck cald for who has attended acording to citation and gave the Church Satisfaction &c 2d Door opend for the Reception of members Receivd one by Experience viz Benjamin fauster on Motion that our next Church meeting be at Mr Carrigers on Watauga Adjourd

February the 14th 1807

The Church met according to appointment after worship Proceeded to Business as follows &c A Door opend for the reception of Members Recevd 2 By Experien viz Abraham Nave Susanna Redmon adjournd

March the 14th

The Church met and after worship proceeded to Business as follows &c 1rst Thomas Woods applyd for Dismission To Join the Cherokee Church as it is more Convenient to him which was granted at his request Adjourd

(P. 20) April the 18th 1807

The Church met and after worship proceeded to Business as Follows--Nothing taken to record adjourd----

May the 16th 1807

The Church met and after Sermon proceeded to Business as follows A Door opend for the reception of members None offerd So adjourd---

June the 20th 1807

The Church met and after Worship proceeded to Business A Door opend for the Reception of members Recd Hannah Humphres by Experience and baptisd ensuing day 2 appointed Samuel tipton as an Deligate to attend our next association at Sinking Creek adjournd &c

July the 18th 1807

The Church met at Sinking Creek according To appointment after Worship proceded to business 1rst a door opend for the reception of members Recevd one by Experience to wit Polley Willot and baptisd the same day Brother John Parker came forward and Confest to the Church He was guilty of offering to fight but was prevent so that he did not commit the fact but Seemd rather to Say that he would fight rather than be called a coward the Church thinking his acknowledgment not to be agreeable with gospel order we do Suspend him from Church privelidge till Church meeting To see wether the Leprosy will spread adjourd

(P. 21) Saturday the 16th of October 1807 &c

The Church met at Sinking Creek according to appointment. after worship proceeded to Business as Follows 1rst the minutes of the association read and approvd 2 Sister Margret Kuhn applyd and obtaind a Letter of Dismission 3d Brothr John parker came forward and gave the Church Satisfaction and was restord to his seat adjournd till tomorrow Met according to adjournment and after Sermon proceeded to Business as follows 1rst a door opend for the reception of members Received Chainey Ginger by letter 2 Sister Sarah Smith cited to next Church meeting to assign the reason why She has so Long Deliquency Sooomon Hendrix Henry Bogart the churches messenger 3 appointed Bro Daniel Stover an assistant Deacon adjournd till meeting in course &c

November the 14th 1807

The Church met at Brother Hendrix after Worship proceeded to Business as follows Brother Bowers and Tipton from a appointment from Last meeting to Look into a matter respecting plank sawd for the use of the meeting house Do report and say that having made Diligent Enquiry therein there is none to be found 2d brn Hendrix and Bogart Reappointed to visit Sister Sarrah Smith 3d an order Issue Letters of Dismission to Sister Elley McNabb 4th adjournd.

(P. 22) Saturday the 19th of December 1807

The Church met at Br Hendrix according to adjournment and after worship Proceeded to Business as follows 1rst the refferance from Last meeting being Call d for The Brethren who were appointed to cite Sister Sarrah Smith Say She Has gave them no special reason why she has Long Delinquent from Church Church meeting She gave no Satisfaction wether She would attend next meeting or no it appears that She Has not attended. We think her crime to be worthy of Excommunication we therefore Declare Her to be out of Fellowship with us Neither are we to be Charged with her futer Conduct 2d adjournd &c &c --

Saturday the 16th of January 1808

The Church met at Br Hendrix according to adjournment after Worship proceeded To Business as Follows 1rst Brother Jonathan Buck appointed to Cite Thomas Buck To next Church meeting 2nd adjournd till next

Saturday the 20th of February 1808

The Church met Sinking Creek acording to adjournment after Worship proceeded to Business as follows 1rst Br Thomas Buck has not attended his Citation it is therefore contimued Bro Jon Buck remains the messenger a Motion is made that Sister Kit be cited to our next Church meeting B Kite Be the Churches Messenger adjournd.

(P. 23) Saturday the 19th of March 1808

The Church met according to adjournment after worship proceeded to Business follows 1rst Br Thomas Buck come forward and gave general Satisfaction 2nd Sister Kite came ford according to citation and gave Satisfaction 3rd opend a Door for the reception of members Receiv,d Two by Verble Testimony to wit- Joshua Edwards & wife one by Experence to wit Martha Patterson 4th adjourned

Saturday the 16th of April 1808

The Church met at Sinking Creek acording To adjournment after worship proceeded to Business follows Nothin taken to record adjornd ---

Saturday the 23rd of May 1808

The Church met acording to appointment after worship proceeded to Business as Follows &c -
The Matter relative to Sister Elisabeth Carriger Taken up and Lade over till next meeting adjord till meeting in Course &c &c

July the 16th 1808

The Church met and after Divine Service proceeded to Business as follows 1rst appointed Brother Jonathan Buck as Deligate to attend the association at bent Creek the Second friday in August next adjournd till meeting in Course--

(P. 24) August the 20th 1808 the Church met at Sinking Creek according to adjournment after Worship proceeded to Business as Follows 1rst Bro Absolom Scott & Br John Parker & Margret Parker his wife applyd for a Dismission to Join the Cherokee Church as it is more convenient for them to attend which was granted accordingly 2d adjor^{d} till meeting in Course

September the 19th 1808

The Church met at Sinking Creek acording to appointment after Worship proceeded to Business as follows 1rst Sister Nancy Hampton applyd for Dismission which was granted accordinly Ajord &c-

(P. 25) January the 14th 1809

The Church met at Br Hendrix and Divine Service Proceeded to Business as Follows 1rst A Door opend for the reception of members Recd one by Experience to wit) Elijah Bucke Adjourd &c ----

February Nothing recorded &c

Mrch the 19th 1809

The Church met at Br Hendrix and after Divine Service proceeded to Business as follows 1rst 4 members applyd for Dismission which was granted to wit Elija Buck Sarra Jane Wood Abraham Bogart and wife adjourd

April the 15th 1809

The Church met at Sinking Creek and after Worship proceeded to Business as follows 1rst A door opend for the Reception of members Recd one by Experience to wit Polly Polin 2d appointed Brethren to wit Jonathan Buck Samuel Tipton to visit Brother Kite to cite him to next Church meeting allso appoint Br Bogart to Cite Sister Little to next Church meeting adjournd

(P. 26) May the 20th 1809

The Church met at Sinking Creek acording to appointment after Worship Proceeded to Business as follows &c 1rst the brethren that visit Brother Kite has not attended the matter was Prospond 2d Sister Little Has not attended but gave Satisfaction by the Churches messenger 3rd A Door oppend for the reception of members Recevd one by Experience to wit Susana Young 4th as there appears a matter of Difficulty between Wm Pugh and his mother they make application to the Church Chose Brn as a Committee which was granted, and Chose to wit) Sollomon Hendrix Samuel Tipton Leonard Bowers John Nave Abraham Odle and to make report at the next Church meeting adjournd &c—

June the 17th 1809

The Church met according to adjournment and after Divine Service Proceeded to Business as follows the Brethren that were appointed Settle Betwen Wm Pugh and Susanna pugh his mother came forward and was Recivd and the Committee Dischargd (P. 27) 2d the matter relative to Br Kite Cald for and Br Kite cam forward and gave general Satisfaction A Door oppend for the reception of members recd by Experience Robert Sanford and Polly Sanford his wife recivd Sister Ervin by recommendation 3rd Solomon Hendrix Jonathan Buck appointed Deligates to attend the Lick Creek association held on 2dFriday in August next adjourd

July Nothing recorded

August the 19th 1809

The Church met according to adjournment and after Worship proceeded to Business an 1rst as the matter Between Br Wm Pugh and his mother seems Not to Be Decided according to the report of the Committee is agreed to Send Brn to visit them and cite them to next Church meeting an get such Satisfaction as may be required Chosen Bren Solomon Hendrix Robert Sanford 2nd on report of some misconduct Transacted by old Black Jem Sent Brother Bower and Br Tipton to cite her to next meeting

(P. 28) October the 19th 1809

the Church met according to adjournment after Divine Service proceeded to Business as Follows 1rst the matter relative to Br Pugh Brough forward the Church agree to Lay him under Censure Br Kinchen Kelly appointed to cite Sister Stevens to next Church meeting 2 adjournd &c-

November the 18th 1809

The Church met according to adjournment after Worship proceeded to Business as follows 1rst the matter as it respects Br Wm Pugh and Sister Pugh Laid over till next meeting 3d Sister Stevins came forward and gave the Church general Satisfaction
4th Brother Hendrix appointed to Cite Jacob Hammer and wife to next Church meeting
5th Also Bro Leonard Bower to cite Daniel Stover
6th adjourd till meeting in Cours

December the 16th 1809

The Church met agreeable to adjournment and after Divine Service proceeded to Business as follows the matter relative to Br Pugh Brought for ward the Church yet agree to wait with him till next meeting
Brother Hammer and wife has not attend the Church agree to wait till next meeting
(P. 29) 3d Daniel Stover came forward and gave Satisfaction
4th A Door oppend for the reception of Members Reced by Experience Martha Denton
6th adjournd till meeting in Course

Saturday the 20th of January 1810

The Church met according to adjournment and after Worship proceded to Business as follows 1rst The Charge as it Concserns Br Pugh Brought forward and that is in regard of his refusing to give his mother the thirds of her Land and then making application to the Church for a Committee to Decide the matter a Grees to what the Committee had done and flees from that and asecond promising the Church to recount his bargain with his Br David and stand to what the Committee first had agreed upon and then did not fulfill his promise The Church Consider his Conduct worthy of Excomminication We therefore Declare him the Said Wm Pugh out of fellowship with us Neither are we to be Charged with his future Conduct.
2 A Charge brought against Sister Martha Whitson in regard of her removal and not applying for a Letter of Dismission we think her Conduct Worthy of <u>Conclusion</u> We Declare her out of Fellowship

(P. 30) February the 17th 1810

The Church met according to adjournment after Divine Service proceeded

to business as follows
1rst Catarine Hammer gave Satisfaction 2nd a door open^{d} for the reception Receiv^{d} one by Letter to wit Levicy Humphres 3^{d} adjourned till meeting in Course

March the 17th 1810

The Church met according to adjournment after Divine Service proceeded to business as follows 1rst after Chosing Br Wm Hiter Moderator Comeing to look into our Situation considering our priveledgeds not as great as a Church ought to be invested with there was a motion made and agreed upon & that by the general voice of the Church to Chose members to go to the Buffoloe ridge to potition for a greater Priveledges Chosen to wit B Solomon Hendrix Samuel Tipton Robert Sanford to be the Churches Messengers
2^{d} adjourn^{d} till meeting in Course &c

April the 14th 1810

The Church met according to adjournment after Worship proceeded to business as Follows 1 Chosen B Hiter Moderator
2 the report of the Brethren was heard that attd. the Buffolo ridg and their petition was reced but no answer (P. 31) The Brethren still continued.
3^{d} A Door open^{d} for the reception of Member Recev^{d} one by Experienc to wit Sabara Hendry
4 adjourn^{d} till meeting in Course &c

May the 19th 1810

Church met a Cording to adjournment af Divin Service proceeded to Business as Follows
1rst Recei^{d} Caty & polly Kelly by letter
2 Rece^{d} Lydia Erwin by Experienc
3 Sister Elisabeth Embree withdrew from this Church because Several of her Brethren were Dissatisfied with her on account of her marriage with Mr Embree who had divorced his former wife because of the sin of adultry therefore she is no more a member of this Churc
4 adjourn^{d} till meeting in Course

June the 20th 1810

Met agreeable to adjournment after Divine Service proceeded to Business as Follows
1rst A Door open^{d} for the reception of Members..Rec^{d} Three by Experience To wit Polly Henry Elender Wright and Polly Erwin
2^{d} adjourn^{d} -&c

(P. 32) July the 16th 1810

The Church met according to adjournment after Worship proceeded to Business as Follows
1rst A Door open^{d} for the reception of members Rec^{d} Three by Experience to wit Clemmy Wilds 2^{d} appointed Brirs Solomon Hendrix Jonathan Buck as Deligates to attend the next association held at the Buffoloe Ridge the Second friday in August next
3^{d} A Motion made a a Greed that their be a Communion Season in August next which Commences on the 17th day

4 Bro Joseph Tipton came forward & gave the Church general Satisfaction and was restord to his former priveledges
adjourn[d] &c

August the 17th 1810

The Church met according to adjournment after Divine Service proceeded to Business as Follows
1[rst] A Door opend for the reception of members rec[d] by Experience Wm Erwin Lucey Scanford
adjour[d]

(P. 33) September The 1810

The Church met after Worship proceeded to Business as follows &c 1[rst] application being made for letters of Dismission to wit- By ----& Rachel Cooper Elisabeth Pugh & Joseph Tipton & Elisabeth his wife which were granted and Isued accordingly Adjourn[d] till meeting in Cours

October the 1810

The Church met and after Worship proceeded to Business as follows Bro Thomas Buck is Excluded for bringing an acc[tt] in forward in Disorder against Brother Tipton and for other Disorders and &c
2[d] Bro Kite cited to attend at the Church meeting Jessee Milsaps the Churches messenger
3[d] application being made for Letters by Edward threewitt and Elisabeth his wife and Cheana Ginger which were granted and Esued accordingly adjour[d] &c

(P. 34) November the [meeting] 1810

The Church met according to appointment after Divine Service proceed to Business as Follow --
1[rst] The matter relative to B[r] Kite attended to and is prospond
2[d] Sis barbara Buck apply[d] for a letter of Dismission and Essued according
3[d] adjour[d] till meeting in Cours at Sinking Creek

December the 15th 1810

The Church met according to adjournment after Worship proceeded to Business as Follows
1[rst] Elisabeth Disney Apply[d] for and obtain[d] a Letter of Dismission
2[d] adjourn[d] till meeting in Course --

January the 19th 1811

The Church met according to adjournment after Divine Service proceeded to Business as follows 1[rst] Sister Elisabeth Bowman apply[d] for and obtain[d] a letter of Dismission adjour[d] &c

February the 16th 1811

The Church met according to appointment and after Worship proceed to Business as follows Nothing Taken to record adjour[d] &c ---

(P. 35) March the 16th 1811

The Church met according to adjournment after Worship proceeded to Business as Follows &c 1rst Sister Barbara Buck gave up her letter which She receid November the last - 2d on motion made and seconded that Sister Zeruiah Buck be cited to next Church meeting to the reason of her long absence John Nave & Jonathan Buck the Churches messengers &c
adjournd

April the 20th 1811

The Church met and after Divine Service proceeded to Business as follows &c 1rst Sister Buck came forward and gave General Satisfaction 2 Sister Chanea Ginger gave up her letter that She receivd 20 of October last 3d on motion made that Sister Barnes be Cited to next Church meeting Br Odle the Churches messenger 4th Sister Kite cited to next meeting by Jesse Milsaps adjournd till meeting in Course

May the 18th 1811

The Church met according to appointment after Worship proceeded to Business 1rst the reference Being Cald for Sister Barnes & Sister Kite came forward and gave general Satisfaction adjourd till meeting in Cour

(P. 36) June the 15th 1811

The Church met according to appointment after worship proceeded to Business as Follow
Sister Barbara buck applyd for a letter of Dismission and Isud acordingly
2d appointed Bro Hendrix as Deligate to the Ensueing association to be held at morelocks meetinghouse the Second friday in August Next. Hawkins County
3d Oppd a door for the reception of Members Receivd a negro woman named Hannah By Experience Recied polly Bogart by Experience 4 adjournd till meeting in Course

July the 20th 1811

The Church met according to adjournment after Worship proceeded to Business as F 1rst Br Jessee Milsaps came forward & Confest that he had got in a very great passion and had made use of profane Language this Church Considerd His Conduct Worthy of Censure by a Unanimous Voice & done adjourd till Meeting in Course &c--

(P. 37) August the 17th 1811

The Church met according to adjournment after Worship proceeded to Business as Follows
1rst Br Jesse Milsaps restord to his Seat
adjournd till meeting in course

September the 14th 1811

The Church met according to appointment after Worship proceded to Business as Follows 1 Chose Wm Grimsley moderator
The mater relative to B Thomas Linvill Prospond till next meeting
2 Sister Leah Parkisson Made application for a letter of Dismission which was granted and Isud accordingly Adjournd &c --

October the 19th 1811

The Church met and after Worship proceeded to Business as Follows 1rst Br Linvill came Forward and gave General Satisfaction adjour^d till tomorrow the church met according to adjournment a^d proceeded to Business Their being a matter of Difficulty Between Lenear Humphres and Polly Willet The Church thought proper to Chose a Committee Chos to wit Solomon Hendrix Wm Grimsley Leonard Bower & Daniel Stover 2^d Sister Ginger apply^d for a letter and obtain^d acordinly
(P. 38) Polly Polin apply^d for a letter of Dismission which was granted and Issue^d accordingly adjourn^d till meeting in Course.

November the 1811

The Church met and proceeded for Business Nothing to be recorded adjourn^d &c

December the 1811

The Church met and after Worship proceeded to Business as Follows Nothing taken to record adjourn^d

January 18th 1812

The Church met and worship proceeded to Business as Follows Nothing to be recorded adjour^d

February the 15 1812

The Church met and after worship proceeded to Business Nothing taken To record adjourn^d &c

March the 14th 1812

The Church met according to appointment af Worship Proceeded to Business follows Nothing Taken to record

(P. 39) April the 18th 1812

The Church met according to adjournment after Worship Proceeded to Business as Follows 1rst a door open^d for the reception of Members Rec^d one by Experience to wit Perter Kuhn 2^d Philemon Lacey & wife made application for letters of Dismission which was granted and Isue^d acordingly
3^d adjourn^d till meeting Course

May the 16th 1812

The Church met according to adjournment after Worship proceeded to Business as follows
1rst a Door opend for the reception of Members Rec^d Martener Hunt by recommendation Rec^d orpha Gibson By Experience
2 adjourn^d till meeting in Course

June the 20th 1812-

The Church met according to adjournment after Divine Worship proceeded to

Business as follows
1rst a Door open^d for the reception of members Rec^d John Wright By Experience 2 Sarah Boring came forward who formerly has Been a member of this Chuch & gave General Satisfaction for her former transgression and was restor^d to her Seat 3^d Bro Tho. Linvill and wife made application for letters of Dismission which were granted
4th adjourn^d till meeting in Course.

(P.40) July the 18th 1812

The Church met according to adjournment after Divine Service proceeded to Business Nothing taken record and adjourn^d &c

August the 15th 1812

The church met according to adjournment after Divine Service proceeded as follows 1rst on motion that their be a Communion Season to Commence on the third friday in October next 2 adjourn^d till meeting in Cours

September the 18th 1812

The Church met according to adjournment after Divine Service proceed to Business as follows 1rst open^d a door for Experience Rec^d Polly Rockhold and Black Jamme and the were baptis^d the following Day 2^d adjourn^d

October the 17 1812

The Church met according to adjournment after Divine Service proceeded to Business as follows 1rst a door open^d for the reception of members receiv^d Prudenc Patterson By Experience the Evening following Rec^d Gideon Phares at B^r Hendrix and they were Baptis^d the following day.

(P. 41) November the 14 1812

The Church met acording to adjournment after Divine Service proceeded to Business as follows a door opend for Experience Received John Dunlap

December the 19th 1812

The Church met acording to adjournment after divine Service proceeded to Business as follows.
1rst a door open^d for Experience Rec^d 4 By Experience To wit Caty Dunlop Cleophe Buck Black Bolk & James Edens
2^d on motion made that Gideon Phares be cited to next Church meeting Samuel Brummit the Churches messenger
3^d adjourn^d till meeting in Course

January the 16th 1813

The Church met acording to appointment after Worship proceeded to Business as follows
The Citation from last meeting brought forward as it Concerns Gideon Phares He has not attended his meeting the Charge therefore as it Stands against him is such that he is guilty of Sriping to fight and beating and runing a foot race. and as he has not attended to give the Church Satisfaction we think his Conduck worthy of Excommunication we therefore Declare him out of

Fellowship 2 a door open^d for reception of members Receiv^d Black Anthony By Experience adjorn^d

(P. 42) February the 20th 1813

The Church meet and after Divine Service proceeded to Business as follows 1^rs receiv^d Bro McCray by Recommendation adjourn^d till meeting course

March the 20th 1813

The Church met and after Divine Service Proceeded to Business as Follows 1^rst application was made for a letter of Dismission for Black Hannah which was granted & Issue^d accordingly 2^d adjourn^d

April the 17th 1813

The Church met according to adjournment and after Divine Service proceeded to Business as follows 1^rst a Door open^d for reception of Members Rec^d George Lacey By Experience and Elisabeth Kuhn By Experience 2 adj^d

(P. 43) May the 15th 1813

The Church met according to adjournment after worship proceeded to Business as follows
1^rst Chose a committee to Enquire into some reports respecting Sister Mc-Fall abusing Caty Harris Chose to wit viz Solomon Hendrix Leonard Bowers David Pugh Abraham Odle Samuel Tipton and after Investigation She was found guilty Whereupon this Church Declars against her the s^d Sister McFall to be no more of us Neither are we to be Charged with her futer Conduct
2 on Motion By Brother Hendrix that Sister Burris be cited to next meeting David Pugh the Churches Messenger 3^d adjourn^d &c

June the 19th 1813

The Church met acording to adjournment and Divine Service procee^d to Business as Follows 1^rst Sister Burres come forward and gave Satisfaction
2^d appointed Br Stover Deligate & Kinchen Kelly to attend next association on Big Pigeon Second friday in agust adjourn^d

(P. 44) July the th 1813

The Church met and after Divine Service Proceeded to Business as follows Nothing Committed to record

August the th 1813

The Church met according to appointment after Divine Service proceeded to Business as follows &c

September No meeting

October the th 1813

the Church met and after Divine Service proceeded to Business as follows (rest of page blank)

(P. 45) December the 18th 1813

the Church met at Sinking Creek and after Worship proceeded to Business as follows Nothing Committed to record adjourn^{d}

January the 14th 1814

The Church met at Sinking Creek and after worship proceeded to Business as follows Nothing committed to record adjourn^{d} &c

February the 19th 1814

The Church met at Sinking Creek and after Worship proceeded to Business as follows 1^{rst} B^{r} Thomas Buck Came forward and made recantation to the Church and was restor^{d} to his former Seat adjourn^{d} &c

March the 19th 1814

The Church met at Sinking Creek and after worship proceeded to Business as follows B^{r} thomas Buck made application for a letter which was Granted and Issued accordingly and adjourn^{d} &c

(P. 46) April the 16th 1814

The Church met and after Worship proceeded to Business as follows Nothing Committed to record adjourn^{d} till meeting in Course &c–

May the 14th 1814

The Church met according to adjournment after worship proceeded to Business as Follows Nothing Committed to record

June the 18th 1814

The Church met according to appointment after Worship proceeded to Business as on motion that B^{r} Jesse Milsaps be Cited to next Church meeting Samuel Tipton the Churches messenger 2 Brin appointed as Delegates to attend our next association to witt Solomon Hendrix & Jonathan Buck which is to be Held at the Double Spring meeting house Hawkins County 2^{d} friday in August next 3^{d} on motion is agreed that our next Coummunion be at our August meeting 4th Bro Wm Ervin & wife & Sister Polly Tilson move to be Dismist from this Church to Join that at Cherokee being more Convenient to them which was granted

(P. 47) July the 15th 1814

The Church met according to appointment after Worship proceeded to as Follows
Bro Milsaps come forward & gave Satisfaction &c &c ---

August the 19th 1814

The Church met according to adjournment after Worship proceeded as Follows 1^{rst} Bro Philemon Lacey & wife were Recev^{d} By Letter &c

September the 16th 1814

The Church met after worship proceed to Business as Follows Nothing recorded

October the 15th 1814

The Church met after Divine Service proceeded to Business as Follows
Nothing recorded

November the 18th 1814

The Church met after worship proceeded to Business as Follows
Nothing Committed to record.

(P. 48) December the 17th 1814

The Church met according to adjournment after Worship proceeded to Business as Follows
1rst Bro Bowers Came forward and gave the Church Satisfaction and was restord to his former Privileges adjournd till meeting in Course

January the 14th 1815

The Church met according to adjournment after Worship Proceded to Business as Follows Nothing Committed to record.

February the 19th 1815

The Church met according to adjournment after Worship proceeded to Business as follows
Nothing committed to record

March the 1815

The Church met according to appointment after Divine Worship Proceeded as Follows Nothing Committed to record

April the 16th 1815

The Church met according to adjournment after Divine Service proceeded to Business as Follows Nothing Committed to record

(P. 49) May the 20th 1815

The Church met according to appointment after Worship proceeded to Business as Follows 1rs Thomas Buck Receivd by Letter 2 Elijah Buck Recevd by Letter 3 William Pugh Restord to his former priveledges and at his request was Dismist adjournd &c

June the 17th 1815

The Church met according to adjournment and after Worship proceeded to Business as Follows
1rst Receivd Kezia Bowman by Letter 2d appointed Br'n as Delegates to our next Insueing association Chose to wit Solomon Hendrix and Daniel Stover adjournd &c

July the 15th 1815

The the Church met and after Worship proceeded to Business as Follows..&c
Nothing Committed to record

(P. 50) August the 18th 1815

The Church met according to appointment after Worship proceeded to Business as follows
Nothing Committed to record.

September the 16th 1815

The Church met according to adjournment after Worship proceeded to Business as follows

October the 14th 1815

The Church met and after Divine Worship proceeded to Business as Follows 1rst Rece[d] Stacey Viney by letter &c

November the 14th 1815

the Church met and after Worship proceeded to Business as follows &c.

December the 16th 1815

The Church met and after Worship proceeds to Business as follows &c

(P. 51) January the 20th 1816

The Church met according to appointment after Divine Service proceeded to Business as Follows Nothing Committed to record

February the 17th 1816

The Church met according to adjournment after Worship proceeded to Business as Follows 1rst a Door open[d] for the Reception of Members Reciv[d] one By Experience To Witt Margret Bogart Adjourn[d] &c-------

March the 16th 1816

The Church met according to adjournment after Worship proceeded to Business as follows Nothing Committed to record

April The 19th 1816

The Church met agreeable to adjournment and after Divine worship proceed to Business as follows Black Winn withdrew Her membership from this Church on acount of Some of the members being Dissatisfied with Her manner of Living with a Black man We therefore Declare against her to be no more of us neither are we to be Charged with her futer Conduct 2[d] Recev[d] Brother Renfro By Letter August the 16 Red and wife also.

(P. 52) May the 17th 1816

The Church met according to adjournment after Worship proceeded to Business as Follows Nothing Committed to record adjourn^{d}

June the 15th 1816

The Church met according to adjournment after Divine Service proceeded to Business as Follows 1^{rst} open^{d} a Door for the reception of Members Recev^{d} Eve Eden By Experience 2^{d} appointed Brother Hendrix and Jonathan Buck Deligates to the next association to be Held at Lick Creek 2^{d} friday in August next 3^{d} adjourn^{d}

July the 19th 1816 The Church met acording to adjournt after Divine Service Proceeded to Business as follows &c
Nothing Taken to record ----

August the 16th 1816

The Church met according to appointment after Worship proceeded as Follows 1^{rst} Recei^{d} Sister Renfro By Letter

(P. 53)   September the 19th 1816

The Church met according to adjournment af Divine Service proceeded to Business as Follows Nothing recorded

October the 16th 1816

The Church met according to adjourment after Worship proceeded to Business as Follows open^{d} a Door for the reception of members Recev^{d} Seily Lansdown By Experience adjourn^{d} till meeting in Course

November the 16th 1816

The Church met acording to adjournment af Worship proceeded to Business as follows &c adjourn^{d} in order Nothing recorded

December 14th 1816

The Church met according to adjournment after Worship proceeded to Business as Follows
Bro Solomon Hendrix & Joseph Renfro app'n to attend the Missionary meeting at bent Creek meeting House ond Crismas day green County.

(P. 54)   January the 19th 1817

The Church according to adjournment after Worship Proceeded To Business as Follows Nothing recorded

February the 15th 1817

The Church met and after proceeded to Business as Follows 1rst a matter of Controversy Betwen Bro Thomas Buck and Several of the Members 2^{d} a motion made and Second that the matter be refer^{d} to a committee and make report to the next meeting appointed To wit.. Joseph Renfro John Dunlap Samuel Brumit Richard Karr & Daniel Stover adjourn^{d}

March the 15th 1817

The Church met according to adjournment after worship proceeded to Business 1rst The report of the Committee was read which was as Follows after Hearing the allegations and Defence of the parties We are clearly of the opinion that Br Thomas Buck Has forfeited his fellowship We therefore Declare S^{d} Buck to be no more of us nor to Be Charged with his futer Conduct adjourn^{d} till meeting in Course.

(P. 55) April the 19th 1817

The Church met according to adjournment after Worship Proceeded to Business 1^{rst} a matter of Controversy that has Taken place between Br Saml Tipton and John Wright respecting Iron Works 2^{d} is a greed By the Parties to Cohose a Committee To Judge the Matter and make report To the next meeting appointed as Follows Br'n Lenard Bowers Solomon Hendrix Jon Nave Dan Stover & Jos Renfro adjourn^{d} till meeting in Course

May the 17th 1817

The Church met after worship proceed To Business as Follows 1^{rst} the report of the Committee was read and a motion was made By Br Renfro that the matter be Continued till next meeting and further Labours be used adjourn^{d} &c.

June the 14th 1817

The Church met according to adjournment after Worship proceeded to Business 1^{rst} Br Uriah Hunt appointed Moderator 2^{d} The Matter relative to Br Tip & B Wright Call^{d} for 3^{d} the report of the former Committee was read again and approv^{d} By the Church which State as Follows We the above mentioned Committee after Hearing both parties are of opinion that Bro Wrigh be Excluded from Fellowship No More to be of us nether are we to be Charged with his futer Conduct adjourn^{d} &c

(P. 56) July the 19th 1817

The Church met according to adjournment after divine worship proceeded To Busness as Follows 1^{rst} appointed Brother Hendrix Moderator
Nothing committed to record

August 29th 1817

the Church met after Worship proceeded to Business Receiv^{d} Sister Hamrick by Letter adjour^{d} &c

September the th 1817

The Church met according to adjournment after Worship proceeded to Business as follows Nothing Committed to record adjourn^{d} &c

October the 19th 1817

The Church met after Worship proceeded to Business as follows Nothing Committed to record adjour^{d} till meeting in Cours

(P. 57) November the th 1817

The Church met and after worship proceeded to Business as Follows Nothing Commited to record adjour[d]

December the 1817

The Church met & after worship proceeded to Business as follows Nothing Committed to record

January the 17th 1818

The Church met and after worship Proceeded to Business as follows Nothing Committed to record adjor[d]

February the 14th 1818

The Church met and after Worship [P]roceeded to Business as follows Nothing Commited to record
adjour[d] &c

(P. 58) March the 14th 1818) Reference made by Henry M. Saylor in year 1903

The Church met and after Worship proceeded To Business as follows 1[rst] Brother John Nave Cited to Church meeting Brother Bowers the messenger on motion made & agreed that Br'n Joseph Renfro & David Pugh be appointed the Churches trustees to Superintend the Procuring a title for one acre of Land Where the meeting House now Stands and the same to be authenticated as the Law requires 2[d] Sister Elisabeth Casaday be cited to next meeting Peter Kuhn the Messenger adjourn[d]

April the 18th 1818

The Church met and after Worship Proceed to Business as follows the reference from last brought forward John Nave attend and give Satisfaction a Door open[d] for the reception of Members Rec[d] one by Letter To Witt Elender McNabb
adjourn[d] &c

(P. 59) May the 15th 1818

The Church met according to adjournment after Worship proceed to Business as follows Nothing Committed to record.

June the 20th 1818

The Church met and after worship proceed to Business as follows Chose Brother Hendrix Moderator 2 appointed B[r] to witt David Pugh & James Edens Deligates to our next association adjour[d] till next meeting

July the 19th 1818

The Church met according to adjournment after worship proceeded to Business as follows Nothing recorded adjourn[d]

August the 18th 1818

The Church met and after prayer Proceeded to Business Nothing recorded

September the 19th 1818

The Church met and after Worship proceeded to business A black man Br James came forward this day and Stated that Some reports about him were false they Church appointed Br Hendrix Pugh & Kuhn to Inquire into the report & make return at next meeting
This Day came Br James Eden & requested the Church to give him leave to Exercise his gift in publick witch was granted (P. 60) Sister Polly McCorcall apply[d] for a letter of Dismission which was granted & Isued accordingly adjour[d]

October the 16th 1818

The Church met according to adjournment after worship proceed to Business the reference from Last meeting Cald for and the report of the Br was heard and the matter Being grounless is Dropt Sister Polly Willet apply[d] for a letter of Dismission which was granted & Issued according adjourn[d] &c

November the 14th 1818

The Church met according to adjournment after Worship Proceeded to Business Nothing recorded adjour[d]

December the 19th 1818

The Church met agreeable to adjournment after Worship Proceeded to Business as follows 1[rs] This day came Elijah Buck and requested the Liberty of the Church to Exercise his gift in Publick which was granted Him 2[d] on motion a greed that Br Joel Cooper Be alow[d] the Sum of Ten Dollars for one acre of Land Where the meeting House now Stands for which he has made a title Here to fore

adjour[d]

(P. 61) January the 15th 1819

The Church met agreeable to adjournment and after worship proceeded to Business as Follows 1[rs] Sister Polly McNabb made application for a letter of Dismission which was granted & Issue[d] accordingly

February the 20th 1819

The Court met according to appointment after worship poceeded to Business as follows 1[rst] Br Joseph Renfro has Informed this Church to day that there are reports in circulation that Sister Pollu Humphres Should have reported against Sister Clemmence Love we therefore think it Duty to send members to Inquire into the reports and see wether they be true & to make a return at the next meeting Chose to witt Joseph Renfro Richard Karr David Pugh Peter Kuhn & Solomon Hendrix as a Committee To Enquire & return 2[d] adjourn[d] &c

March the 20th 1819

The Church met agreeable to adjournment after Divine Service proceeded to Business as follows 1[rs] The report of the Committee was read on the case of Sister Humphres which say the are groundless reports
adjourn[d] untill meeting Course

(P. 62) April 17th 1819

The Church met agreeable to adjournment after Worship procceded to Business as follows 1rst Motioned & Seconded that We Become a Constituted Church 2d Appointed Br Joseph Renfro trustee of this Church

May the 12th 1819

The Church met agreeable to adjournment after Worship proceeded to Business as follows 1rst Motioned & a greed that this Church send a petition to the Body to Become a Constitution
2d adjournd

June the 19th 1819

The Church met agreeable to adjournment af Divine Service Proceeded to Business as follows 1rst our petition for a Constitution from last meeting being granted agreeable to our request was brought forward & the answer read and after some Debates the matter is as not Concluded 2d on motton is & agreed to be Continued 3d Chose Delegates to our next association to witt, Jonathan Buck James Edens 4th orderd By the Church that Joseph Renfro Issue $1-50 cents for use of the association fund Adjourd

(P. 63) July the 17th 1819

The Church met agreeable toadjournment after Worship proceeded to Business as Follows 1rst the matter as respect a Constitution taken up 2d Continued the same till next meeting 3d adjournd till meeting in Course &c --

September th 1819

The Church met agreable to appointment after worship proceeded to Business as follows 1rst a door opend for the reception of Members Recd Jonathan Lipps & wife By letter 2d adjournd in order &c ---

October the 16th

The Church met agreeable to adjournment after worship proceeded to Business as follows 1rst Br Mulkey moved that the matter of Br Hendrix be reconsidered in moving him from being Treasurer after Some Deliberation the Church agreed that he be restord to his former priveledges the Constitution still Continued adjourned

(P. 64) November the 20 1819

The Church met and after worship proceeded to Business as follows 1rst The matter as respects the Constitution agreed to be Continued untill our next may meeting 2d a door opend for the reception of Member Recd By Letter Mark Holtsclaw Phebe Hart & Easter Daugherty
adjournd in order

August the 14- 1819--

The Church met agreeable to adjournment after worship proceeded to Business as follows 1rs the Constitution taken up and Still continued adjournd &c

December the 18th 1819

The Church met according to adjournment after worship proceeded to Business as follows Nothing Committed to record adjourn[d] in order

January the 15th 1820

The Court met and after worship proceeded to business as follows Nothing recorded.

February the 19th 1820

The Church met acording to adjourment after worship proceeded to Business follows 1[rst] Sister Hendry apply[d] for a letter of Dismission which was granted and Issued accordingly
adjourn[d] in order

(P. 65) March the 18th 1820

The Church met after worship proceeded to Business as follows 1[rst] a door open[d] for The Reception of members Rc[d] one by Experience To wit Polly Hart Dismist in order

April the 15th 1820

The Church met and after worship proceeded to business as follows 1[rst] Br Jonathan Buck apply[d] for a letter of Dismission which was granted and Issued accordingly Dismisst in order &c ---

May the 20th 1820

The Church met agreeable to adjournment after Worship proceeded to Business as follows 1[rst] a reference from Last November meeting Call[d] for as respected a Constitution after Some Deliberation the arm of this Church has unanimously agreed to Enter into Constitution and to become a Body Distinct Body from the Buffoloe Ridge Church and accordingly were constituted By the Rever[d] Br[n] to wit 2[d] Jonathan Mulkey & Uriah Hunt and Chose Jonathan Mulkey to take pastorial care of this Church
3[d] adjourn[d] &c

(P. 66) June the 18th 1820

The Church met agreeable to adjourment after Worship proceeded to Business as Follows
1[rs] Chose B[r] Mulkey moderator of this Church when present with us
2[d] Daniel Stover appointed Clerk of this Church
3[d] Appointed Brn Sl Hendrix & Stover Deacons of this Church
4th A motion made By Bror Lipps that Bros Mulkey & as many of the members as saw it convenient to attend on Stony Creek at Thomas Evens the first Saturday in July to set as a Church to receive members if any Should offer To which motion this Church Cuncur

July the 1[rst] 1820

The Brethren met at thomas Evens agreeable to appointment and after Divine Service oppen[d] a door for the reception of members and Rec[d] By Experience

Henry Nave & wife and Polly Ivy and Baptised the same day
adjourn^d &c-

(P. 67) July the 15th 1820

The Church met according to adjournment after Worship proceeded to Business as follows
1^rst appointed B^r Hendrix & B^r Edens Deligates to attend Ensueing association
2 order by the Church that there be 9/S put in their hands for the use of the association fund
3^d Adjourn^d in order

August 19th 1820

the Church met & after Divine Service proceeded to Business as follows 1^rs Sister Prudence Bailes formerly Prudence Patterson Excommunicated for the sin of fornication

September the 16th 1820

The Church met agreeable to adjournment after Worship proceeded to Business as follows 1^rst application made by B^r Hendrix that Sister Easter Doherty have a letter of Dismission which was granted and order^d to be Issued appointed Elijah Buck to Cite Sister Burris & Sister Whitson to attend next meeting adjourn^d in order &c

(Note written in Pencil as follows: the June 1820 minute show the organization of the Baptist Church on Stony Creek, Henry M. Saylor Clerk this June 15. 1916)

(P. 68) October the 14th 1820

The Church met agreeable to adjournment and after Worship proceeded to Business as follows
1^rst the references as respect Sis Burris and Sis Whitson Contimued
2^d a motion made & greed that theit Church meeting held on Stony Creek at Thomas Evens the first Saturday in November
Dismist in order

November the th 1820

The Church met at Thomas Evens on Stoney Creek agreeable to appointment after Worship open^d a door for the reception of members and Recev^d three By Experience to Wit Joseph Cobb Elexander Moten and Elender Evens and Baptised them the following day by the Revd B^r Rees Bailes and dismist in order

November the 1820

The Church met at Sinking Creek agreeable to meeting in Course and after Worship proceeded to Business as follows 1rs Sister Whitson came forward and gave satisfaction to the church 2 on motion it was agreed to hold Church meeting on Stony Creek Wednesday and thursday before the meeting at Sinking in Course next.

(P. 69) December the th 1820

The Church met at Thomas Evens on Stony Creek according to appointment after Divine Service opend a door for the reception of members Recev[d] two by Experience to witt Valentine Bower & Geney Moten and Baptised them the following Day By the Rev[d] B[r] Rees Bailes
Dismist in order &c--

January the 20th 1821

The Church met according to adjournment after proceeded to Business as follows 1[rst] To Hear Br Elijah Buck preach agreeable to his own request wether or not he does posess the gift of preaching but give him the privilodge of Singing, praying and Exorting" after hearing him this Church doth say by a unanimous voice that he doth not posess the gift of preaching

his fellow creatures 2[d] Sister Rachel Whitson does request a letter of Dismission from this Church which was granted & Issued accordingly
3[d] Motion[d] and agreed that this Church write a few lines to Br Mark Holtsclaw to let him know that this Church has taken notice of his Conduct in leaving this Church in Disorder and further agree to wait with him till our May meeting to come and make his recantation
4th Motion[d] agreed that our next meeting be on Stony Creek adjourn[d]

(P. 70) February the 17th 1821

The Church met at Thomas Even[s] agreeable to adjournment after Worship proceeded to Business as follows 1[rst] A Door open[d] for the reception of members Recev[d] By Experience James Peters Abigail Bowers & Lydia Taylor & adjour[d] the following day Received Thomas Evens and all were Baptis[d] the Same day by rev[d] B[r] Rees Bailes 3[d] Dismist in Order

March the 17th 1821

The Church met and Divine Service proceeded to Business as follows Nothing to be recorded &c-

April the 14th 1821

The Church met according to adjournment after Worship proceeded to Business as follows a Citation from September meeting call[d] for as respects Sister Burres non attendance She has disobey,d the call of the Church and further more has removed away from this Church without making application for a Letter of Dismission the Church think her Conduct has forfeited Her Fellowship therefore declare against her the s[d] Sister Bussis no more to be of us Neither are we to be Charged with her futer Conduct. (P. 71)
Brother Miens made application for a letter of Dismission for Sister Boyd which was granted & Issued accordingly.
3[d] Brother Buck gave up his letter of dismission

April the 28th 1821

The Church met at Stoney Creek meeting House according to appointment after Worship proceeded to Business as follows oppen[d] a Door for the reception of members receiv[d] Margret Musgraves by Experience
2 adjourn[d] in order &c &c

May the 19th 1821

The Church met and after Divine Service proceeded to Business as follows 1rst Jno Hampton & wife Joind this Church by letter 2d Thomas Buck moved for membership but was not recied

(P. 72) June the 16th 1821

The Church met according to appointment after Worship proceeded to Business as follows 1rst Brother Bucks Inform the Church that that he Cited Brother Mark Holtsclaw agreeable to the Churches request and that he cannot attend till August meeting this Church agrees to wait with him 2d on motion agreed that our next Church meeting be held at Stony Creek Meeting House 3d appointed Brethren to witt Jonathan Buck Jame Edens & Solomon Hendrix as Deligates to attend our Insueing association to be held at Bent Creek the 2d friday in August next 4th orderd By the Church that their be 9s/ deposited in in the hands of the Deligates for the use of the association fund 5th adjournd & --

July the 14th 1821

The Church met at Stoney Creek Meeting House according to appointment of Divine Service proceeded to Business as follows &c-
1rst The address to the association Read and approvd 2d oppend a door for the reception of members and receivd by Experience Sarrah Musgraves Elisabeth Nave Ann Buckels Rebekah Nave Nancy Berry Levicy Carriger
3d a greed that our Communion season be at our next August meeting
4th Adjournd in order &c --

(P. 73) August the 17th 1821

The Church met after worship proceeded to Business as follows Nothing recorded Adjournd in order

September the 15th 1821

The Church met and after worship proceeded to Business as follows
1rst the Referance as respects Bro Mark Holtsclaw Brought forward the Church Still agrees to wait longer as Br Buck Expects to See him Shortly and to re cite him to this Church
adjournd &c &c

October the 19th 1821

The Church met at Stony Creek Meeting House acording to appointment after Divine Service proceeded to open a door for Experience None came forward adjournd till tomorrow
the following day the Church met after worship opend a Door for the reception of Members Red by Experience Jacob Cable Seily Cole Elisabeth Hataway adjourd
The Church set the following day & gave oppertunity for the reception of Members Recd Experience Clearissa Evens Samuel Musgrave and by Recommendation Sarrah Gentry and were Baptisd the same day by the Revd Br Rees Bailes adjournd &c

(P. 74) November the 17th 1821

The Church at Sinking Creek Meeting house according to appointment after Worship proceeded as follows 1rst Susannah Mcfall Restord 2d Dismisst her by letter 3d on application by Br John Nave in behalf of Br Jacob Cobb for Dismission which was granted and Issued accordingly

December the 15th 1821

The Church met at Sinking Creek after Worship proceeded to Business as follows Nothing recorded Adjournd &c--

January the 19th 1822

The Church met at Sinking Creek after Worship proceeded to Business as follows 1rst Sister tiner Hunt applyd for letter of Dismission which was granted and Ussued accordingly 2d Adjournd in order

February the 16th 1822

The Church met at Sinking Creek after worship proceeded to Business as follows 1rst the matter as respects Br Holtsclaw Still Contimued (P. 75) 2 Sister Elisabeth Danniels applyd for a letter of Dismission which was granted and Issued accordingly 3d was moved by Br Jonathan Lipps that they Stony Creek members Do petition for Constitution after some deliberation the matter is prespond till next meeting for further consideration 4th Motiond and agreed that their be Church meeting on Stony Creek the Second Saturday in March Adjournd

March the 9th 1822

The Church met at Stony Creek Meeting House according to appointment after Worship proceeded to Business as follows opend a Door for Experience Recd Rebekah Cable adjournd

March the 16th 1822

The Church met at Sinking Creek Meeting house according to appointment af Worship proceeded to Business as follows the reference from last meeting calld for as respects the Constitution after some deliberation the matter was freely given up that they Stony Creek members to become a constituted body & as many as feel free are at Liberty to Join them
Dismist in order

(P. 76) April the 20th 1822

The Church met according to appointment after worship proceeded to Business as follows Nothing recorded &c &c

May the 18th 1822

The Church met according to appointment after Worship proceeded to Business as follows 1rst Bro Joshua Edwards and wife moved for Dismission from this Church to Join the Buffoloe ridge Church at Muddy Creek be more convenient which was granted adjournd &c

June the 16th 1822

The Church met according to adjournment after Divine Service proceeded to Business as follows 1rst appointed Br James Edin Richard Carr & John Dunlap to attend our association as Deligates 2d Orded by the Church that their one dollar put in the Hands of the Deligates for the use of the association fund. Adjournd &c

July the 20th 1822

The Church met and after Divine Service proceeded to Business 1st read and approvd the Latter to the Asso: 2 the matter as respects Br Holtsclaw taken up this Church Excludes him from fellowship no more to be of us Neither are we to be Charged with his futer Conduct. (P. 77) 3d the Church had under Consideration br Eden gift referd till next meeting 4 receivd John Carty by Experience 5 our next meeting to be a Communion Season
Dismist in order

August the 17th 1822

The Church met according to appointment after Divine Service proceeded to Business as follows
1rst Was Movd by bro Hendrix that John Carty should give up his Licence to which he agreed and requested Licence from this Church to preach in the bounds of the Church which was granted
2d the matter as respects Br Eden taken up after some Deliberation the matter was freely given up that he should have Licence to preach where So Ever the Lord may cast his Lot
Dismiss in order

September the 14th 1822

The Church met according to agreement after worship proceeded to Business as follows 1st Br Jesse Milsap applied for a letter of Dismission & is granted and Issued. 2d this Church agrees to Meet at James Laceys on Doe river the 2d monday in octr
3d John Hampton Dd Pugh & Jos Rentfro appointed to Superentend the repairing the meeting House
4th the Church Hav agree that the Church record Shall be put in hands of Br Hendrix and to brought to Every meeting
adjournd

(P. 78) September Sunday the 15th 1822

The Church set and gave oppertunity to hear Experience & Receivd Wilmoth Sommerly and her Baptism Deferd till the Second Monday in October at James Love (?) in the Doe River Cove & the Church met agreeable to appointment and performed the above Deference

October the 19th 1822

The Church met according to appointment after worship proceeded to Business as follows 1rst Bro Jonathan Buck applied for a letter of Dismission which was granted and Issued accordingly adjournd in in order

November the 16th 1822

The Church met according to adjournment after Worship proceeded to Business as follows 1rst Sister Martha Paterson applyd for a letter of Dismission which ~~was~~ Granted and Issued accordingly 2d Br John ~~Darty~~ Dlarty applies for a Written Licence which was granted him to preach the gospel Wheresoever the lord Might Cast his Lot

December the 14th 1822

The Church according to appointment met after Divine Service proceeded to Business as follows
Nothing Committed to record adjournd in order &c ---

(P. 79) January the 18th 1823

The Church met according to agreemant after Worship Proceeded to Business as follows Nothing Committed to record.

February the 14th 1823

The Church met acording to adjournment after Worship proceeded to Business as follows Nothing Committed to record adjournd

March the 14th 1823

The Church met Nothing worthy of record adjourned

April the 19th 1823

The Church met Nothing to be recorded Adjournd &c

May the 17th 1823

The Church met & proceeded to Business in order Nothing recorded

June the 14th 1823

The Church met agreeable to adjournment & proceeded to Business 1rst appointed Br'n James Edén Solomon Hendrix to at attend our Next association as Deligates from this Church 2d the Clerk appointed to Write and adress to the association and present at next meeting for Inspection.
Adjournd in order —

(P. 80) July the 19th 1823

The Church met agreeable to adjournment after worship proceeded to Business as follows the letter to the associ read abd approved 3d this Church has receivd Information from Reports that James Hunts Black man is guilty of Some Mis Conduct We think proper to Cite him to next meeting Br Hampton the Churches messenger 4th this Church has agreed that the Clerk take the record home with him and keep it in possession and to Bring it when Calld for adjournd in order

August the 15th 1823

The Church met agreeable to adjournment of Divine Service proceeded to Business the refrence as respects Br Jame Brought forward Br James attended ang gave Satisfaction adjournd &c

September the 20th 1823

The Church met according to appointment after Worship proceeded to Business as follows a Petition from Cobbs Creek Church for helps to see into the standing of sd Church for sd purpose we have Chosin our beloved Br James Eden Soomon Hendrix Peter Kuhn James Peters Daniel Stover Joseph Rentfro & David Pugh adjourd

October the 18th 1823

The Church met agreeable to adjournment after worship proceeded to Business as follows Br Mulkey no being present Chose Br Hendrix Moderator 1rst Sister Love applyd for a letter of Dismission was granted and Issued the same Adjournd in order

(P. 81) November the 15th 1823

The Church met after Worship proceeded to Business as Follows.

December the 20th 1823

The Church met after Worship proceeded To Business as Follows Nothing recorded

January the 17th 1824

The Church met after Worship proceeded to Business as follows 1rst (large blank space follows)

February the 15th 1824

The Church met after Worship proceeded to Business as follows 1rst Moved By Br Edens that their be a Church meeting Calld to attend at Nicholas Smiths at the Crab orchard on Doe river the --

(P. 82) February the 28th 1824

The Church met at Nicholas Smiths on Doe river acording to appointment after Worship proceeded to Business as follows 1rst Chose Br Rees Bailes Moderator opend a Door for Experience Recd 3 to wit Nancy Miller Sarah Bedley & Nancy Briant & Baptisd the the following day By the Revd Rees Bailes

March the 20th 1824

The Church met after worship proceeded to Business as follow

April the th 1824

The Church met after Worship proceeded to Business

May the th 1824

The Church met ater Worship proceeded to Business as follows 1rst Br Abraham Odle and wife applyd for a Dismission and was granted 2d opend a Door to hear Experience Recd Elisabeth Kuhn & Gean Barker
Adjournd in order

(P. 83) June the 19th 1824

The Church met and Worship proceeded to Business as follows 1rst appointed Brn James Eden & Joseph Rentfro to and attend the Insueing asso as Deligates and order[d] By the Church the their be one Dollar put in the hands of the Deligates for the use of the asso.. fund.

July the 17th 1824

The Church met and after Worship proceeded to Business as follows Br Eden Moves that Their be a Church meeting appointed at the Crab Orchard to Set the Saturday before the fifth Sunday in august which was Granted agreed the Communion be at our next meeting in Course

August the 14th 1824

The Church met after worship proceeded to Business as follows 1rst a petition from Cobbs Creek Church to this Church presented By Br John Dugger that this Church take in Consideration the gifts and qualifications of Br Edens to the minestry the Church accepted the above petition and Deferd the answer for further Consideration 2d opend a door for Reception of members Re[d] Edward Hendry By Experience

(P. 84) August the 28th 1824

The Church met at the Crab Orchard on Doe river acording to appointment after worship proceeded to Business open[d] a Door for Experience Re[d] Sarah Whitehead Susannah Purkins Rebekah Hammit the Church set the following day and Rec[d] James Jones By Experience and Batism administered By the Rev[d] Rees Bailes adjourn[d] &c

September the 17th 1824

The Church met according to appointment after Worship proceeded to Business as follows the matter as respects the Cobbs Creek petition Taken up and Still Continued as reference 2 Mov[d] Br Hendrix and Seconded By Br Kuhn that Br Stover had Serv[d] as a Deacon without ordination after Some Examination this Church agrees to ordain S[d] Stover which was done the following day By the Rev[d] Brn Jonathan Mulkey and Joseph Crouch 3[d] Mov[d] By Bro Hendrix that this Church take in Consideration the Conduct of Sister Nancy Bailes s[d] Sister being present and Examined refusing to give the Church the Satisfaction She requires we therefore take Cognizanc of her Conduct and by the request of her husband only Censure her from Church privaledges untill a gospel recantation.

(P. 85) October the 16th 1824

The Church met according to adjournment and after worship proceeded to Business as Follows a door open[d] for the reception of Members R[d] by Experience Josiah Parker James Miller & Nancy Puck 2 the matter as respects the Cobs Creek petition Taken up after some debate the Church appears not to be unanimous the matter is dropt.

November the 14th 1824

The Church met according to appointment after Worship proceeded to Business

as follows the reference as respects Sister Nancy Bailes Still Contimued 2d proposition movd by Br Mulkey wether the Laying on of hands on new Baptised members should be contimued yea or nay after Some Debate on the Subject the Church agrees to Discontimue the practice 3d opend a Door for the reception of Members Receivd fanny Rentfo By Experience and agreed that her Baptism Be Deferd till till the Second Sunday in december and to be admind By the Revd Rees Bailes
Adjournd in Order &c--

November the 18th 1824

The Church met according to adjournment after worship Proceeded to Business as Follows the Case of Sister Nancy Bailes take up. 3d Sister Came forward and gave Satisfaction and was restord to her former previledges.
(P. 86) 2d proposition moved by Br John Hampton Respecting Sister fanny Rentfres Baptism as She has not Complyd with the requisitian of this Church but one week previous to the appointment of the Church has Been Baptised by Jeriel Dodge This Church then taken in Consideration wether the Baptism Be Valued yea or nay as it appear that Sd Dodge is not of our union after Some Debate on the Subject it appeares that the Church not being unanimous in Sentiment the Matter is prospond till next meeting for further consideration adjournd till meetin Cours

January the 15th 1825

The Church met according to appointment after Worship proceeded to Business as follows 1rst a door opend for the reception of members Recevd Jemima Tipton by Exper 2d the Case as respects Sister fanny Rentfro Baptism Contimued adjournd

February the 20th 1825

The Church met agreeable to adjournment after Worship proceeded to Business as follow the case as respects Sister fanny Renfro taken up again after Some Debate on the Subject the Matter was put to a motion in the Church as it appears the Church is divided in Sentiment is agreed that the matter be contimued till the Church think proper to take it up again adjournd &c

(P. 87) March the 16th 1825

The Church met agreeable to adjournment after worship proceeded to Business as follows 1rst--The Case as respects Sister fanny Renfro taken up again after Some Debate on the Subject (it was) motioned and agreed that this Church Should Send for help to the different Churches as follows Buffoloe ridge Cherokee Indian Creek Cobs Creek & Stoney Creek & for ther helps to attend at our next Church meeting as a Select Committee 2d & we have further agreed to a Bide by the Decision of this Committee &c 3d appointed Brn to Bear petitions to the different Churches Br Mulkey to the Buffoloe ridge Del Bayles to Cherokee Rees Bayles to Indian Creek James Edens to Cobs Creek D Stover to Stoney Creek
4th adjournd in order &c

April the 16th 1825

The Church met according to agreement after Worship proceeded to Business as follows 1rst the record of last meeting read as respects the case of fanny Renfro the brethren who were appointed by the different churches before mentioned being present to wit Buffoloe ridg Thomas Hunt Nathan Shipley Cherokee Samuel Bayles Wm Bayles Rees Bayles Joseph Hunter John Murr Jon Hunter & Elijah Brown Indian Creek John Rose Abram oDle Jno Edwards Joseph Longmires Cobs Creek Isaac Campbell John Whitehead Stony Creek Sl. Tipton Leod Bowers Jon Nave Henry Nave Benjamin White after Some Debate on the Subject this Church has agreed to Leave the Matter to a Unanimous Decision of the above committee

WM McGimsey Thomas Edwrads

(P. 88) and after this Committee being put in full possession of the matter as it Stands By the Revd Brother Mulkey do withdraw and at their return do report and Say as Follows

We the above Committee met according to appointment at Sinking Creek Church and Chose Rees Bayles Moderator & Nathan Shipley Clerk on examination of the Case of Fanny Rentfro We do unanimously agree that the Baptism administerd by Jariel Dodge is not agreeable to Gospel order as practisd by the Baptist Churches We further Do also advise the Church at Sinking Creek to hold Fanny Renfro in the Same Situation that She Stood in the Church before She was Baptisd by the Sd Jariel Dodge

Signed by order of the Committee Saturday the 16th 1825

Rees Bayles Md
Nathan Shipley C C K

James Miller applyd for a letter of Dism which was granted and Issud accordingly

adjourd

May the 14th 182 The Church met after Worship Proceeded to Business as follows Nothing recorded

(P. 89) June the 18th 1825

The Church met according to appointment after worship Proceeded to Business as Follows 1rst Br Renfro Movd to this Church that he be releast Serving as one of the trustees to Superintend the repairing of the meeting House which was granted him 2d adjournd &c

July the 16th 1825

The Church met according to appointment of Divine Service proceeded to Business 1rst apointed Brn to wit James Eden John D Carty Delegates to the association 2d appointed the Clerk to write the adress to the asso and to be read the following day which was granted & done accordingly & adjourd &c

August the th 1825 No Meeting.

SepR, the 17th 1825

The Church meet according to appointment after worship proceeded to Business as follows 1rs Br John D Carty applyd for a Letter Dimission after Some Debate respecting his baptism this Church agrees to give him a Letter with this Exception Stating the manner of his baptism as being Baptisd by a people who Calld themselves Christian Body adjournd &c &c

(P. 90) Blank (P. 91) December the 17th 1825

The Church met according to adjournment after Worship proceeded to Business as follows 1rst Chose Solomon Hendrix moderator & John Dunlap Clerec pro tem 2 Br Josiah Parker came Forward and made recantation For Transgression the Church Rd it 3d in answer to a request From hopewell Church Monroe County Verbaly by Sister Patterson respecting Prudence Bailes we agree to Submit the Case to that Church to act as think proper 4th the Committee who were previous appointed to settle a matter of Controversy between Br John Hampton & br rentfro went into an Investigation of the matter and deferd the report till next meeting in Course

Adjournd in order

January the 14th 1826

The Church met and after Due Solemnity performed of the day performed interd on Business as follows the report of the Former Committee was read and approved by the Church which reads as Follows

We the Committee appointed to Settle the allegiations brought against Br John Hampton by Br Rentfro after Due Examination we do not find Br Hampton guilty of the Charge Brought again him given under our hands this 17th day of December 1825

John Dunlap
Elijah Buck
Peter Kuhn
Josiah Parker
David Pugh

(P. 92) February the 18th 1826

The Church met according to adjournment after Worship proceeded to business as follows Nothing recorded Adjournd in order.

March the 18th 1826

The Church met acording to adjournment after worship proceeded to business as follows Nothing Committed to record adjournd in order

April the 15th 1826

The Church met after Worship proceeded and Nothing recorded adjournd &c

May the 20th 1826

The Church met after Worship proceeded and Nothing recorded adjournd

June the 17th 1826

The Church met after Worship proceeded to Business Nothing recorded

July the 15th 1826

The Church met after Worship proceeded to Business as follows 1rst appointed Solomon Hendrix and Daniel Stover Deligates to our next asso- 2 orderd that there be one Dollar put in their hands for the asso. fund. (P. 93) 3d Orddrd that the Clerk prepare to address to the asso- Adjournd &c

August the 15th 1826

The Church met after Worship proceeded to Business as follows 1rst Chose

Brd Eden Moderator 2d Sister Bradly made application for a letter of Dismission which was granted and Issued accordingly Adjord &c

September the 16th 1826

the Church met after Worship proceeded to Business as follows Nothing to be recorded adjournd &c

September the 26th 1826

The Committee appoind by the asso Met at Sinking Creek meeting house according to appointment Namely-- Caleb Witt Joseph Crouch & James Poindexter Enquird into the difficulties in Sink Creek Church find them to be a divided People both in principle and practice Therefore we do autherise that part of the Church which hold the principles on which they were Constituted & act agreeable to the rules of our asso..to be the Church & hold the keys of the Church and avise them to Exclude all those who have publickly declard against the Government of this Church and in favour of the Arian Principles and as many others as will not comply with the advise of the asso.. after due Co Coars to restore them
assind by the above Committee

State

Caleb Witt
Joseph Crouch
James Poindexter

(P. 94) October the 14th 1826

the Church met and after worship Proceeded to Business nothing recorded &c

October the 18th the Church Met at Br John Dunlaps having Laboured a long time under Certain difficulties thought it Expedient to appoint a private meeting and proceed to Business Chose Br Rees Bayles Moderator the first Case taken up is Br Hendrix and unfellowship declard against him for Charges as follows 1rst is for advocating the baptism of fanny rentfro and saying it mattered not who administerd the ordinance so the subject had faith in it 2d is after agreeing that a dicision might be made by a Committee Calld for by the Church and afterwards remonstrated against the dicision of that Committee 3d We likewise declare an unfellowship against Molly Hendrix Joseph Rentfro David Pugh Richard Karr Edward Henry and Elly McNabb for Justifing Solomon Hendrix and advocating the same cause we also declare against Molly Humphres for Joining Millers Church 4th proceeded to appoint trustees Chose John Dunlap & John Hampton to procure and hold the title of the land on which the meeting house now Stands
5th We Unanimously agree not to Invite any of the people calld Arians Socinians Unitarians or Symatics or any that will not write their Creed preach in our houses or meeting houses &c adjord in order

(Inserted page follows) (INSERT Betwen P. 94 & 95)

October the 18th 1826

The Church of Christ at Sinking Creek having long laboured under such difficulties that we could not decide on any pointe thought it Necessary to apoint a private meeting at Br Dunlaps after worship proceeded to buisness as Follows 1rst Chose Br Rees Bailes Moderator
2d the case as respects Bre Hendrix taken and unfellowship declard against

him for Charges as follows 1st for advocating the Baptism of Fanny Rentfro and saying it matterd not who aministerd the ordinance So the Subject had faith in it 3rd after agreeing that a decision might be made by a Committee Called for by the Church and afterwards remonstretied a Gains the decision of that Committee so We likewise declare an unfellowship agains Molly Hendrix Joseph Rentfro David Pugh Richard Karr Edward Hendry and Sally McNabb for Justifying Socomon Hendrix and advocating the same cause 4 Proceeded to apoint trustees John Dunlap & John Hampton trustees to hold the title of the land on which Sinking Creek meeting house now stands 5th We unanimously agree not to Invite any of the people Called arians, Socinians Unitarians or Sysmaticks or any other that will not wright their Creed to preach in our meeting house or private &c

adjourned in order

October the 18th 1826

The Church of Christ at Sinking Creek Having long labourd under Such difficulties that we could not decide on any point thought it nessesary to appoint a private meeting at Bro Dunlaps, after Worship proceeded to Buisness first, Chose Br Rees Bailes moderator 2 the Case of Br Hendrix taken up and unfellowship declard against him for Charges as follows first for advocating the Baptism of fanny Rentfro and Saying it matterd not who administerd the ordinance so the subject had faith in it 3d after agreeing that a decision might be made by a Committee Called for by the Church then remonstrated against such a decision of that Committee 2d We likewise Declare an unfellowship against Molly Hendrix Joseph Rentfro & David Pugh Edward Henry Richard Karr and Elly McNabb, for Justifying Solomon Hendrix and advocating the same cause.

4 We proceeded to appointed trustees to hold the title of the land on which our the meeting house now stands appointed John Dunlap John Hampton

5th We unanimously agree not to invite any of the people called arians Socenians Unitarians or Sysmatick or any that will not wright their creed preach in our meeting house or private houses

adjournd in order

November the 1826 The Church met acording to appointment After Worship proceeded to Business as follows
Nothing committed to record adjournd in order &c ---

(P. 95) December the 16th 1826

The Church met according to adjournment after Worship Proceeded to Business as follows Chose Br Stover moderator 2d this Church have adapted a rule that is at our Church meeting days a door shall be open Induring the time of Business unless Immideately Concernd in Business for the reception of members 3d Joseph Rentfro came forward and made a recantation the Church not being fully satisfied have referd it &c -- Sis rockhold and Sister Kelley come forward and declared the were disatified with this Church and would wish to withdraw their fellowship this Church grants their requst and declares against them to be no more of us 5 was made that this Church take in Consideration the Gift and quallification of Bro Edens to the ministery

January the 20th 1827

The Church met according to appointment after worship proceeded to Business 1rst the reference as Respects Br Edens gift after some debate this Church set him apart for ordination 2d BR John Dunlap appointed Deacon and set

apart for ordination 3d this Church agrees to petition Br to Witt Richard Murrel Joseph Crouch & Rees Bayles to attend at our next meeting as in order to ordain the above mentioned Brn 4 Br Hampton to be the Churches Messenger to Bear the above petition
adjournd in order

(P. 96) February the 17th 1827

The Church met according to adjournment after Divine Service proceeded to Business as Follows 1rst a door opend for the reception of members Recd Risba Hatcher by Experience 2d the presbetyra attended accordingly proceeded and after Examination perford the Solemn duty adjournd in order &c --

March the 17th 1827

The Church met after Worship proceeded to Business as follows Nothing committed to record

April the 14th 1827

1rst Moved by Br Kuhn that Joseph Crouch be fornisht with a copy of record from the asso.. Committee who attended at Sinking some time Previous which was agreed to &c 2 Recd Elisabeth Owens by Experience adjourd &c--

May the 19th 1827

the Church met after worship Proceeded as follows and Nothing Comitted to record

June the 16th 1827

The Church met after worship proceeded to Business as follows 1rs agreed that Br Eden act as moderator in this Church # - appointed to witt James Eden & John Dunlap 3d Moved wether a division in the asso.. Yea or Nay agreed no division 4th agreed that their be one Dollar appropreated in the hands of the above Delegates for the use of the asso.. fund # appointed delegates to our next assoc Brn
5th this Church has reconsider the act of Washing feet and agreed to practice the same (P. 97) Immediately after supper
6st Sister Carriger by Br Stover aplyd for a letter which was Granted accordingly 7 Brn appointed Kuhn and Hapton to Laber with Sister Stevens and Cite her to next meeting &c adjournd &c

July the 14th 1827

the Church met after worship proceeded to Business as follows the Brn appointed to visit Sister Stevins report and say that she gave them Satisfaction to which the Church Concur 3 the address to the asso.. Read and approvd adjournd &c --

September the 14th 1827

The Church met according to appointment after Worship proceeded to Business as follows 1rst This Church being informd this day that Jemima Tipton being in a State of pregnancy We therefore declare an unfellowship with her she is no more of us &c &c

2d ~~This Church has agreed to adopt the practice of washing feet after the Lords Supper~~ 3d this Church think it duty to take notice of Some Conduct that old Br Jonathan Buck is Guilty of and appoint Brn to witt John Hampton Peter Kuhn & Daniel Stover to inquire and make report at next meeting &c (P. 98) 4th adjournd till tomorrow
The Church accordingly meet and receivd Ephraim Morehead by Experience the following day recd his wife by Experience adjournd &c

October the 20th 1826 (?)

The Church met according to appointment after worship proceeded to Business as follows 1rst took up the case of Bro Buck as respects him and deferd it till next meeting 2d Sister polly heart applied for a letter of Dismission which was Granted and Issued accordingly 3d agreed that this Church have a Sample of letter of Dismission recorded in the Church Book
4th appointed Brn John Dunlap & peter Kuhn to visit Sister polly Bogart
5th appointed Elijah Buck & John Hampton to visit Sister Elisabeth Casada respecting some reports that are in Circulation adjournd.

November the 17th 1827

The Church met after worship proceeded as follows 1rs a Copy of a letter Dismission Read & approvd and oderd to be recorded in the Church Book for and Exsample
2d the Case as respects Br Jonathan Buck taken up after hearing the alegation which is as follows 1rs intoxacation of liquor 2d making use of profane Language &c this Church Consider the Conduct unbecoming a preacher of the Gospel Declare against him no more to be in fellowship with us untill a Gospel recantation (P. 99) 4th Brn that visited Sis polly Bogart report and say She stated to them that She had Joind the Methodist this Church Immediately declare an unfellowship with her to be no more of us & 5th the case as respects Sis Casada taken up Sis Casada being present gave general Satisfaction 6 Recd a petition from the Buffoloe Ridge praying us to send them help for which this Church Concur and send James Eden John Hampton Elijah Buck John Dunlap Peter Kuhn and Daniel Stover &c-

December the 15th 1827

The Church met after worship proceeded to Business as follows 1rs appointed Brn James Jones and Peter Kuhn to visit Sister Brient and report at next meeting

January the 18th 1828

The Church met and after Worship proceeded to Business as follows 1rst the case of Sister Brient taken up 3d Sister being present gave Satisfaction 2d proposition is the case of Brother Casar Respecting his marriage as he Desired to know the mind of the Church after Some Debate on the subject the matter is prospond further Consideration 3d appointed Eden & John Dunlap to Cite Sister Hammet to next meeting.

(P. 100) February the 16th 1828

The Church met according to agreement. After Worship proceeded to business &c The matter as respects Br Cesar taken up and referd till next meeting 2d Old Br Buck writes to this Church and Wishes this Church to answer him for which purpose the Church appoint Elijah Buck to write him and answer and likewise to the Church in that Vacinity respecting his Common Deportment &c

March the 15th 1828

The Churc met after worship proceeded as follows 1rst took up the case of Cesar and there agreed to Cite him to next meeting Br Ephraim Morehead & John Dunlap the messenger 2d agreed to have a Communion next meeting 3d Recd The Churches bounty which is $1-90 cents

April the 18th 1828

The Church met according to appointment after worship proceeded to Business 1rst the Case of Cesar taken up he being present Rather Wishes to withdraw his membership to which the Church Concurs 2d case as this Church this day hath recd information that Sister Briant has conducted herself very disorderly in that she went off with a man in disorder the Church declare unfellowship with her &c &c

(P. 101) May the 17th 1828

The Church met and after worship Proceeded to business as follows 1rst Motioned and agreed to cite Sister Nancy Casada to our next meeting Brn Peter Kuhn and Elijah Buck the messengers &c 2d agreed to cite Sister Mary Rockhold & Sister orpha Tompson to next meeting John Dunlap and John Hampton the Churches messengers 3d adjourd in order &c by prayer

June the 14th 1828

The Church met and after worship Proceeded to Business as follows 1rst The Sister Cited at last meeting came forward Namely Nancy Casada and orpha Tompson 2d the minutes of the asso.. Recd Read and approvd 3d Chose Brn John Dunlap & Peter Kuhn as Delegates to the asso.. 4th ordered that there be one Dollar put in the hand of the delegates for the use of the asso.. fund 5th Recd Sarah Dunlap by Experience

July the 19th 1828

The Church met according to appointment after worship Proceeded to Business as follows 1rst Sister Catharine Smallen applyd for a letter of dismission which was Granted and ordered to be Isued accordingly. (P. 102) 2nd appointed Br Peter Kuhn trustee in the room of Br Hampton Deceasd 3d Motiond and agreed that Br Rees Bayles Be Celicited to attend at Br John Dunlaps on Monday the 28th of this Instant in order to baptise old Sister Dunlap Br Parker appointed to Inform him of the Same 4th Sister Polly Rockhold came and gave Satisfaction for her non attendance at Church meeting 5 adjord in order

August the 16th 1828

The Church met and after worship Proceeded to business as follows 1rst Motiond and agreed the their be a nether letter sent to Spring Creek Church respecting old Br Buck and Br Stover to write the same
2d agreed to Cite Sister Milly Peters to next Meeting Peter Kuhn & John Dunlap the Messengers
3d Was Motion and agreed that we petition for the next Union meeting and

B^{r} Dunlap write the same 4th adjourn^{d} in order by Prayer &c

(P. 103) September the 20th 1828

The Church met according to appointment after Worship proceeded to Business as follows 1^{rst} the B^{rn} appointed to Cite Sister Peters report her Comissions for non attendance the Church Recive^{d} it &c Sister Peters makes application for dismission which was granted the Clerk order^{d} to Issue the Same
2^{d} B^{r} Joseph Rentfro come forward and made a Satisfactory recantation and was restor^{d} to his former privilledges
3^{d} B^{r} John Dunlap makes application for letters of dismission for him and wife was granted and Issued accordingly
4th B^{ro} Stover apply^{d} for a letter of Dismission for him and wife which was granted &c
5 appointed B^{rn} Peter Kuhn and Elijah Buck Deacons to fill the place of B^{r} Dunlap and Stover &c
6st adjourn^{d} in order &c
When this you see remember me Daniel Stover

(P. 104) October the 17th 1828

The Church met according to adjournment after Worship Proceeded to Business as follows 1^{rst} Br Elijah Buck appointed one of the trustees of this Church adjourn^{d} till tomorrow
18th Met according to adjournment and proceeded to Business as follows 1^{rst} Agnes Hatcher came forward and was receiv^{d} by Experience 2^{d} The minutes of last meeting of Asso.. Read & Approv^{d} adjourn^{d} in order The following day the B^{rn} who were appointed Deacons were Legally ordained

November the 15th 1828

The Church met according to appointed and proceeded to Business as follows Nothing Committed record

December the 20th 1828

The Church met and after Worship proceeded to Business as follows 1^{rst} This Church again hath agreed to petition B^{r} Rees Bayles to take the Pastorial Care of this Church B^{rn} Elijah Buck & Peter Kuhn the messengers to Carry the Same &c Dismist in order

January the 17th 1829

The Church met and after Worship proceeded to Business 1^{rst} The messenger appointed to Carry the Petition to B^{r} Bayles report and say that he will attend our meeting and &c
adjourn^{d} in oder

(P. 105) February the 14th 1829

The Church met and after worship proceeded to Business as follows 1^{rst} this Church agree to have a Communion in may the fifth Sabbath

March the 14th 1829

The Church met and after worship proceeded to Business 1^{rst} the Church has agreed to give B^{r} Joseph Renfro a leter of dission 2^{d} the Church has appointed Brother Elijah Buck & Peter Kuhn to Cite Sister Nancy Bayless to our nex meeting and inquire into Some reports respecting her conduct dismissed in order

April the 18th 1829

the Church of Christ on Sinking Creek met and after worship proceeded to Business 1^{r} the case of Nancy Bayles taken up and after some altercation this Church declars an unfoleship with her for disobeying the call of the Church and for some immorral Conduct Dismiss in order

May the 16th 1829 the Church met acording to appointment and after worship preceded to Business as fellows 1^{rs} appointed Bro Peter Kuhn Clark for this Church Dismiss^{d} in order

May the 29th 1829 the Church of Christ at Sinking Creek met acording to apointment and after worship preceded to business as follows 1^{rs} Recev^{d} a petition from Stony Creek Church praying us to send them helps which was granted &c and appointed as Elijah Buck Peter Kuhn & Ephrim Morehead to fill the petition 2^{d} motion^{d} and Seconded that Brother Casaday be Cited to next meeting as their appers to be reports in Circultion respecting his immoral Conduct &c appointed B^{ro} Elijah Buck and Peter Kuhn the Churches messengers Dismiss^{d} till Saturday the 20th the Church again met and after worship proceeded to Business as follows 1^{rs} Recev^{d} three by letter to it Charrity Ross Franky Allen Rachel Mays ajorn^{d} til meeting in Cors

(P. 106) June the 17th 1829 the Church met and after worship proceeded to business as follows 1 the case of Bro Casaday taken up and referd 2^{d} the Church has Chose heir deligats to the asso to it James Edens and Peter Kuhn 3^{d} agreed that we scend 1$ to the asso Dismis^{d} in order

July the 18th 1829 the Church met and after worship proceded to business as follows 1! the case of bro Casaday agane taken up and refer^{d} and appointed Brethren Elijah Buck and Ephrim Morehead to invit him ~~agreed to~~ to attend at our September meting 2^{d} agreed to petition the next asso to be held at this place 3^{d} the letter prepar^{d} to the asso Red and approv^{d} adjorn^{d} in order

August the 15th 1829 the Church met and after worship proceded to business nothing recorded ajorn^{d} in order

September the 18th 1829 the Church of Christ at Sinking Creek met and after worsip proceded to business as follows 1^{d} recev^{d} Thomas Dilard Love by experans
2^{d} the cas of brother Casaday taken up and after an investigation this Church declarse an unfelleship with him for disobaying the Call of the Church.
3^{d} Elisabeth Kuhn applyed for a letter of dismission wich was granted also sister Sary Dunlap apply^{d} for a letter and it was granted 4 the minutes of the asso red and approvd 5th agreed that Baptism be administer^{d} on the lords day ajorn^{d} in order
Saturday the 19th the Church met and after worship proceded to business as follows 1^{d} a greed that this Church writ a letter to the Church at Mount rhewhama and Bro Love to writ the same and the letter to be red at the next meting ajorn^{d} in order til meting in Cors.

October the 17th 1829 the Church meet acording to ajornment and after worship proceded to Business as follows 1rs Mary Hampton came forward and gave a relation of the work of grace on hir mind and was recavd and also Rebecca Stevens and was recevd and also Fanny Matterson and was recevd 2d Hannah Bogart came forward and gave Satisfaction and was recevd 3d Sister Rachel Mays applied for a letter of dismission and it was granted and also Hannah Bogart applid for a letter and it was granted 4th agreed to send messengers to see sister Milly Peters and inquir of hir (P. 107) whi she holds his letter and invite hir to attend the the next meting and bren Josiah Parker and Peter Kuhn the Churches messengers ajornd in order NB Rebeca Stevens fanny Matterson was baptized on the lords day

November the 14th 1829 the Church meet and after worship proceeded to business as follows 1d the messengers appointed to see sister Peters report that on inquiry we find hir to hold hir letter and that she has taken the love fest with the methodis and on motion agree refer it til next meeting 2d agree to Call Bro Whit to administer the ordinance of Baptism on tomorow be attended and Baptizd Mary Hampton 3d a greed that Bro Elijah Buck be liberated to preach the gospel in the bounds of this Church ajornd in order

December the 19th 1829 the Church meet acording to ajornmet and after worship proceeded to business as follows 1: the reffeance from last meeting taken up as it respects Sister Peters and we declar an unfellowship with hir for disobeying the Cawl of the Church and for retaining hir letter and saing that she intended to keep it 2 a greed that Bren Peter Kuhn and Josiah Parker to go and demand hir letter 3 bro Ephraim Morehead and wife applide for letters of dismission and granted hirn and referd his case and a greed to send messengers to see him and apoint Thomas D Love and Elijah Buck messengers and also Charrity Ross and Franky allen applid for letters of dismission and tha was granted and also sister Orphy Thomson applid for a letter and it was granted 4 Recevd Elisabeth Kuhn by letter ajornd in order

January the 16th 1830 the Church meet acording to ajornment and after worship proceded to business as follows 1 the messengers returnd no letter 2 the messengers to see Bro Morehead report tha saw him and got no sadisfaction and the matter referd til next meeting a Jornd in order

February the 20th 1830 the Church meet and after worship proceded to business as follows 1 Chose Bro Buck moderator 2 the refference from last meting taken up respecting Bro Morehead and this Church declars an unfelloship with him for disobeying the call of the Church anfor immorral conduct 3 motiond and a greed to have a Communion season on the 5 Sabbath in May the meting to begin on friday aJornd til meting in cors.

(P. 108) March the 20th 1830 the Church met and after worship proceded to business as follows 1rs John Wright came forward and gave satisfaction and was recevd 2d Brother Elihah Buck and wife came forward and applid for letters of dismission and it was granted and issued acordingly ajornd in oder

April the 17th 1830 the Church met and after worship proceded to Business as follows 1 s apointed Brother Thomas D Love a trustee of this Church in place of Bro Buck Dismisd in order

May the 15th 1830 the Church at Sinking Creek met and after worship proceded to business as follows 1nd Motioned and agreed that Bro Kuhn be alowed to exercise in exertation ajornd til metin in Cors

May the 28th 1830 the Church met and after worship proceded to business as follows ajornd till tomorrow 11 oclock
Saturday the 29th the Church agane met and after worship proceded to business as follows ajornd til meting in Cors

June the 19th 1830 the Church met and after worship proceded to Business as follows 1 Chose Bro Parker Clark protem 2 apointed our deligats to the asso to it Bro James Edens and Josiah Parker 3 agree to send 1 dolar to the asso.

July the 17th 1830 the Church met and after worship proceded to Business as follows 1: agree to report Milly Peters to the association as holding her letter in disorder 2: the letter to asso red and aprovd 3 recevd Margret Profit which now Cooper by letter
4 recevd 2 by experanc vis Orphy and Aseneth Hatcher 5 agree that it is not right to call for an administrater when we hav one among us a Jornd in order

September the 18th 1830 the Church met and after Worship proceded to Busieness as follows 1 Chose Bro Kuhn moderter 2 minuts of the asso red and recevd aJornd in order

October the 16th 1830 the Church met and after Worship proceded to business as follows 1 the letter from Thomas Buck taken up and and after some altercation agree to send a letter Stating the facts and refer the Case to the Church where he lives 2 motiond and agreed that Brother Love ade in writing the Same and the letter to be red at the next meeting 3 agree to have a Communion on the 5 sabath in this month the meting to commence on friday 4 Sister Whithead hath maid application by Bro Edons for a letter of dismission which was granted (P. 109) 5th agreed that Brother Peter Kuhn be alow,d to preach the gospel in the bounds of 4 Churches to it Sinking Creek Buffalow ridge and Cherokee Stony Creek
ajornd in order

Oct the 29th 1830 the Church met after worship proceded to business as follows 1 the letter to Thomas Buck red and recevd 2 a pointted Bro Writ to Settle with the Clark and reporte to next meting Saturday the 30 Chuch a gane met and after worship proceded to business as follows 1 agreable to the order of yesterday Bro John Wright report his settlement with the Clark and is discharg'd ajornd in order

November the 20th 1830 the Church met and after worship proceded to business as follows 1 motiond and agred to send messiongers to see Sister Susannah Perkins and in vit her to come and fil her seat and inquire into Som reports Bren James Edons Peter Kuhn messengers 2 Bro John Wright made application for a letter of dismission which was granted
ajorned in order

December the 18th 1830 the Church met and after Worship proceded to Business as follows 1 the messengers to see Sister Sussan Perkins report that tha saw her and She a greed to fill her Seat and on failing to attend agree to refer the matter till next meting ajornd in order

January (Blank)

Febary the 19th 1831 the Church met and after worship proceded to business as follows 1 the referance from December meting taken up and refer'd til may meting 2 agree to hav a Communion on the 3 Sabbath in April the meting to commence on friday a Jornd til meting in Corse

March the 19th 1831 the Church met and after worship proceded to business as follows 1 Sister Elisabeth Kuhn came forward and applid for a letter of dismission which was granted and also Sister Ann and Mary Hampton applid for letters of dismission and tha was granted ajornd in order

April the 15th 1831 the Church met and after worship proceded to business as follows a Jornd til to morrow 11 O,clock Saturday the 16th the Church agane met and after divine Service proceded to business as follows 1 by request of Brother Kuhn our former Clark we agree to releas him from that office and apoint Bro Thomas D Love to fil the Same 2 a gree to give Bro Peter Kuhn a writen lisons to preach the gospel whetherso ever God in his providence may cast his lot Peter Kuhn aJorned in order

(P. 110) Sunday the 17th the Church agane met and after worship Sat for business David Pugh came forward and gave Satisfaction and was restord to his former priviledge agane aJornd

May the 14th 1831 the Church meet and after worship proceeded to Business as follows 1 chose Brother Peter Kuhn Clark protemary--2 the referince from febuary meetting concerning Susanah Perkins taken up & after some altercation she came forward and withdrew her membership- 3 motioned and a greed that our Communion Season be held in May and October hereafter
aJorned in order Thos D Love Clerk

June the 18- 1831-

the Church of Christ on Sinking Creek meet according to its regular monthly meeting and after divine worship proceeded to business 1 on motion & a greed to that the Church Chose its delegation for the association for the Second friday of August next and that two be chosen and after Balloting Brothers James Edens and Peter Kuhn were chosen--the 2 motion and greed to that the Clerk prepare a letter for the association by the next Church meeting it is greed that the Church send one Dollar to the association- 3 motion that it is refered to the next meeting for a Deacon to be Chosen and that Saturday be set apart for fasting and prayer the Church then adjorned in order

Thos D Love
Clerk

(P. 111) July the 16- 1831- the Church of Christ on Sinking Creek meet according its monthly meeting & after worship proceeded to business- first the letter that was prepared by the Clerk was read and approved of 2 motioned and agreed to that the Chois of Deacon be refered to the next meeting John & Elizebeth Cashdys come forward and both were receivd by experience into the Church and also Robert Cashdy came forward and was receivd by recantation and baptism were administred on Sunday nothing more appearing the Church adjorned in order

Thos D Love Clerk

August the 20- 1831 the Church of Christ at Sinking Creek meet according to adjornment & after worship proceeded to business--on motion and Seconed that the Choise of deacon be refered to next meeting- Solomon Hendrix and Mary

Hendrick came forward and was receivd into Church by recantation nothing appearing the Church adorned-- Thos D Love Clerk

September the 18th - 1831 the Church of Christ at Sinking Creek meet according to adjornment & after worship proceeded to business; on Motion and Seconded that brother Solomon Hendricks & wife be restored to their former Deacon Ship & it was agreed to by the Church that they be restored to all the priveledges of that offices- Sister Elizabeth Kuhn produced a letter from Mudy Creek being of the same faith & order & was receivd into this Church Sarah Hatcher came forward & was received on experience brother Kuhn moved to be released from the office of deacon & it was refered to November (P. 112) meeting nothing appearing the Church adjorned to its next meeting -- Thos D Love Clerk --

October the 14th 1831 the Church of Christ at Sinking Creek meet according to its adjornment and after worship proceeded to business minutes of the assosiation was read and apprvd the Church then adjorned untill tomorrow 11 Oclock Saturday the 15 the Church of Christ meet according to their adjornment yesterday the Church Covenant was produced and read & it was motioned Seconded that the referance in it to the Philadelphia confession of faith be expuged from the Church Covenant the Church then adjorned
Thos D Love

November the 18- 1831 the Church of Christ at Sinking Creek meet according to adjornment & after worship proceeded to business the reference of brother Peter Kuhn was taken up & it was ordered by the Church that brother Peter Kuhn be released from being Deacon the Church then adjorned untill meeting in course-- Thos D Love Clerk

December the 17- 1831

the Church of Christ at Sinking Creek meet according to their former adjornment and after Worship proceeded to business, & nothing appearing it adjorned untill meeting in Course--
Thos D Love Clerk

January the 14- 1832--

Church of Christ at Sinking Creek meet according to their former adjornment and after Worship proceeded to business it was motioned Seconed that the former refference for the Choice of a deacon be taken up and after brother David & Sister Rachel Pugh were Chosen Deacon and Deaconist & it was motioned & seconed brother Pughs ordination be reffered untill May meeting it was motioned & Seconed that Church (P. 113) petitioned for help from other Churches to come for the ordination of brother Pugh at may meeting and that brother R Baels B White J Pointdexter and L Bowers be request to aid in the ordination of brother Pugh and that brother Parker, Eadens & Kuhn is appoined messengers to the before named brothers for to git their assistance to ordain brother Pugh nothing more appearing the Church adjorned untill meeting of Course-- Thos D Love Clerk

february the 18 -- 1832

the Church of Christ at Sinking Creek meet according its adjornment after worship proceeded to business Sister feby Boren produced a letter from Roane Creek Church & was received into this Church motioned and seconed

that the former reference respecting the Choise of a paster be withdrawn and refered to March meeting and that then a choise be made it was motioned and seconed that brother Pugh and Love be appointed to settle with brother Kuhn the former Treasurer of this Church on Saturday of our next meeting, & report the same nothing more appearing the church adjorned-
Thos D Love Clerk --

febuary the 19- 1832--

this day the Church of Christ at Sinking Creek meet and recived brother John D Carty by letter from Medow Church in Montgomery Virginia
Thos D Love Clerk

March the 17th 1832 the Church of Christ at Sinking Creek meet and after worship proceeded (P. 114) to business as follows first Chose Bretheren Bayless and Kuhn moderator and Clerk protem 2 the reference from last meeting was taken up respecting the Choise of a Paster and it was a greed that Brother Rees Bayless be and was Chosen Paster the Church was then adjorned in order until meeting in course--Thos D Love Clerk --

April the 14- 1832-

the Church of Christ at Sinking Creek meet according to its former adjornment after worship proceeded to business it was motioned & agreed that brother Kuhn be appointed moderator protem. the report of the committee Composed of brother Love & Pugh respecting the Settlement with the Treasurer be confirmed. Motioned & agreed to that we petition for the next union meeting motioned & agreed to that brothers Kuhn, Hendrix & Pugh be appointed a Committee to beare the petition for the union meeting and that brother Love write the same motioned & agreed to that the Church adjorn untill meeting in cours-- Thos D Love Clerk

May the 18- 1832--

the Church of Christ at Sinking Creek meet according to adjornment and after worship proceeded to business as follows first the petition prepared by our Clerk brother Thos D Love was read and approved of as & Seconly it was moved and agreedto that enquiry be made into the conduct of Sister Jane Parker on a charge of fornication and from the evidence produced it appeared that she was dilivered of an eligitmate child it was therefore ordered by the Church and agreed to withdraw their fellowship from her then the Church adjorned untill tomorrow. Thos D Love Clerk --

(P. 115) (Refferance 1903 In Pencil)

Saturday May the 19th 1832

the Church of Christ at Sinking Creek meet according to it adjornment yesterday after Worship proceeded to business as follows first it was moved and agreed to that the washing of feet be refered for further Consideration and then nothing more appearing the Church adjorned untill tomorrow
Thos D Love Clerk ---

Sunday May the 20- 1832--

the Church of Christ meet according to it adjornment yesterday and there appearing a sufficient number of ordained Preachers the Church proceeded to the ordination of brother David Pugh as one of the Deacons of this Church than it was done and approved of by the Church then the Church adjorned untill meeting in Course Thos D Love Clerk

June the 16th 1832

the Church of Christ at Sinking Creek meet according to its former adjornment after worship Proceeded to business as follows first Chose brother Peter Kuhn moderater protem motioned and agreed therefore it was ordered by the Church that messengers be sent to ~~[illegible]~~ invite brother John D Carty to fill his seat & brethren Solomon Hendrix and David Pugh be appointed to invite him to attend at the next meeting then Leonard Hart came forward and was recieved into the Church by experience and Sarah Nave was also received by experience motioned & agreed therefore it was ordered by the Church that we appoint two delagats for to represent this Church in the association by ballot which was done and resulted in the Choise of bretheren David Pugh & Peter Kuhn also agreed that this Church send one Dollar to the association & also it is ordered by the Church that the Clerk prepare the letter for the next assosiation to be read at the next Church (P. 116) meeting agreed to send this as a quеary has a Church a right to call on an ordained authority to fill his seat at the monthly meetings of his Church or not the Church then adjorned untill meeting in Course

Thos D Love Clerk

July the 14 - 1832--

the Church of Christ at Sinking Creek meet according to its adjornment and after worship proceeded to business as follows first motioned and agreed that the referance of washing feet be refered untill the minuets of the association come to hand- Secondly that brother James Edens and Sister Eve Edens have letters of dismission from this Church and that brother Love our Clerk write the letters at a more convenient time the messengers that were sent to invite brother Carty to his seat returned with him and he took his Seat accordingly also the letter for the association was produced by the Clerk was read and approved by the Church nothing more appearing the Church adjorned Thos D Love Clerk

August the 18- 1832--

the Church of Christ at Sinking Creek meet according to its adjornment and after worship proceeded to business as follow, - first the account of Brother Solomon Hendrix of the Church funds was prodused and adjusted and there appeared to be nine cents in favour of the Church in the hands of the treasurer nothing more appearing the Church adjorned

Thos D Love Clerk

\- September the 15th 1832

the Church of Christ at Sinking Creek met and after worship proceded to business as follows
1st the minuts of the association red and approvd 2 the referance from a former meting taking up respecting washing the Saints feet and to practice the same 3 motioned and agree that Brother Peter Kuhn be ordaind and Call for a prisbatary to attend at our next meting for that purpose 4 Sister

Rebecah Stephens applid for a letter of dismission and it was granted and Brother Edens to wright the Same aJorned

Oct the 19th 1832 the Church met and after worship proceeded to business as follows 1 brother Kuhn movd to be raleast from being trustee and it was agreed to and Bro David Pugh to fill the vacancy 3 Sis nancy Price applid for a letter of dismission by bro Pugh and it was granted 4 Margrat Threewitts came forward and gave a ralation of a work of grace on heir mind and was recev,d Saturday the 20th the Church agane met and after 2 sermon and an exertation Sat for business 1 Thomas Perry Came forward and gave a relation of the works of grace upon his mind and was recev,d and also Mary Perry came forward and was recev,d 3 according to the call of the Church the Presbytery met and after examination Proceded to the ordination of Brother Kuhn to the ministary to wit Rees Bayless James Edon Jerimiah Hail and John D Carty and thos recev,d was all Baptized the day following

November the 17th 1832 the Church of Christ at Sinking Creek met and after worship proceded to Business as follows 1 our Clarke being absent we have Chose brother Peter Kuhn Clark pro tem 2 John Broiles came forward and gave a relation of a work of grase on his mind and was recev,d and also his — Eliza Broiles and Simaon Broiles and Nancy Pary and Wm Pugh and was recev,d and was all Babtized the next day 3 we are call,d to inscert the Deth of our beloved Brother Thomas D Love he Deceast 16th of this instant 4 motion,d and a greed that Brother Hendrix attend at brother Loves and appli for the ledger and bring it to the next meeting in Cors a jorn,d

December the 15th 1832

the Church of Christ at Sinking Creek met and after worship proceded to business as follows 1 WM Pary came forward and gave a relation of a work of grace on his mind and was receved the referance of last meeting respecting the Coise of Clark continued (P. 117) Brother Hendrix has agreeable to the order of last meeting brought the lager and gave it up to the Church motion,d and a greed that we that we insert in the Church lager the Deth of all our members a greed that John Broiles be our trustee in place of Thos D Love
We are call,d upon to insert the Deth of our beloved Brother Joel Cooper ho Decest the 29th of this instant a Jornd

January the 19th 1833 the Church of Christ at Sinking Creek met and after worship proceded To business as follows 1 the referance of last meting respecting the Choise of Clarke taken up and unanimously agree that Brother William Pugh Fill the place 2 received Tennessee Nave by letter 3 Brother Peter Kuhn and wife Elizabeth Applied for letters of dismission and it was granted a Jornd as following

February the 16th 1833 the Church of Christ at Sinking Creek met and after worship proceded To business as follows 1 Received Brother Isaac Gilbert and Cassie his wife by letter 2nd Receivd Charlety Ellis by Experience adjornd till the meting in Corse

March the 16th 1833 the Church of Christ at Sinking Creek met and after worsh Proceded to business as follows first Brother John D Carte applied for a letter of Dismission and it was granted the Church then adjorned until to morrow Wm Pugh Clerk

April the 20th 1833 the Church of Christ at Sinking Creek met and after worship Proceded to Business as follows & nothing appearing it adjorned until meting in cors-- William Pugh Clerk

May the 17th 1833 the Church of Christ at Sinken Creek met and after worship prosded To buisness as follows
1 William Wheeler came forward and gave a relation of a work of grace on his mind and was received--
2 Hannah Ensor came forward and gave a Relation of a work of grace on her mind and was received
3 James Peoples Came forward and was received by letter 4 the Church Being informed by a letter from Cherokee That they disaprobate a pamphlet in circulation the title of which is dream or Dialogue between a baddon and his Clergumen we fell to join them and have apointed our Brothern Solomon Hendrix and David Pugh to meet them of Sister Churches on Saturday of our next meting to form a Piece to be put into the formers Journal and nothing more appearing we adjorned until tomorrow

Wm Pugh Clerk

June the 15th 1833

The Church of Christ at Sinking Creek met and after worship proseded To business as follows 1^rst^ Receiv^d^ Thomas Hampton and Any his wife by Letter 2^d^ Received Nancy ford by Letter 3^d^ unanimously agreed that Simeon Broyles Be dismiss by letter 4th the (P. 118) Church agreed to Ballot for Deligates To the Asosiation and Chose Solomon Hendrix and David Pugh and agreed to Contribut one Dollar to the asosiation then nothin more appearing we adjorned until to morrow--

Wm Pugh Clerk

July the 20th 1833 the Church of Christ at Sinking Creek met according to adjornment and after worship proseed to business as follows and nothing appearing we adjornd until tomorrow

Wm Pugh Clerk

August the 17th 1833

The Church of Christ at Sinking Creek met according To adjournment and after Divine Service proceeded To business as follows first Chose David Pugh to Act as Clerk protem 1st a Door was opened for the Reception of members no won Coming forward William Pugh made application for a letter of Dismission and it was then Granted adjorn^d^ untill the next meeting in Cours

David Pugh Clerk
Protem

September the 14th 1833

The Church of Christ at Sinking met according to adjournment after interducing the worship of God by Singing and prayd Proceded to business first opened a Door for the reception of members 2 The Church took the Circumstance of Cassia Bowman under Consideration and hath made up Seven Dollars in Clothing for hair 3 the Church hath Sent Mary hendrix and Rachel Pugh and Sarah Nave to See the Sister and report to the next meeting adjournd till meeting in Cours

(P. 119) October the 18th 1833

The Church of Christ at Sinking Creek hath met according to adjournment and after worship proceded to Business first opened a Door for the Reception of Members-- 2 and this being a union meeting Received a letter of Corrispondence from the fourth Devision by their deligats Brother Benjemin White Brother Vollentine Bowers and invited them to Seats with us which They Cordially accepted 3 and appointed Brother Tennessee Nave to write a letter of Corrispondence To them then Dismisd in order

~~David-Pugh~~
~~Clerk-Protem.~~

Till tomorrow met according to adjournment after worship proceded to business 4th Muddy Creek Church Petioned for the next union meeting to be held with them no opposition we say that our next meeting Be at Muddy Creek meeting house in Suliven County Commencing on friday before the Ceconed Sunday in October adjournd till the next meeting in Cours

David Pugh Clerk
Protem

November the 16th 1833

The Church of Christ at Sinking Creek met according to adjournment Nothing recorded

David Pugh Clerk
Protem.

December the 14th 1833

The Church of Christ at Sinking Creek met according to adjournment after Divine worship preceded to business as follows 1 first Sister Elisabeth Helton came fd joined the Church By Letter from the Baptist Church of Sherroun in North Carrolina
Elisabeth hatcher came foward (P. 120) and gave a ralation of a work of grace on her mind and was Received into the Church then Dismissed Untill the next meeting in Course---

David Pugh Clerk
Protem

January the 18th 1834

The Church of Christ at Sinking Creek met according to adjournment nothing Recorded adjournd till Meeting in Cours

David Pugh Clerk
Protem

February the 15th 1834

The Church of Christ at Sinking Creek met acording to there adjournment and after Divine Worship Proceded to Business as follows first a Door was opened for the Reception of members Second 2 Brother Solomon Hendrix made application to the To Releis him from his Deacon Ship Moved and Seconed to be refered till the next meeting 3 Brother Joshua Adams Came forward and joined The Church by letter from the Watauga Church Nothing more appearing adjourned till next meeting in Cours--

David Pugh
Clerk Protem

(P. 121) March 15th 1834

The Church of Christ at Sinking Creek met according to adjournment and after Divine worship Proceded to Business first took up the Refference of last Meeting Respecting Brother Hendrix Being Released of his Deacon Ship 2 motioned and agreed on that the Reference Respecting brother Hendrix Being Released from his Decon Ship Be Contimued till next meeting in Cours-2 a door opened for the Reception of members Sister Tabitha Adams come forward and joined the Church by letter from the Wattauga Church Then Dismisd untill the next meeting in Cours

David Pugh Clerk
Protem

April the 19th 1834

The Church of Christ at Sinking Creek math met according to there adjournment and after divine worship Proceded to Business first took up the Reference Respecting Brother Hendrix being Released of his Deacon Ship unanimously agree by the Church to Release Brother Hendrix —
2 after Brother Hendrix was Releasd by the Church of his Deacon Ship Through the Request of brother Pugh be offered to assist Brother Pugh at the communion table if not otherwise Supplyd which was cordially accepted of the Church nothing more appearing Adjournd in order

David Pugh
Clerk Protem

May the 16th 1834

The Church of Christ at Sinking Creek hath according To there adjournment after Divine worship proceded To Business 1 first it was moved that the Church Make Choice of her Deccon 2 motiond and Seconed (P. 122) That it be Refered till to morrow nothing more appearing at present adjournd till to morrow Saturday the 17th The Church met according to her adjournment third Received Brother Matthias Broils and Anna Broils his wife By letter from the Wattauga Church 4th Refferance of last meeting Calld for and taken up Respecting a Dacon and after Balleting By the Church Brother Solomon Hendrix and Sister Mary Hendrix was Reelected into there former offices again By the Church nothing more appearing adjournd in order

David Pugh Clerk protem

June the 14th 1834

The Church of Christ at Sinking Creek hath met according to there adjournment and after worship Proceded to Business 1 first it was motioned and agreed that the Church Choose her Deligates by Balleting which was Done and Resulted in the Choice of Brn Solomon Hendrix and David Pugh to Represent her in this association also agreed that this Church Send one Dollar to the association and also it is ordered By the Church that the Clerk Prepare a letter to be inspected at our next meeting to send to the association
2 it was motioned and agreed that we Send messengers to labour with Sister Wright to know the Cause of her long absence from the Church and Solomon Hendrix and David Pugh be the Churches messengers and make ther report to the next meeting Nothing more appearing adjourned in order

David Pugh Clerk
protem

July the 19th 1834

The Church of Christ at Sinking Creek Hath met according to there adjournment after Divine worship Proceded to business (P. 123) First the case respecting Sister Wright calld for The Messengers of the Church failing to Do there Duty the Citation continued till next meeting in cours

2 the letter to the association calld for and read in the preasence of the Church and approved of 3 A Door was opened for the reception of members No one came forward adjourned in order

David Pugh Clerk

August the 16th 1834

The Church of Christ at Sinking Creek hath met according to there adjournment after worship Proceded to business as follows 1 first the Referance Respecting Sister Wright Called for and Continued 2 Brother James Jones made application for a letter of Dismission by Brother James Edens and it was granted and ishued accordingly 3 it motioned and greed that this Church Send Messengers to the Wattauga Church to make Enquiry of that Church to know The Cause of there Retaining Brother Adams Licence and make report at our meeting next for which we have Chosen our Beloved Brethren Josiah Parker Wm Perry and David Pugh 4th Brother Thomas Perry made application For letters of Dismission for him and his wife which was granted and issued accordingly nothing more appearing adjourned

David Pugh Clerk

September the 16th 1834

The Church of Christ at Sinking Creek met according to adjournment after Divine worship proded to business 1 first the Case Respecting Sister Wright called for and Taken up and Prefered till next meeting in Cours ---
2d The Case of Brother Adams Respecting his Licence taken up after Due Consideration (P. 124) of the Church they think it most expedient to let it Rest where it is a while longer 3d a Door opened For the Reception of members 4th Sister Charlette Ellis made application for a letter of Dismission which was granted adjourned in order

David Pugh Clerk

Friday the 17 of October 1834) the Church of Christ at Sinking Creek met according to there adjournment after Divine worship Proceded to Business 1 first the Referance Called For and taken up Respecting Sister Wright motioned and agreed to Refer it till to morrow 2 a Door being opened For the Reception Members no one came forward Adjournd till to morrow at Eleven oclock 3 met according To adjournment after Divine woship Prceded to business
The Case respecting Sister Wright taken up and the Church Do Declare an unfellowship with her for Leaving her own church and joining another Church and Disobeying the Call of the Church when Sent for 4 fourth a Door was opened for the Reception of members Brother richerd Carr came forward and Exprest a Desire to,live with us and was Cordially received
Nothing more came forward we adjournd in order

David Pugh Clerk

November the 15th 1834

The Church of Christ at Sinking Creek met according to There adjournment after interDuceing the worship of God By Singing and prayr Proceded to business first Chose Brother Robert G Kimbrew Moderater nothing came Before the Church adjournd in order)

David Pugh Clerk

(P. 125) December the 19th 1834) The Church of Christ at Sinking Creek Hath met according to there adjournment after worship Proceded to

Business not anything more appearing worthy of Record adjourd in order --
David Pugh Clerk.

January the 17 1835

The Church of Christ at Sinking Creek hath met According to there adjournment after Divine worship Proceded to Business a door ware opened for the reception of members Received Sister Temperance Hale by letter From Pig river Baptist Church Virginia 2d --Brother Gilbert mad application for letters of Dismission which was granted and ordered by the Church that the Clark Should wrte them which ware Don accordingly 3d--Old Sister Ervin made application for a letter of Dismission By Br Baylis if her name ware found in the Book ordered by the Church that the Clerk Serth the Church Book and if her name is in to write her a letter of Dismission and Send it to her by Br Baylis 4th from Reports that is in Circulation respecting Sister Mary Perry The Church think proper to Send messengers to See the Sister and labour to reclaim the Sister if Possible and make There report at next meeting for which we have Chosen our beloved brethren Wm Wheelor Josiah Parker John Broyls 5th Brother David Pugh made application for to be released from being Clerk which was Don accordingly and Chose Brother Richard Karr to fill the place)
Nothing more appearing adjournd in order
David Pugh Clerk

(P. 126) February 14th 1835

The Church met according to appointment and after worship proceded to Business 1st the Referance Concerning Sister Polly Perrys case taken up - it was motioned and Seconded that theare be a Committee appointed and the following Brethren were appointed (to wit) Solomon Hendrix David Pugh John Broiles Wm Whelor Josiah Parker Tennessee T Nave Richard Carr and after Due Examinnation no positive proff of the Charges made against her though the sister acknowledged she had done wrong although she thought God had forgiven her and she wished the forgiveness of the brethren also we thearefore feel to acques with the sistter - nothing more appeared the Church adjourned in order
Richard Carr Clk

March 14th 1835 The Church of Christ at Sinking Creek Carter County met according to adjournment and after worship proceded to Business 1st old Brother Ceasor came forward and was restord to his former priviledges in this Church by Recantation
2nd a Doore was opened for the Reception of members by Experience or letter none came forward
3rd The Churches Contribution was handed in amounting to \$0..87½
Richard Carr Clerk

April 18th 1835 The Church met according to appontment and after Divine servis prosed to Business 1st a door was opened for the Reception of members none came forward 2nd Sister Nancy Miller by Brothe Eaden pertioned for a letter of dismition which was granted and Issued accordingly
(P. 127) 3d the Churches Contribution was handed in amt \$0..97½
adjournd in order 0..12½
Richard Carr Clk

Friday 15th of May 1835 The Church met according to apointment and after worship proceded to Business 1st Nothing Committed to Record adjournd in order &c

Richard Carr Clk

Saterday 16th of May 1835

The Church met according to apointment and after Divine worship proseded to Business 1st the subject of feet washing at our Communion seasons was taken up and after some debate it was determd that the practice Should be followed 2nd Brother Seasor applyed for a letter of Dismition which was granted and Issued accordingly adjournd in order &c

Richard Carr Clk

June 20th 1835

The Church of Christ at Sinking Creek met according to appointment and after worship proceded to the Church to be Released from his Deacon Ship which was granted by the Church
2nd it is agreed by the Church to Refer the Choice of a Deacon til next meting in course
3rd the Church agreed to Ballet for deligates to Represent her in the Insuing association and the Choce Resulted as follows (to wit) Solomon Hendrix William Wheeler David Pugh (P. 128) also agreed to send one Dollar for the use of the association 4th it is Requested by the Church that the Clerk prepare a Letter against the next meting to send to the association adjournd in order

Richard Carr Clk

July 18th 1835 The Church met according to appointment and after worship proceded to business 1st the letter to the association was read by the Church 2nd the Reference of Chusing a Deacon was taken up and after Balleting by the Church the Choice fell on Brother ~~Matthias Brei~~es 3rd it was motioned By Brother Thomas Hampton to know whether this Church will agree to have a protracted meting at the time of thear next Communion Season which was agreed to by a unanimous vote
Nothing more appearing the Church adjound in order

Richard Carr Clk

~~Sept 19th 1835 The Church met according to adjournment and after Devine servis proceded to Business and theare appearing nothing worth Recording the Church adjourned in order~~

~~Richard Carr Clk~~

(P. 129) September 19th 1835 The Church met according to appointment and after worship proceded to business 1st the Churches Contribution to defray the Expence of thear next Communion meting Called for and the following Sumes handed in to wit

Robert Casaday — — —	$0..25
Solomon Hendrix	0..25
Wm Whelor	0..25
Richard Carr	0..25
Hannah Ensor	12½
	1..12½

and theare appearing nothing more worth Recording the Church adjourned in order

Richard Carr Clk

October 16th 1835 The Church met according to appointment & after divine worship proceded to Business 1st a doore was opened for the Receiption of members by letter or Experiance John Carty Joined by letter from Watauga Church and 2nd Wm Pugh came forward and Joined by letter Both was Cordially Received nothing more appearing worth recording the Church adjourned in order

Richard Carr Clk

This Being a protracted meting and theare being a Church meting held on the next Wednesday following the following members was Received vz Joel Cooper David Wright Sarah Wright James Casaday Elizabeth Whelor Mahala Kuhn Franklin Casaday Robert Casaday Junr.. (P. 130) Rachel Vanne ----- Wilson John Swinney ------Brumit -----Broyles Mary Tipton of color and all weare baptised done by order of the Church and Susannah Swinney by Letter

Richard Carr Clk

November 14th 1835 The Church met according to appointment and after worship proceded to Business 1st a doore was openned for the Reception of members by letter or Experience we received William Hatcher Samuel Tipton George T Hale Thos Hatcher John Hatcher all by Experience adjourned till to morrow
the Church agane met and set for Business 1st a doore was opened for the reception of members Madison Ensor came forward and was Received by Experiance Church Business waa adjournd and the others duties of the day attended to
Signed by order of the Church

Richard Carr Clk

The 19th of December 1835 the Church of Christ at Sinking Creek met according to appointment and after worship proceded to Business 1st a doore was opened for the Reception of members Elizabeth Ann Hopper came forward and was Received by Experiance (P. 131) 2nd Brother Mathias Broyles applyed for liberty from this Church to Exercise his gift in the diferent Churches compaing the Holstoh Baptist association which was granted to him by the Church though not lisoned
nothing more appearing the Church adjourned in order
Richard Carr Clk

Saturday 16 of January 1836 The Church of Christ at Sinking Creek met according to adjournment and after worship proceded to Business 1st a door was opened for the Reception of members by letter or Experiance Hampton Hyder came forward and was Recd By Experiance nothing more appearing the Church adjourned in order

Richard Carr Clk

Feb.. 20th 1836 the Church of Christ at Sinking Creek met according to appointment and after divine worship proceded to Business 1st a door was opened for the Reception of members none came and nothing more appearing the Church adjourned in order

Richard Carr Clk

Saturday 19th of March 1836 The Church of Christ at Sinking Creek met according to adjournment and after worship proceded to Business theare not appearing any thing worth Recording the Church adjourned in order
Richard Carr Clk

(P. 132) Sunday 20th of March 1836 after preaching by Brother Bayles the Church sat for Business
1st a doore was opened for the Reception of members Brother Daniel Buckner and his wife Polly came forward and Each of them presented a letter which was Excepted nothing more appearing the Church adjourned in order
Richard Carr Clk

Saterday 16th of April 1836

The Church of Christ at Sinking Creek met according to appointment and after Divine worship proceded to Business 1st a door was opened for the Reception of members by letter or Experiance Nancy Casada came forward and was Received by letter 2nd a ~~Charge was brought against Brother Thomas Hampton for uncharitable Conduct towards George Hayes on the same nite of his death and after some altercation on the subject the mater was laid over til next meting in course~~ 3rd The Church then made her contribution for the Church purposes (to wit) in the folowing manner

Solomon Hindrick --- --- ---	$0.25
Daniel Buckner -------------	0.25
(P. 133) Josiah Parker ------	0.10
Pheby Boring	0.10
Margaret Threewit	0.12½
Robert Casada	0.25
Sarah Wright	0.12½
Thos Hatcher	0.10
Wm Whelor	0.25
Richard Carr	0.25
Mathias Broyles	0.25
Sister Hale	0.12½
Saml Tipton	0.06¼
John Hatcher	0.06¼
Mary Tipton of couler	.12½
amounting to --------	2.58¾

Richard Carr Clk

Friday 13th of May 1836 The Church met according to appointment after worship proced to business as follows 1st Br Hendrick Requested to be Released from his Deaconship the Church unanimously agreed to his Request nothing more appearing the Church ajorned in order
Richard Carr Clk

Saterday 18th of June 1836 The Church met according to adjournment after worship proceded to Business 1st Br Bayles not being preasant Br Bucner was chosen Modarator protem 2nd a door was opened for the Reception of members none came forward
3rd Brother Buckner John D Carty and Richard Carr was Deligated to the association and send one dollar (P. 134) 3rd Br Hendrix our Treasurer made a surrender of the Churches fund which ammounted to $2.22½
4th Brother Whelor was Elected for the office of Deacon and Brother Whelor not approbating the Churches Choice fully the matter was laid over til next meting nothing more appearing worth Recording the Church adjourned in order --------- Richard Carr Clk

Saterday 16th of July 1836

The Church of Christ at Sinking Creek met according to adjournment and after worship proceded to Business to Business 1st a doore was opened for the Reception of members Rachel Price came forward and was Received by Experience 2nd the Referance of Bro Whelor taken up and he not being present the matter was Continued until the next meting in course Adjourned in order.

Richard Carr Clk

August 19th 1836 The Church met according to appointment and after worship proceded to Business 1st a door was opened for the Reception of members none came forward thearefore theair not appearing anything of Importance the Church adjourned in order

Saturday August 20th 1836 the Church again Sat for Business Br John Broyles applyed for a letter of Dismition for himself and wife which was granted and Issued accordingly nothing more appearing the Church adjourned in order

Richard Carr Clk

(P. 135) Sept. 18.. 1836 the Church met according to appointment and after worship proceded to Business and theare not appearing anything worth Recording the Church adjourned in order

Richard Carr Clk

Friday Oct 14th.. 1836 the Church met according to appointment after worship proceded to Business 1st the Case as Respects Br Whelor acting as Deacon was taken up after some altication Br Whelor was Released from the same 2nd Sister Nancey Ford applyed for a letter of dismition which was granted and Issued 3rd a doore was opened for the Reception of members Catharine Barnes came forward and was Received by Experiance
4th Madison Ensor applyed for a letter of Dismition which was granted and Issued adjourned in order

Richard Carr Clk

Nov 19th - 1836 The Church met acording to appoint and after worship proceded to Business 1st agreed upon by the Church that Bro Hampton Hider be Cited to attend the next Church meting and Bro David Pugh and Bro Tennessee Nave be the Churches Mesengers and Report to next meting 2nd that Bro Robert Casaday & John Casaday Cite Bro John Swenney to attend next Church meting and make Report to the same Richard Carr Clk

(P. 136) January 14th 1837 The Church met according to appointment after worship proceded to Business as follows 1st a Referance from Nov meting as Respects the case of Bro John Swinney's Citation to attend the next meting and being Cited by the Brethering apponted by the Church (to wit) Brethering Robert and John Casada and the having Citted him he did not attend and theare being Evedance of his having a horse Race after his Citation the Church thearefore declares an unfelloship with him and that he is no more of us
2nd agreed that Bro George Hale be Cited to attend next Church meting and Brethering Robert Casada and Richard Carr be the Churches messengers and Report to next meting.

Feb 18th 1837 The Church met and after worship proceded to Business as follows 1st the Referance Respecting Bro Hale taken up and Continued til next meting
2nd Sister Orpah Hammer moved for a letter of Dismition which was granted and Issued accordingly
3rd Sister Mary Eliza Hampton was Received into this Church by letter

ajournd in order Richard Carr Clk

March 18 1837 The Church met and after business worship Sat for Business 1st took up the referance of Bro George T Hale and after finding no Reformation and an Entire neglect of the call of the Church thearefore the Church dose Entirely disown him for the sin of intoxication and disobaying the Call of the Church adjourned in order

Richard Carr Clk

(P. 137) April 15th 1837 the Church met and after worship Sat for business 1st Brother Hampton Hider applyed for a letter of Dismition which was granted and Issued accordingly nothing more appearing the Church adjourned in order

Richard Carr Clk

May 19th 1837 the Church met after worship Sat for Business 1st a door was opened for the Reception of members Micajah Owens and his wife Dorcus was Recvd by letter 2nd moved by Brother Hendrix that our Communion be in May and Sep.. which was agreed to 3d Bro Thomas Hatcher was Elected to serve this Church as Deacon 4th agreed by this Church that Bretheren Solomon Hendrix Richard Carr David Pugh Josiah Parker Joel Cooper Stand as a Committee to apoint who shall fill the Stand at their monthly metings for the term of one year the Church adjournd in order

Richard Carr C C

June 17th 1837 The Church met according to appointment after worship proceded to Business 1st a dore was opened for the Reception of members none came forward 2 appointed Bretheren Richard Carr and Josiah Parker deligates to our assosiation and sen one Dollar adjournd in order

Richard Carr C C

July 15th 1837 the Church met and after worship Sat for Business 1st a door was opened for the Reception of members Mary Morgan came forward and was Received by letter 2nd Brother D Buckner applyed for aletter of dismition for himself and wife which was granted

Richard Carr Clk

(P. 138) August 19th 1837 The Church Met after worship Sat for business 1st a door was oppened for the Reception of Members James White came forward and was Received by Experiance 2nd Bro Matthias Broyles and wife applyed for a letter of Dismision which was granted and Issued accordingly 3rd Sister Rachel Cooper applyed for a letter of dismission which was granted the adjourned in order

Richard Carr Clk

September 15th 1837 The Church met and after worship sat for Business 1st by a unanimus voices of this Church Bro Joshua Addams will go to Wattaugau Church with three or four others and make a gospel asknoledgement that Request his lisance that Church took from him.
adjourned in order

Richard Carr Clk

October 14th 1837 The Church met after worship Sat for Business 1st the Referance from last meting Respecting the Case of Bro J Adams was taken up and after some altercation on the matter it was agreed that thear be a Commitee appointed to Enquire into a Charg in Circulation against Bro Adams and that the following Bretheren Compose that Body David Pugh Tennessee

T Nave & Richard Carr and that they attend at Jessee Junkins the fourth Saterday of this instant and Report to next meting
2nd Sister Mary Rockhold applyed for a letter of dismision which was grand and Issued accordingly
3rd theare was a doore opened for the Reception of members Sister Susannah Nave Came forward and was Recvd by letter adjournd in order

Richard Carr Clk

(P. 139) Nov 18th 1837 The Church met after worship proceded to Business 1st our moderator and clk not Being present we Chose Bro John D Carty Moderator and Tennessee T Nave Clk protem 1st the Referance Respecting Bro J Adams taken up and Refered til next meting
adjournd in order

Tennessee T Nave Clk protem

December 16th 1837 The Church met after worship Sat for Business 1st the Case of Bro Adams taken up and the Report of the Commitee given in who sayes sister Junkins affirms that the Report of intoxication against Bro Joshua Adams is true the question was taken and by a unanimous voice he was Excluded for the sin of Intoxication and deming the same to be true 2nd Sister Mary Morgan applyed for aletter of dismision which was granted and Issued accordingly adjournd in order

Richard Carr Clk

January 20th 1838 The Church met after worship sat for business 1st it being Communicated to the Church that theare are som Evil Reports on sister Rachel Cooper the thinks it nessasary to inquire into the truth of said Reports and to try to stir her up to her duty and Br Richard Carr and Br R Casada be the Churches messengers and Report to next meting
2nd agreed by this Church that Br Whelor and Bro Carr Cite Br Franklin Casada to attend next meting and to acquaint him of same Evil Reports on him and to Report to next meting
adjournd in order

Richard Carr Clk

(P. 140) Feb 17 1838 The Church at Sinking Creek met after worship proceded to business 1st Chosse Brethern J D Carty Moderator protem and Ten T Nave Clk protem 2nd Cald for the Commitee the Thethern not attending we Contimued the Case til next meting ----adjourned in order

Ten.. T Nave Clk
protem.

April 14th 1838 The Church of Christ at Sinking Creek met after worship sat for business 1st the Referance Respecting sister Cooper was Continued til next meting and that Bro Henry Nave and sister Nave are Requested to Enquire whether he former husband is yet alive or whether he was living at the time of her mariage with Cooper 2nd the case of Bro Franklin Casada was taken up and Contimued til next meting
3rd Sister Assineth Edwards applyed for a letter of dismission which was granted and Issued
adjournd in order

Richard Carr Clk

Friday 18th of May 1838 The Church met after worship Sat for Business 1st the Referance Respecting Sister Cooper was taken up and after the Evedence was Examined She was found gilty of Marring a nother man while her husband was yet living and for which she was Excluded from the Christian fellowship of this Church 2nd the Referance Respecting Bro Franklin Casada was taken up and was Excluded from their Christian fellowship for not filling his seate at our Church meting days and (P. 141) not obeying the Churches Call and some other Immoral Conduct 3rd agreed by the Church that John D Carty be cited to attend next Church meeting and bring the Certifycate which he gave to Joshua Adams after his Exclution with him and that Bro Wm Pugh and Bro Tennessee T Nave be the Churches messengers and report to next meting -----

Saterday 19th of May 1838
the Church sat for Business 1st Brethern Leonard Hart and Wm Whelor Thos and John Hatcher Robert Casada and Richard Carr are appointed to enquire wheare Rachel Cooper is and to demand her letter of dismision which she obtained from this Church previous to their knoledge of her last Mariage while her former husband was yet living
2nd a door was opened for the Reception of members and Tinsa Brit came forward and was Received by Experiance
Signed by order of the Church

Richard Carr Clk

June 16th 1835 The Church met after worship sat for Business 1st Choose Br Lion Moderator 2nd a door was opened for the Reception of members Bro Henry Nave and his wife Mary was Received by letter 3rd Brethern Henry Nave and James White are appointed deligates to attend our next association adjournd in order

Richard Carr Clk

July 14th 1838 the Church met after worship sat for Business 1st Bro Henry Nave was Chosen for our Deacon adjourned in order

Richard Carr Clk

Bro Robert Casada Junr..departed this life July 4th 1838

(P. 142) August 18th 1838 The Church of Christ at Sinking Creek met after worship sat for business 1st Bro Owens applied for letters of dismission for himself and his wife which was granted 2nd a door was opened for the Reception of members and William Hampton Came forward and was Received by letter adjournd in order

Richard Carr Clk

Friday 14th of September 1838 The Church met after Divine worship Sat for business 1st a door was oppened for the Reception on members none came forward
2nd Sister Elisabeth Helton applyed for a letter of dismission which was granted and Issued accordingly nothing more appearing the Church adjournd in order

Richard Carr Clk

October 20th 1838 The Church met after worship Sat for Business 1st theare was letters of dismision applyed for and granted to the following members (to wit) Tennessee T Nave and his wife Sarah Susanah Nave David T Wright John Casada and his wife Elizabeth all of which was Issued accordingly, nothing more appearing worth Recording, the Church adjournd in order

Richard Carr Clk

(P. 143) December 15th 1838

The Church met after Divine worship Sat for Business 1st Sister anna Hampton applyed for a letter of dismistion from the Church which was granted and Issued accordingly nothing more appearing the Church adjournd in order
Richard Carr Clk

January 19th 1839 The Church met after worship Sat for business 1st a doore was opened for the Reception of members when Susan Nave came forward and was Received by letter nothing more appearing the Church adjournd in order

Richard Carr Clk

Feb.. 16th 1839 The Church met after worship sat for Business nothing appearing worth Recording the Church adjournd in order
Richard Carr Clk

Sister Margaret Stevens departed this life March 8th 1839

March 16th 1839 The Church met after worship Sat for business 1st Chose Br H Nave moderator and nothing appearing worth Recording the Church adjourned in order

Richard Carr Clk

April 20th 1839 The Church met after worship Sat for Business 1st a doore was opened for the Reception of members when sister Orpha Hammer Came forward and was Received by letter nothing more appearing the Church adjournd in order

Richard Carr Clk

May 17th 1839 The Church met after worship sat for business nothing appearing worth Recordin adjournd in order
Richard Carr Clk

(P. 144) June 15th 1839 The Church met after worship sat for business 1st our moderator not being present Bro Henry Nave was Choose modarator protem 2nd the Church went into the Choice of Deligates to Represent them in the next assosiation and after Balleting the Choych seemd to be Brethren Hanery Nave and Richard Carr 3rd Bro Richard Carr made application to be Released from acting as Clk for this Church which was granted and Bro Wm Pugh was appointed to fill his place nothing more appearing the Church adjournd in order

Richard Carr Clk

Brother John Poland Departed this life June 8th 1839

July the 20th 1839 The Church of Christ at Sinking Creek met acording to ajornment and after worship proceded to business -----
1rst Jemima Marten came forward and Joined the Church By letter give a letter of adress to the next assotion Brought forward and read and aproved of nothing more Appear the Church adjorned in order
William Pugh Clk

August the 19th 1839 The Church at Sinking Creek adter worship set for business 1st received brother Mason R Lyon by letter from the Wattaga Church 2d this Church gives Brother Mason R Lyon the Liberty of excerziseing his gift from a text or otherwise whear ever God may cast his Lot nothing mor appearing the Church adjournd in order
William Pugh Clk

(P. 145) September friday the 13th 1839
The Church of Christ at Sinking Creek met acording to apointment and after devine worship sat for buisness 1rst the Case of brother thomas hatcher as serving this Church as a deacon was taken up and it was agreed by the whooe Church That brother hatcher be ordained on to morrow a day of our proseeding meeting and set apart to the work him and His wife sister hatcher 2nd the minute from our Last association to this Church was brought Forward and distributed nothing more appearing The Church adjourned until tomorrow 3rd The Church met acording to her ajournment and after devine worship sat for buisness 4 the ordination of brother hatcher and his wife was attended to 5 motioned and Seconed that sister Marrey Parry be sited to attend our next meting and fill up her seat and that Brother David Pugh and Brother Parker be the Church messengers to invit the Sister to attend the next meeting Nothing more appearing the Church ajorned in order

William Pugh Clerk

October the 20th 1839

The Church at Sinking Creek met acording to Apointment and after devine worship the Church Set for buisness 1irst the refference from last meting called for and taken up the Church agree That the refference be Continued until next meeting Nothing more appearing the Church ajourned in order until next meeting in Cours

William Pugh Clerk

Sister Mary Hendrix Departed this life on friday the first Day of November in the year of our Lord 1839

(P. 146) November the 16th 1839

The Church met at Sinking Creek acording to apointment and after devine worship seat for buisness 1rst taken up the refference from last meeting as Respecting the case of polly perry and the Church Declare an unfellowship with her for abscorning From her husband and not living with him and Disobaying the call of the Church when sent for and we now say she is no more of us ---
2nd the Church being informed of some unfavourable Reports being in sirculation against brother Wm Perry and the Church think it proper to apoint two of the Brether to visit Brother perry to attend our next Meeting in Course and fill up his seate and - Answer its Charges against him and do apoint Brother Hanry Nave and Brother Thomas Hatcher to Be the Churches messengers to invite the Brother To meeting nothing more appearing the Church ajorned In order -------

William Pugh Clk

December the 14th 1839

The Church at Sinking Creek met and after worship The Church seat for buisness 1rst our Moderator not being present the Church Chosen Brother Henry Naye for to act as moderator protem
2nd the refferance from our last meeting Call For and the Brother that was sited to meeting attended and fille up his seat and rendered Full satisfaction for all the Charges a ledge Against him and the Church now — Retains him in full fellowship Nothing more appearing the Church adjorned in order

William Pugh Clerk

(P. 147) January the 18th 1840

The Church at Sinking Creek met and our moderator not being present and the day being verry Cole and disagreeable and but fue of us in number brother Henry Nave opened meeting by singing a hymn and praying and Set as our moderator protem the members Seated them selves as a Church for business 1rst inquired for Business no matter of refferance it was then motioned and Seconed that the Church Covenant be brought to every Church meeting day and read when requested nothing More presenting itself to the notice of the Church we ajorned in order -- --- ---

William Pugh Clerk

February the 15th 1840

The Church at Sinking Creek met and divine worship The Church set for buisness 1rst the Church Covenant was Red by the request of the Church 2nd the Church received A letter from brother Samuel P Tipton that left this Church some time ago and moved to where he now lives in Cherokee County State of North Carolina requesting a letter of dismission From this Church and it was granted nothing more appearing The Church ajorned in order --

March the 14th 1840

The Church at Sinking Creek met and after devine worship The Church then set for business 1rst a doore was opened For the reseption of members Either by letter or Experence None came forward 2nd this Church appoint Brother Richard Carr and Brother James White as trustees to act for this Church in adition to Brother David Pugh for the deed for this land whear this meeting house now stands on and for to hole the donation of this Church nothing more Presenting self to notice of Church adjorned in order til next meeting in Course ----------

William Pugh Clerk

April the 18th 1840

The Church at Sinking met and after devine worship The Church set for buisness 1rst a doore was opened for The reseption of members Either by letter or Experience

2nd Brother Granville T Kite came forward and Joind this Church by letter nothing more presenting it self to the Church we ajorned in in order til meting in Course

William Pugh Clerk

(P. 148) Friday the 15th day of May 1840

The Church at Sinking Creek met and after devine worship the Church Set for buisness 1rst a doore was opened for the reseption of members Either by Experience or letter nothing presenting it self to the notice of the Church we ajorned until to morrow

Saturday the 16th of May 1840 The Church at Sinking met and after devine worship the Church set for Buisness 1rst a doore was opened for the reseption of members Either by letter or Exsperence 2nd bro David T Wright came forward and Joined the Church by letter 3rd Brother Solomon Hendrix came forward and gave a donation of one hundred Dollars in Silver to this

Church for the use of Building a good meeting house which was paid over in to the hands of the trustees Brother David Pugh holds thirty three dollars of the Donation and Brother Richard Carr holds thirty Three and a half dollars of the donation and Brother James White hold thirty three dollars and a half of the donation 4th this Church gives Brother Henry Nave the liberty of exersising his Gift where ever the Lord may Cast his lot Nothing more appearing the Church ajorned in order

William Pugh

June the 20th 1840 ----

The Church of Christ at Sinking Creek met and after devine Worship set for business 1rst our moderator not being presant Brother Henry Nave sat as our moderator protem 2 and Antony Tipton came forward and Joined the Church by recantation 3rd The Church Chosen Brother James White and Brother David T Wright for her delegates to the asociation ~~nothing more appearing the Church ajorned in order~~ 4th Sister Winsa ann Hopper applyed for a letter of dismission which was granted The Church then ajorned in order

William Pugh Clerk

(P. 149) July the 18th 1840 The Church at Sinking Creek met and after worship the Church set for buisness 1rst our Moderator not being present the Chosen Brother Henry Nave To act as moderator protem 2nd the Letter brough forward and read to the Church and aproved of 3rd this Church apoint Brother Mason B Lyon and Henry Nave as Deligates to the association insdition to the former Deligates apointed from our last meeting this Church send one dollar to the association
ajorned in order

William Pugh Clk

September friday the 18th 1840

The Church at Sinking Creek met and after worship Proseeded to business 1rst our moderator not being presant the Church then Chosen brother Henry Nave to set as our moderator Protem 2nd the minutes from our last association was brought forward read and received and distributed then ajorned until To morrow 11 Oclock-- Saturday the 19th met acording to ajornment and after devine service the Church set for business 3rd motioned and sectioned that the Corrisponding minutes from the differant associations be filed away in the Clerk office and also a coppy of minutes of our last association be filed away with the afore said minutes also for the furture 4th this Church give Brother Henry Nave the Liberty to Exerescise his gift from a text or in any way that he feel Like or other wise where ever God in his proveidence may Cast his Lot then ajorned

William Pugh Clerk

October the 17th 1840

The Church at Sinking Creek met and after devine worship set for business 1rst our moderator being absent the Church Chosen Brother Henry Nave to act as our moderator protem 2nd a doore was opened for the reseption of members Either By letter or Exsperance none came forward 3rd the Church Being informed that Brother William Perry had inrolled his name on the books for horse raseing as having entering a horse in the ensueing this Church appoint Brother Henry Nave and Brother William Hatcher to be the Church Messengers to go and examion the horse book to see whether His name be on the Booke for having entering a horse for raising or not and also to site the Brother to attend our next meeting in Course and fill up his seat then in order

(P. 150) November the 14th 1840 the Church at Sinking Creek Met and after devine worship the Church seat for buisness 1rst the refferance from our Last meeting takeing up as it respects the case of William perrey and the Brother failed To attend meeting and to fill up his seat this Church Declare an unfellowship against William perrey for horse raseing and disobeying the Churchs call when sent for and say that he is no more of us the Church then ajorned in order

William Pugh Clerk

December the 19th 1840

The Church at Sinking Creek met and after devine worship proseeded to business as follows 1rst a Doore was opened for the reseption of members; Either By letter or Exsperance none came forward the Church then ajorned in order -------

William Pugh Clerk

January the 16th 1841

The Church at Sinking Creek met and after devine worship the Church seat for business 1rst a doore was opened for the reseption of members Either by letter or Exsperence 2nd Brother Madson T Ensor came Forward and Joined this Church by letter nothing els presenting its self to the notice of the Church we ajorned in order

William Pugh Clerk

February the 20th 1841

The Church of Christ at Sinking Creek met and our moderator not being Pressent the Church Chosen Brother Henry Nave as moderator protem 1rst a door was opened for the Reseption of members either by letter or Exsperance none came forward nothing els appearing the Church ajorned in order

(P. 151) March the 20th 1841 the Church at Sinking Creek met and after devine worship the Church Seat for business 1rst a door was opened for The Resiption of members either By Letter or Exsperance

2nd Received and read a Letter from The tucke Leeckey Church blunt County tnn The Church granted full approbation to the Request of that Letter and appointed Brother Rees Bayless to answer the Letter

3 the Church then ajorned in order

William Pugh Clerk

April the 17th 1841

The Church of Christ at Sinking Creek met and after devine worship proceed to business 1rst our - Moderator being absent the Church Chosen Brother Henry Nave as moderator protem 2nd no business occuring the Church ajorned in order

William Pugh Clerk

Friday the 14th day of May 1841 The Church of Christ at Sinking Creek met and after devine worship the Church Seat for business nothing occuring the Church then ajorned in order until to morrow 11 Oclock ---

Saturday the 15th day of May 1841

The Church of Christ at Sinking Creek met acording to appoinment And after Devine worship the Church seat for business 1rst a door was opened for the ressption of Members Either by Letter or Exsperence 2nd Sister Nancy Mayton came forward and was Received By Letter 3rd Sister Mary Jackson came forward and was Received by Letter 4 the Church then ajorned in -- --

William Pugh Clerk

(P. 152) June the 19th 1841 the Church of Christ at Sinking Creek met and after devine worship the Church set for business first our moderator being absent Brother Peter Kuhn was Chosen Moderator protem 2nd a door was opened for the reseption of members Either by letter or Exsperence none came forward 3rd our Brother David T Wright came forward and informed the Church of the Course That he had been persueding in the ministry 4th the Church after makeing some inquire into this matter finding that brother David T Wright had gone out preaching without asking liberty from this Church and that among a people of a different faith and order after some altercation the Church Contimue this matter as a refference til our next meeting in Course — --

5th Brother Henry Nave James White & William Hatcher as deligates to our next association and the church send one dollar and fifty cents for the use of the association--

6th This Church unanimously gives her decenting voices against a constitution in her letter of adress to the association then ajornd in order til our next meeting in course

William Pugh Clerk

July the 17th 1841

the Church of Christ at Sinking Creek met and after Devine worship the Church set for business 1rst a door opened for the reception of Members Either by letter or Exsperience none came forward 2nd the refference from our last meeting call for as it respects the Case of David T Wright and after some altercation we find that the brother has disobeyed the Church by praching whil under Censure Before aquited of the Charge that the Church held against him and among a people of a different faith and order therfore we say that we do not approbate the Course that the brother has taken 3rd the Church being informed that David T Wright has Joined another society of a different faith an order therfore we think it proper to bring this matter to a decision this Church now declair an unfellowship against David T Wright for disobeying the rules of the Church and say that he is not more of us 4th the letter of adress to our next association brought forward red and aproved of the Church then ajorned in order.

William Pugh Clerk

Friday September the 17th 1841

The Church of Christ at Sinking Creek met and after devine worship the Church set for business 1rst a door opened for the Resseption of members Either by letter or Exsperance 2nd Vaentine B Nave came forward and joined the Church by Exsperance 3rd the minutes from our last association Brought forward read & received and distributed 4th Brother William Hatcher ask liberty of this Church to exsercise gift in public 5th this Church gives Brother William Hatcher the liberty of exsercising his gift by way of exertation or to comment from a pasage of scripture tehn ajornd in order until to morrow 11 Oclock

(P. 153) Saturday September the 18th 1841
the Church at Sinking Creek met according to an apointment and after Devine Worship the Church set for business 1rst a door opened for the reseption of members either by letter or exsperence none came forward 5th baptism was then attended to the Church then ajorned in order - William Pugh Clk

October 16th 1841 the Church of Christ at Sinking Creek met and after devine worship the Church set for business 1rst a door opened for the reseption of members Either by letter or Exsperance none came forward the Church then ajorned in order
N b Brother John Hatcher petitioned this Church for a letter of dismission which was granted

William Pugh Clerk

November the 20th 1841

The Church of Christ at Sinking Creek met according to an appointment and after devine worship the Church Seat for buisness 1rst our moderator being absent the Church Chosen Brother James Eden To set as her moderator protem 2nd a door was opened for the reseption of members Either by Letter or Exsperence 3rd Sister Anny White a member of the Buffalo Ridge come forward and requested to have her fellowship here with her husband in this Church and was Received into our Christian fellowshup 4th Brother Jonathan H hyder Came forward and wished to have fellowship with This Church the Brother was a member some years ago in this Church and when he left here and went to Blount County To go to Colledge he got a letter of dismission and with this letter he joined the six Mile regular Baptist Church in Blount County since he has returned and is living in the bounds of this Church he states that some time after he Left there and came here he rite to Henry f buckner a scool mate of his and also to the Church for a letter of dismision which letter was granted Rite and put into the hands of Henry f buckner for the safe conveyance to the brother and the brother states he under stands the letter was obtained by buckner and got misplaced in his hands the Church under these Considerations Receive Brother Hyder into her Christian fellowship the Church then ajorned in

(P. 154) Wednesday the 24th of November 1841
The Church at Sinking Creek met and after devine worship the Church seat for business 1rt a door opened for the reseption of members either by letter or exspereance --
2nd Sister delceney Crouch cam forward and joind this Church by letter
3rd Ruben Hatcher came forward and Joined this Church by Exsperence
the Church then ajorned in order----

January the 15th 1842

We the Batists Church of Christ Sinking Creek met and after devine worship the Church set for business 1rst a doore opened for the reseption of members either by letter or Exsperence 2nd Asariah Peoples and his wife Eliza came forward and gave a Relation of the worke of grace on there mind, and was Received into our Christian fellowship--
3rd moved that brother Henry Nave be called to ordination
4th motioned and seconed that this matter be laid over until our next in course for the Churches further Consideration
5th Mary Barnes request to have fellowship with this Church which was granted and the sister was restored into our Christian fellowship the sister now

request a letter of dismission and it was granted the Church then ajorned in order til next meeting in Course
N B Received Brother Stephen Boman by letter
William Pugh Clerk

February the 19th 1842

We the Baptist Church of Christ at Sinking Creek met according to an appointment and after devine worship set for business 1rst a door was opened for the reseption of members either by letter or exsperence 2nd agnes Hatcher came forward and gave a relation of the worke of grace on her mind to this Church and was received into our Christian fellowship 3rd Sister Elizabeth Montgomery applyed for a letter of dismission and it was granted 4th Brother Thomas Hatcher & family applyed for a letter of dismission and it was Them Viz Sarah his wife and Wrispey tilson & agnes hatcher & Elizabeth Patten & Ruben Hatcher & Rebecka Hatcher these are the names of Brother Hatchers family that are dismissed from our Church 5th the refference from our last meeting Call for as it respects the case of Brother Henry Naves ordination and unanimously agreed by the Church that this matter be Droped the Church then ajorned in order
William Pugh Clerk

(P. 155) March the 19th 1841

The Church of Christ at Sinking Creek met and after worship the Church seat for business 1rst our moderator being absent Brother Henry Nave was Chosen to Set as our moderator protem 2nd a door was opened for the reseption of members Either by letter or Exsperance none came forward nothing als appearing to the notice of the Church we then ajorned in order ---
William Pugh Clerk

Saturday the 16th day of April 1842

We the Church of Christ at Sinking Creek met acording to an a pointment and after divine worship The Church Set for business 1rst a door opened for The resseption of members Either by letter or Exsperance 2nd the Church taken under Consideration the vakency of a deacon and after some altercation upon it agreed by The Church that it be laid over until our next meeting in cours as a refference 3rd Brother Bayles petitioned The Church for letters of demission for Sister Temperance Hail & also for Sister phebey Boren which letter was granted the Church then ajorned in order
William Pugh Clerk

Friday the 13th day of May 1842

We the Church of Christ at Sinking Creek met and after Devine worship the Church Set for business 1rst a door open for the reseption of members Either by letter or Exsperence
2nd the refference from our last meeting Call for as it respects the vakency of a deacon and agreed to be laid over until to morrow 3rd Brother Henry Nave petitioned the Church for a letter of dismission for Sister Mary Jackson and it was granted the Church ~~then ajorned in order until tomorrow Eleven oclock --4 Received delency Crouch by letter into our Christian fellowship --5th Received Stephen Boman by letter into our Christian fellow ship~~

(P. 156) Saturday the 14th of May 1842

We the Church of Christ at Sinking Creek met and after Devine Worship set for business 1rst a door opened for The reseption of members Either by letter or Exsperence 2nd the Refference from yesterday taken up and unanimously agreed By the Church that Brother James White fill the place of a Deacon and be called to ordination at our next meeting in June the Church then ajorned in order
3rd Brother Mason R lion & lenard Hart & wife was dismissed by letter
William Pugh Clerk

Saturday the 18th day of June 1842
The Church of Christ at Sinking Creek met and after Devine The Church set for business 1rst a door opened for the Reseption of members Either by letter or Experance 2nd Sister Sarah Mitchel came forward and wish to unite with this Church and was received into our Christian fellowship
3rd Brother James White was called forward and ordained to offce of a deacon and Set apart to the work 4th Brother Henry Nave and Brother James White and Brother William Hatcher ar delegated to our next association
5th this Church send one dollar and fifty Cents to the association then ajorned in order
William Pugh Clerk

Saturday the 16th of July 1842 the Church of Christ at Sinking Creek met and after devine worship the Church set for business 1rst opened for the reseption of members Either by letter or Exsperence non came forward 2nd the letter of adress from this Church to the association was forwarded and red and approved of nothing more presenting itself to notice of Church then ajorned in order
William Pugh Clerk

(P. 157) August the 16th 1842 We the Church of Christ at Sinking Creek met and after devine worship the Church set for business 1rst opened for the reseption of members Either by letter or Exsperance non came forward the Church then ajorned in order
William Pugh Clerk

Friday the 16th day of September 1842

We the Church of Christ at Sinking Creek met and after devine Set for business 1rst a door opened for the reseption of members Either by letter or Exsperance 2nd Sister Mary Emett petitioned for a letter of dismission and it was granted, the Church then ajorned in order until tomorrow at Eleven O,clock

Saturday the 17th day of September
the Church met- ajornment and after devine worship the Church set for business 1rst a door opened for the reseption of members Either by letter or Exsperence
2nd Brother Josiah Parker and wife petitioned the Church for the liberty to move their membership to the Cherokee Church and it was
the Church then ajorned in order til tomorrow Eleven oclock
Sunday the 18th met acording to ajornment and devine worship Received Rachel Rowe and Mary Moore by Exsperance then ajorned in order
Wm Pugh Clerk

Saturday the 15th day of October 1842 We the Church of Christ at Sinking Creek met and after devine worship the Church set for business 1rst a door opened for the reseption of members Either by or Exsperance non cam now the Church ajorned in order

William Pugh Clerk

November the 19th 1842 The Church of Christ at Sinking Creek met and after devine worship Set for business nothing occurinf to the notice of the Church then ajorned in order William Pugh Clerk
N B William White came forward and was Received into her Christian fellowship also Sister Nancy White came forward and was Received into our Christian fellowship

William Pugh Clerk

(P. 158) December the 17th 1842 The Church of Christ at Sinking Creek met and after worship the Church set for buisness lrst a door opened for the reseption of members Either by letter or Exsperance
2nd Sister Rebeka Casaday and Sister Rebecka Young and Sister Mary Smith came forward and wish to unite with this Church and was Received into our Christian fellowship
3rd Sinking Church gives Brother Jonathan H Hyder the Liberty to Exsercise his gift in public when ever Called on and particular in the bounds of this Church and as often as he posible can then ajorned in order

William Pugh Clerk

January the 14th 1843 The Church of Christ at Sinking Creek met and after devine worship the Church set for business lrst a door opened for the reseption of Members Either by letter or Exsperance non came forward The Church then ajorned in order til meeting in Course

William Pugh Clerk

February the 18th 1843 We the Baptist Church of Christ at Sinking Creek met and after devine worship The Church set for business lrst a door opened for the Reseption of members Either by Letter or Exsperance non came forward nothing els presenting it self to The notice of the Church then ajorned in order

William Pugh Clerk

March the 18th 1843- We the baptist Church of Christ at Sinking Creek met and after devine worship the Church set for business lrst a door opened for the Reseption of members Either by Letter or Exsperance none came forward the Church ajorned in order

William Pugh Clerk

(P. 159) April the 15th 1843 We the Baptist Church of Christ at Sinking Creek met and after Devine Worship the Church set for business lrst Brother William Pugh made application to This Church for to Releas him from serving this Church as a Clerk any longer which request was granted By this Church Brother William Pugh is released by This Church of being there Clerk any longer and Brother William White held in nomination
2nd Sister Rachel Smalling desires to have her membership with this Church now Receives Sister Rachel Smalling into her Christian Fellowship 3rd this Church now discovers that there is not as many members in the bounds of this Church as in number as she formily have claimed and presented in her letter of adress to association the correct number at this time is only fifty one members in the bounds of this Church 51 members

Saturday may the 20th 1843 the Church of Christ at Sinking Creek met accord-

ing to appointment after worship proceeded to business first our moderator being absent Chos broth henry Nave to act as moderator this meeting 2 haveing released brother William Pugh from being Clerk
the Church then ajorned in order

William White Clerk

Saturday June the 17th 1843
the Church of Christ at Sinking Crek met according to appointment after divine worship proseeded to business as follows first nominated the deligates to the association brother Henry Nave & brother James White & brother William Hatcher second nominated the deligates to sed to the Convention brother Henry Nave & brother James White then adjorned in order

William White Clerk

(P. 160) Saturday July the 15th 1843 the Church of Christ at Sinking Creek met according to appointment and after Divine worship Preseeded to buisness first our moderator being absent Chose brother Henry Nave moderator for this meeting Second the letter of adress to the association was red before the Church and was approved of then adjorned in order

William White Clerk

Saturday august 19th 1843 the Church of Christ at Sinking Creek met according to appointment and after divine worship proseeded to buisness first the dor of the Church was opened for the reception of members either by experience or by letter none came forward the Church then ajorned on order

William White Clerk

Saturday September 17th 1843
the Church of Christ at Sinking Creek met according to appointment and after Divine worship proceeded to business 1st nothing was presented worth the attention of the Church then ajorn[d] in order

William White C C

Friday the 13 of October 1843
the Church of Christ at Sinking Creek met according to appointment and after Divine Worship proceded to buisness 1st nothing was presented to the churches notice then ajorned untill to morrow eleven Oclock. the Church met again according to appointment and after Divine worship proceeded to buisness nothing presented itself the m ajornd in order

William White C C

Saturday November 18th 1843 the Church of Christ at Sinking Creek met according to appoint and after Divine Worship proceed to Buisness first the door was opened for the reception of members either by letter or experience Brother Alfred Car Came forward and Joined by Experience and Brother Thomas Ensor and Brother John L Roe and Sister Mary Emmert and Sister Mary Pew and Sister Jane Boren and Sister Nancy Ann Jefferson the Church then ajorned in order

William White C C

(P. 161) Brother Richard Carr Departed this life on Sunday the 29th Day of October in the year of our Lord 1843

Brother Madison Ensor Departed this life on Sunday the 5th day of November in the year of our Lord 1843

Saturday December the 16th 1843 the Church of Christ at Sinking Creek met according to appointment and after Divine worship the Church set for buisness first the door was opened for the reception of members either by leter or by experiance 3 sister E. D. Lyon came forward and joined by letter the Church then ajorned in order

William White Clk

January the 20th 1844 the Church of Christ at Sinking Creek met according to appointment and after worship procedd to buisness then ajorned in order

William White C C

Saturday february the 17th 1244
the Church of Christ at Sinking Creek met according to appointment and after Devine worship proceeded nothing was presented before the Church ajorned in order

William White

Saturday March the 14th 1844 the Church of Christ at Sinking Creek met according to appointment and after Divine Worship proceeded to buisness then ajorned in order

William White C CLK

Saturday April the 20th 1844
the Church of Christ at Sinking Creek met according to appointment and after Devine Worship proceeded to buisness
then ajorned in order William White C Clk

(P. 162) Friday the 17th of May 1844
the Church of Christ at Sinking Creek met according to appointment and after Divine worship the Church set for buisness nothing was presented to the Churches notice then ajorned in order until to morrow The Church met again and after worship Set for busnes first it was moved and a few words said about nomination to the Convention it was moved and Seconed that it be laid over till the next meeting ajorned in order

William White C Clk

Saturday June the 15 1844
the Church of Christ at Sinking Creek met acording to appointment and after Devine worship the Church set for buisness first the door of the Churc was opened for the Reception of members either by letter or experience one came forward and joined by Experience Second balletted to delegate to the James White Thomas T Ensor & William Hatcher (written in pencil-Brother Jesse duncan come forward and joined By Experience)

William White C Clk

Saturday July the 20th 1844 the Church of Christ at Sinking Creek met according to appoint ment and after Divine worship the Church set for buisness first the letter to the association was red and approved of second motioned and seconed that brother Hider and Cartee be sent for to fill up their seats the September meeting third brother Nave and brother Hatcher was appointed as messengers to tell them to attend the September meeting fourth the letter to the Convention was was red and approved of ajorned in order

William White C Clk

Saturday august the 17th 1844

the Church of Christ at Sinking Creek met according to appointment and after Divine worship the Church set for buisness first the dor of the Church was opened for the Reception of members Either by letter or by Experience none came forward then ajorned in order

William White C Clk

Friday September the 13th 1844
the Church of Christ at Sinking Creek met according to appointment and after Divine worship the Church met according to appoint ment and after Divine worship the Church Set for buisness nothing was presented before the Church ajorned in order until to morrow the Church met again acording to apointment and after worship set for buisness nothing was presented before the church then ajorned in order

William White C Clk

(P. 163) Saturday october the 19.. 1844
the Church of Christ at Sinking Creek met according to appointment and after Divine worship the Church set for buisness first was motioned and Seconed that Brother Alfred Car act in his fathers Stead seconed Brother David Pugh moves that he be Released from acting as trustee and brother Thomas Ensor act in his stead then ajorned in order

William White C Clk

Solomon Hendrix departed this life November 1844

William White C Clk

Saturday august the 17th 1844
the Church of Christ at Sinking Creek met according to appointment and after Divine worship the Church set for buisness first the dor of the Church was opened for the Reception of members Either by letter or by Experience none came forward then ajorned in order

William White C Clk

Friday September the 13th 1844
the Church of Christ at Sinking Creek met according to appointment and after Divine worship the Church met according to appointment and after Divine worship the Church Set for buisness nothing was presented before the Church ajorned in order until to morrow the Church met again acording to apointment and after worship set for buisness nothing was presented before the Church then ajorned in order

William White C Clk

The names of those that joined at the protracted meeting in november 1844
John A Swaner Joshua Swaner Mary A Swaner Mahaley Matin William Matin Washington Matin Henry Jefferson Andrew Kughn Joel McFall John Kuhn D. J. McFall Mary ann McFall Susannah Cross John Balys Abraham Job Jackson Cres Elizabeth Loudermilk Elizabeth Maten

William White C C K

November the 16th 1844 the Church of Christ at Sinking Creek met according to appointment and after Devine worship the Church set for buisness first nothing was presented to the Churches notice then ajorned in order

William White C. Clk

Sat December the 16th 1844 the Church of Christ at Sinking Creek met according to appointment and after Divine worship the Church Set for buisness first the door of the Church was opened for the reception of members either by letter or exsperience none came forward the Church then ajorned in order

William White

Saturday february 1845 the Church of Chris at Sinking Creek met according to appointment and after Divine worship the Church set for buisness first the door of the Church was opened for the reception of members either by letter or experience none came forward then ajorned in order

W White C. Clk.

The names of those that joined at old Bankharts
William Nave Mary Hart William Taylor of Color

(P. 164) Saturday March the 15 1845
the Church of Christ at Sinking Creek met according to appointment and af Divine worship the Church set for buisness first the door of the Church was opened for the reception of members either by letter or experience none came forward then ajorned in order

William White C. Clk

Saturday April the 19th 1845
the Church of Christ at Sinking Creek met according to appointment and after Divine worship the Church set for buisness first the door of the Church was opened for the reception of members either by letter or experience first John W. Maten Came forward and joined by letter the Church then ajorned in order

William White C. Clk

Friday may the 16th 1845 the Church of Christ at Sinking Creek met according to appointment and after Divine wor the Church set for buisness first the door of the Church was opened for the reception of members either by letter or experience none Came forward then ajorned in order until to morrow eleven Oclock the Church met again according to appointment and after Divine worship the Church set for buisness first the door of the Church was opened for the reception of members either by letter or experience 1rst Sister Catharine Kelly came forward and was restored into full fellowship again with this Church 2 Nancy Carethers came forward and joined by experience 3 Brother Thomas T. Ensor and wife was chosen and ordained as deacons to serve this Church

William White Cl

Saturday June the 14th 1845
the Church of Christ at Sinking Creek met according to appointment and after Divine worship the Church set for buisness first appointed the Delegates to the association our beloved Brethren Henry Nave and James White and Thomas T Ensor and Alfred Car this Church agrees to send one dollar the Church also agree that at the July meeting there be a public Collection taken for the use of the association ajorned in order

William White

(P. 165) Saturday July the 19th 1845
the Church of Christ at Sinking Creek met according to appointment and after Divine worship the Church set for buisness first the door of the Church was opened for the reception of members either by experience or letter second Brother Richard Car and wife wishes to unite with this Church third the let-

ter of adress to the Association was red and approved of fourth Sister Phebe Prophet requests a letter of dismission from this Church then ajorned in order

William White Cl

Saturday August the 16th 1845 the Church of Christ at Sinking Creek met according to appoint and after Divine worship the Church set for Buisness first the Door of the Church was opened for the reception of members either by letter or experience then ajorned in order

William White C Clk

The Number of members belonging to the Sinking Creek Church at this time is seventy nine 79

Saturday September the 20th 1845
the Church of Christ at Sinking Creek met according to appointment and after Divine worship the Church set for Buisness first the door of the Church was opened for the the reception of members either by letter or experience then ajorned in order

William White C Clk

Friday October the 17th 1845 the Church of Christ at Sinking Creek met according to appointment and after Divine worship the Church set for Buisness first the door of the Church was opened for the Reception of mem- either by letter or experience then ajorned until to morrow the Church met again according to appointment and after Divine worship the Church set for Buisness first the door of the Church was opened for the reception of menbers either by letter or experience Second Mary More and William hampton made application for a letter of Dismission which was granted then ajorned in order

William White C. Clk

(P. 166) the name of those that joined at the Protracted meeting in october 1845 Susannah Hampton Anna A Hampton Fanny C Hampton Rebecca Scalp Thomas Carter Mary Carter Eli Swinney

Saturday November the 15th 1845
the Church of Christ at Sinking Creek met according to appointment and after Divine worship the Church set for buisness first the door of the Church was opened for the Reception of members either by letter or experience second the Church agree to send a Committee to wit Henry Nave and John W Maten to go and inquire of Thomas Carter to know whether he has two wives or not and then persue as they think best third the church think it duty to appoint a Committee to wit William Hatcher and William Nave to site brother Cartee and brother hider to tend the next Church meeting fourth the Church agrees to send a letter to the lorrel fork Church and state the acknowledge ment that sister Jane hampton has made to this Church and that Brother William Hatcher write the letter then ajorned in order

William White C C

Saturday December the 20th 1845
the Church of Christ at Sinking Creek met according to appointment and after Divine worship the Church set for buisness first the door of the Church was opened for the reception of members either by letter or experience Second brother John D. Carter made application for a letter of Dismission from this Church and it was granted then ajorned in order

William White C Clk

Saturday January the 17th 1846
the Church of Christ at Sinking Creek met according to appointment and after Divine worship the Church set for buisness first the Door of the Church was openedfor the reception of members either by letter or experience Second this Church declares unfallowship against Thomas Carter and wife the Church agrees to wait until next Church meeting on brother hider and that brother Nave bear the message to him then ajorned in order

William White C. Clk

Saturday february the 14th 1846
the Church of Christ at Sinking Creek met according to appointment and after Divine worship the Church set for buisness first the door of the Church was opened for the reception of members either by letter or experience second the Church agres to send brother Nave and brother maten to inform brother bowman that this Church wishes him to ten the next Church meeting third Sister Mary More received a letter of Dismission from this Church but has returned it again and is received into our fulfellowship then ajorned in order

William White C. Clk

(P. 167) Saturday March the 14th 1846 the Church of Christ at Sinking Creek met according to appointment and after divine worship the Church set for buisness first the Door of the Church was opened for the reception of members either by letter or Experience Second the Case of brother bowmans be left as a referance until next Church meeting and that brother White and brother Carr is appointed to inquire into the of brother Barbery and report it to this Church then ajorned in order

William White C. Clk

Saturday April the 18th 1846 the Church of Christ at Sinking Creek met according to appointment and after divine worship the Church set for buisness first the door of the Church was opened for the reception of members either by letter or experience then ajorned in order

William White C Clk

Saturday May the 16th 1846
the Church met again according to appointment and after Divine worship the Church set forbuisness first the door was opened for the reception of members Second Sister E. D. T. Lyons made application for a letter of Dismission and it was granted then ajorned in order

William White C. Clk.

Friday June the 19th 1846 the Church of Christ at Sinking Creek met according to appointment and after Divine worship set for buisness first the door of the Church was opened for the Reception of members either by letter or experience Second brother Job and brother Pew nominate the Delegates to the association third brother Ensor and brother Car is appointed Delegates from this Church fourth this Church agrees to send one dollar fifth brother John Bayless Requests a letter of Dismission from this Church and it was granted than ajorned in order until tomorrow
Saturday June the 20th 1846 met again according to appointment and after worship the Church set for buisness first the Door of the Church was opened for the reception 6f members either by letter or experience Second brother Hampton Mulkey came forward and joined by letter third Sister Eliza Mulkey came forward and Joined by experience fourth the Church has given their present Clerk up and appointed William Hatcher in his stead then ajorned in order

William White C Clerk

(P. 168) June the 21st 1846 Brother Leonard hart and sister Phebe hart came forward and Joined by letter and was recieved into our Christian fellowship---

William White Church Clerk

ORBITURY

Sister Margaret Threewit Departed this life the 17th day of June 1846---
Sister Mehala Kuhn Departed this life the 25th day of June 1846

Saturday July the 18th day 1846
The Church of Christ at Sinking Creek met according to a Journment and after Divine Worship the Church set for business first the door of the Church was opened for the reception of Members either by letter or experience Seconly the letter to the association was forward and approved of them ajourned in order

William White Clk protem

Saturday August 15th day of 1846
The Church of Christ at Sinking Creek met according to a Journment and after Divine Worship the Church set for buisness; a Door was opened for the reception of members none came forward

William Hatcher Clerk

Friday Sept 18th day 1846

The Church of Christ at Sinking Creek me according to Ajournment and after Divine Service the Church set for business; a door was opened for the reception of members, two came forward by Experience, Michael Smithpeters and Mary his wife
(P. 169) Secondly William Hatcher moved to be released from acting Clerk which was granted, and Brother Robert H Mulkey appointed Church Clerk ---
Saturday 19th --the Church again met and after Devine Service Sat for Business, first a door was opened for the Reception of Members, one came forward by Experiance William Jobe a man of Colour. Second this Church agrees that they will not fail to fill up their seats for the next Twelve Months unless Providentially hindred the Church Ajorned in order --

William Hatcher Clerk

Saturday Oct 17th 1846

Wee the baptist Church of Christ at Sinking Creek met according to ajournment and after divine worship The Church Sat for buisness, first the Church opened the door for the reception of members none came forward,- Second the minits of the association came to hand
Ajournd in order - - - -

Robert H Mulky
Church Clerk

Saturday Nov 14th 1846

Wee the baptist Church of Christ at Sinking Creek met according to adjournment and after Divine worship the Church Sat for buisness. the door was opened for the reception of members - Sister Penelopy Allen was rec by Baptism Adjourned in order

R. H. M. CC

(Note Written in Pencil)

Saturday Nov 17, 1847.

the baptist Church of Christ at S. C. met according to adjournment & after Divine worship sat for buisness A Door was opened for the rec of mem Brother Mayton wife & daughter requested a letter of Dis which was granted

(P. 170) Saturday Dec 19th 1846 — — —

Wee the Baptist Church of Christ at Sinking Creek met According to Ajournment & after Divine worship the Church set for Buisness
1 A Door was opened for the reception of members Sister Nancy hix Joined By experience 2 the Church Agrees to with draw her fellowship from rebecca Scelp for joining the methodist Church & other Charges 3 Brother John Mayton & wife & daughter requests a leter wich was granted
Ajourned in order

Robert H. Mulkey
Church Clerk

Saturday January 16th 1847 the Baptist Church of Christ at Sinking Creek met after Divine worship Proseeded to Buisness 1st a Door was opened for the reception of members rebecca Scelp made aplication to get back into the Church Brother H. Nave & brother T. inser & brother Wm Hatcher was A pointed to further Investigate her Case 2 the mimuite of the Generel association Came to hand — — —
Ajourned In order

Robert H Mulkey
Church Clerk

four Joined By Experience
Three Dismissed

(P. 171) Saturday February 20th, 1847

The Church at Sinking Creek met according to appointment & after worship Sat for buisness — —
1st a door was opened for the reception of members. Mary Ann Price was rec By experience Jesse Humphreys & Eliza his wife By letter also Ann France was rec By letter.
Ajourned in order

R. H. M. C. Clerk

Saturday March 20th 1847

the baptist Church of Christ at Sinking Creek met according to apointment & after Divine worship Sat for buisness 1st Brother Henry Nave & Brother David Pugh are appointed to site Brother Wright & Brother Washington Mayton & Brother Joshua, & Brother Jefferson Swanner to the Church on the next Church meeting Day ajorned in order

Robert H Mulky
Church Clerk

(P. 172) Saturday April 17 1847

the Baptist Church at Sinking Creek met according to A pointment & after Divine Worship the Church sat for buisness A Door was opened for the Reception of members Them came up that was sent for at the March meeting &

made their acknowledgement the Church forgave them.
then Ajourned in order

Robert H Mulkey
Church Clerk

Saturday May 15th 1847

the Church at Sinking Creek met A cording to A pointment & After Divine worship the Church sat for buisness first A Door was opened for the reception of members None Came foward then ajourned in order

R. H. M. C C --

Saturday July 19, 1847.

the Church of Christ at Sinking Creek met acording to adjournment & After Divine worship Sat for buisness a door was opened for the rec of members. Brother Rich Jefferson Joined & was rec by baptism 2d brother Wm Hatcher & brother Alford Car are apointed by the Church to sit in the association ajourn in order

R. H. Mulkey

(P. 173) Saturday July 17 1847

The Church of Christ at Sinking Creek met & after Divine Worship Sat for buisness 1st A Door was opend for the rec of members 2nd the for the association was forwarded & rec 3d the Church agrees to refer the September meeting & our Communion Seson to be in October 4 the Church agrees to liberate Brother R Jefferson to hold prare meeting & to exort for six months 5 the Church also agrees to give Brother Wm Hacher written licens to preach
Ajourned in order

Robert H Mu
Church Clerk -- -- --

October the 16th 1847

the baptist Church in Christ at Sinking Creek met acording to ajornment and after divine worship the Church sat for buisness excluded Brother Robert H. Mulky for improper conduct as a maried man with a girl and for treating the Church with Contempt Dismissed Brother George (Bean, Bown, Brown ?) in order for the purpose of Joining Union Church

Jesse Humphreys Church Clerk

November the 20th 1847

the baptis Church in Christ at Sinking Creek met acording to adjornment and after Divine worship proseaded to buisness first restoared Brother Robert H Mulky to the fellowship of the Church again upon giving Satisfaction to the Church for the Charges aledged against him
(P. 174) Dismisses Brother Hampton Mulky & Sister Eliza G Mulkey by letter

Jesse Humphreys Church Clerk

Dec 18th 1847

the baptis Church in Christ at Sinking Creek met acording to adjornment and after divine Service proseaded to buisness first took up the case of brother

Jefferson and granted him the priveledge of exhorting the same as formerly
Jesse Hamphreys Church Clerk

Jan the 15th 1848

The Baptist Church in Christ at Sinking Creek met acording to ajournment and after Divine worship Proseaded to buisness first took up the Case of Brother Steaven Bowman & Sister Alphy Bowman on the Subject of granting them a letter and owing to Charges brought against Brother Bowman for falshood and defraud excluded him from the Church but granted sister Alphy bowman a letter in full fellowship with us Brother John Maton wife & daughter returned the leter that the Church had granted them and received them Back again in fellowship with us

Jesse Humphreys Church Clerk

N. B. On Sunday A door being opened for the reception of members Sister Margaret Hathaway Joined by leter

J Humphreys C C

(P. 175) february 19 1848

the baptis Church of Crist at Sinkinging Creek meet acording to apointment and after worship first the Church sat for bisness firs Chose brother Jesse duncan for the time being to act as Cleark 2nd took up the diffacult betwin brother Jessa umphris and Sara Laws and refurd to the nex meeting 3rd appointed brother William hatcher and Alfred Carr to visit Sister Laws and requeat her to attend the next meeting adjourned in order

March the 18 1848

Church meet at Sinking Creek meeting house after worship first excluded Jessa Umphris for imprudent Conduct towards Sarah Laws a member of Watauga Church and acnoledged to in presence of Mikel Smithpeters and wife and then denied in whole when brought in presence of the Church.

Jessa Duncan
Rees Bayles

this requisted by Sinking Creek Church
this mattor is refurd with regard to Choosing a Clark

(P. 176) April the 15 1848

the baptist Church at Sinking Creek meet acording to apointment and after worship the Church sat for buisness first the Church unanimously agred to dismiss Sister Mary Nuel 2nd Chose Alfred CarrChurch Clerk by ballet the Church then adjorned in order

Sister Penelopy Allon Departed this life february 21st 1848

Friday May 19th 1848

The baptist Church of Christ at Sinking Creek meet acording to apointment and after worship sat for buisness 1st Chose Bro H Nave moderator nothing came before the Church worth recording the Church adjourned in order

Sattorday 20 the Church after worship Sat for buisness first the case of sister Alpha Boman was was taken up and granted sister Boman a lettor in full fellowship then adjourned in order

Alfred Carr C Clerk

(P. 177) Sattorday 17th of June 1848

the baptist Church at Sinking Creek met Acording to adjournment after worship sat for buisness 1st a dore was opened for the reception of members by letter or Experance none came forward 2nd Agreed to elect delligats to the assosciation elected Alfred Carr and Henry Knave 3rd agreed to send 100 dollar to the association 4 Sunday the 18 the Church unanimously A greed to dismiss our beloved sister boman by letter as a member in good standing with us when joind to some other Church of the same faith and order adjournd in order

Alfred Carr C C K

July 15th 1848

The Church at Sinking Creek meet A Cording to apointment and aftor Worship Sat for bisness 1st a dor was opend for the reception of members by lettor or expers and 2nd Sistor Deborah Johnson Came forward and goined by lettor 3rd A pointed Bro ~~William Nave and Volentine~~ Pugh and Volintine Nave to invite Bro Washington Maton to attend next Church meeting
4th The lettor of address to the association was red and appoved
Then adgornd in order

Alfred Carr C C K

Names of members Joind at the protracted meeting at Sinking Creek meeting in august 1847

Joined by exsperence

Hisire McFawl Marier Umphris Mary Holston Jane Oar Louisa Swinney Sarah Helton Zurah Addoms

(P. 178) Sattorday August the 19th 1848

The Babtist Church at Sinking Creek met Acording to Agornment after worship Sat for Byseness first a dore was opend for the receptton of members by lettor or Exsperns none Joind 2nd tuck up the refferns of last meeting Respecting Bro Washington Maton and agreed to lay it over until next meeting in corse then Adjornd in order

Alfred Carr C CK

Sattorday 16 day of September 1848

The baptis Church at Sinking Creek meet a Cording to Agornment and after worship Sat for buisness 1st a dore was opend for the reception of members either by lettor or experience none came forward 2nd twok up the Case Br Washington M aton and Layed ofver untill next meeting then adjourned in order

Alfred Carr C C K

Sattorday October 14 1848

The baptist Church at Sinking C reek meet A Cording to agornment and after worship the Church sat for B uisness firs a dor was opend for the reception for members either by letter or Exsperence none came forward 2nd took up the case of Bro M aton and requited him and restord him to full fellowship again then adgournd in order A C C H K

Sunday 15th day of October 1848

Aftor worship B ro Thomas E ansor and wife Rebeca Ensor petishend for a lettor of dismision whish was unanimous granted

Alfred Carr C C K

(note in pencil) Refference made by H. M. Saylor in the year 1903

(P. 179) Sattorday 18th day of December 1848

T he B aptist C hurch at Sinking Creek meet A Cording to Apointment aftor worship the C hurch sat for buisness 1st a door was opend for the reception of members by letter or exsperens Sistor Nancy Reed Joined by Lettor 2nd Br Joshua Swoner and Sister Mahala T Swoner his wife petishend for Leters of dishmishion wish was granted the adgornd in order

Alfred C arr C C K

Sattorday the 20th day of January 1849

T he Baptist C Hurch at Sinking Creek met A cording to apointment aftor worship the Church sat for buisness nothing worth of recording the Church then adgourned in order

Alfred Carr C C K

Sattorday 17 day of March 1849

The Baptist Church at Sinking C reek meet A C ording to Apointment and aftor worship sat for buisness 1st a dor was opend for the reception of members by lettor or exsperance 2nd mad A move for Chois to A lect 2 deacons and was left for Consideration untill next meeting 3rd mooved by Br Jefforson that Br Hampton Hyder be ordaned and was left for the Churchs Consideration untill next meeting --
adgourn untill nex meeting

A Carr C C K

(P. 180) Brother Eli Swinney departed this life March 28 day 1849

Sattorday April 14 day 1849

The B aptist Church at Sinking Creek meet a cording to Apointment and after worship Sat for Buisness 1st a dor for the Recepttion of members by Lettor or Exsperence 2nd Sister Jamima Nave Joined by Lettor 3rd Sistor Mary Newel Joind by Letter 4th Bro Newell RecvD under the wash cear of this church 5th tuck up the Refferenc from Las meeting Balleted for deacons and Elected Bro Alfred Carr and Bro Richard V Carr as deacons 6th tuck up the Refferns from last meeting the ordination of Bro H HyDer and a majority of the Church was in favour of his ordination and agreed to have him ordained next meeting 7 apointed Bro William Wheellor and Bro John Kuhn trustees with Alfred Carr for Sinking Creek meeting hous and land 8th Sister Margerit Hathaway applyed for a letter of dismishion through Bro Bayles which was granted then agournd in order

A. C. Clk

Friday 18 day of May 1849

The Baptist Church at Sinking Creek meet A Cording to A pointment and aftor worship the Church sat for buisness 1st tuck up the reffernse of Last meeting 2 Chose Br Richard Carr Decon and wife.
(P. 181) 3rd Exscluded Br John Maton from our fellowship for drunkenness and runing a way with a nother mans wife

4th Exscluded B r Washington Maton for runing aftor Bad woman and useing profain Langaig Languae absenting himself from the Church
4th the Church Apointed A Committee of five to William Hatcher and A C arr Joel Mcfawl J Hampton Hyder H Nave to wait on Jessa Humphris and Br Humphris gave the Committee full sadisfaction the A gorned in order
Alfred Car C Clark

Sattorday the 19th day of May 1849

the Church met after worship Sat for buisness 1st Ordained Br Johnathin H Hyder to the ministry 2nd Recve B r Jessa Umphris by recantation adgornd in order

A Carr C Clark

Sattorday 19 day of June 1849

the B aptist Church at Sinking Creek meet A Cording to apointment aftor worship Sat for buisness 1st A dor was opend for members none came forward
2nd went into the chois of delagats by ballet to the association 3rd Chose Br William Hatcher and Alfred Carr delagates
4th this C hurch agrees to send 75 cents for the printing of minites adjournd in order

Alfred C arr C Clark

(P. 182) Sattorday 14 day of July 1849

the Baptist /Church at Sinking Creek meet after worship proseded to Buisness first the Lettor to the association was brot forward and red and approve nothing more worth of recording adgournd in order
A C Church cl

Sattorday August 18 day 1849

The Baptist Church at Sinking Creek meet A cording to A pointment aftor worship proseed to buisness first a dor was opend for the reception of members by letter or exsperence none came forward- 2nd tuck up the case of Br Richard Jefferson and was talked over in the Church and the Church unanimously agreed to withdraw thar fellowship from him and was exspeld for drunken ness adgournd in order

A. C. Church Clark

friday 14 day of September 1849

the B aptist Church at Sinking Creek meet A Cording to A pointment aftor worship sat for Buisness first B r Jessa Humphres wanted to now whether or not this Church Lowed him to bee restord to his deconship or not Agan the Church agreed to Leave it as A mattor of Refferns then adgournd in order
A C Church C

S Attorday 15 day of September 1849

the Church meet aftor worship proseed to buisness first invited B ro Bayles to attend us A nother yaar and be agreed to do so nothing more agreed to adgourn adgournd in order

A Carr Church Clerk

(P. 183) Satorday 20 day of October 1849

the Church met A Cording to apointment aftor worship sat for Buisness first tuck up the Case of Sister Rhua Addams Respecting of keeping of a Bad hous and Apointed A Cometee of two Br John Khun and Bro Joel McFawl to visit her and Request her to attend next meeting nothing more adgournd in order

Alfred Carr C C

Sattorday 17 day of November 1849

the B aptist Church at Sinking C reek met A Cording to Apointment aftor Worship the Church sat for Business first Dissmist Sister ~~Louisa Swinnet~~ Debory J ohnson by Lettor--
2nd the Church unanimously withdrew ther fellowship from Sistor Louisa Swinney for disorderly leaving the Church the C hurch then adgournd in order

A Carr C C K

Sattorday 16 day of December 1849

the Baptist Church met A Cording to A pointment after worship the Church sat for buisness first our former Clerk being absent A pointed Bro William Pue pro tem no buisness Came before the Church of notice then adgornd in order

Alfred C arr C C L

(P. 184) Sattorday 19 day of January 1850

the Baptist Church at Sinking Creek met A C ording to A pointment aftor worship the Church sat for bisness
first dismissed Br other Jackson own by Lettor nothing mor worth recording then adgornd in order

A Carr C C lark

Sattorday 16 day of March 1850

it being the time of our regler meeting day and owing to the rane and hy wator there was no meeting.

A Carr Church Clark

Sattorday 16 day of April 1850

the Baptist Church at Sinking Creek meet A Cording to Apointment and aftor worship Sat for buisness 1st A dor was opend for the reception of members by Lettor or Exsperns Sistor ibba Duncan Came forward and Joind by giving a relation ship of her mind
2nd the Church withdrew ther fellowship from Br Henry J efferson for drinking Swaring and fiting 3rd dismiss Sistor Nancy Reed by Lettor 4th the Church with drew ther fellowship from Sistor Rhua Addams for disorderly Conduct----- adjournd in order

A Carr Church Clerk

(P. 185) M ay Sattorday 11 1850
Names of persons Joind at a potraced meeting at Sinking C reek held by M V Kitzmiller and W C Newel with the pastor
thuseday 14th day Susanna Saylor Joind by Exsperns
Wensday 15 day Elbert Rang J oind By Exsperns and Mary Wolf By Exsperens
Martha J ane Lysenby by Lotter allso on the same day Mary Lib By Exsperens
James taylor By Exprns

friday 17 day Being Church day aftor worship the mattor of Refferns from the february meeting was taking up respecting the decon ship with A Carr and agreed to Lay it over untill Sattorday then adgornd

Sattorday M ay 18th 1850

Aftor worship the Church sat for Business first opend A door for members and Washington Orrens Joind by ex making in all during the meeting 7 and was all Baptist 2nd By or der of the Church Alfred Carr was ordained to the office of Deacon Elders Rees Bayles and M V Kitzmiller and Wm C Newel officiating as presbytry then adgond in order

Alfred Carr Church Clark

Sunday 19 of May dismissed Br Wm C Newel and wife by Lettor in good standing and in full fellowship with us

(P. 186) Sattorday 15 day of June 1850

The Baptist Church at Sinking Creek met A Cording to A pointment aftor worship sat for Buisness 1st Chose Br Wm C Newel Moderator Br Bayless not present 2nd the Church Sends Br Wm Phue and Br H Nave as a delagation and requist Br Joshua Sowner (Swoner) and wife to attend next meeting and assine thear reasons for absenting them selvs from the Church So Long as we understand tha Still hold the lettors of dishmishion from this Church 3rd Apointed A Carr J H Hyder and Wm Hatcher delegates to the next meeting of the Holston association which mets at Inden Creek Church 2nd friday in August nex 4th Agrees to send 1 00 dollar to help defray associational Expences 5 instructs the Clark to insert in the Letter that we are pleasd with the past years plan of misenary operation then adgournd in order

A Carr Church Clark

Sattorday 20 day of July 1850

The Baptist Church at Sinking Creek meet acording to adjournment after worship Sat for buysness first the Lettor of address to the the association was red and approve 2nd Robert H Mulkey and wife Joind by Lettor Then adgournd in order

A Carr Church Clerk

(P. 187) Sattorday 17 day of August 1850

the Baptist Church at Sinking Creek met A Cording to Apointment aftor worship Sat for Buisness first tuck up the case of Br Joshua Swoner and the Church unanimously with drew ther fellowship from him for disorderly conduct and holding up his lettor and not attending his meeting
2nd Dismissed hour be Love Sister Mahaly Swoner in full fellowship with us
3rd Apointed Br Henry Nave and William Hatcher to demand Br Swoner Lettor of him adgorned in order

A C Church Clerk

friday 13 day of September 1850

the Baptist Church of Christ at Sinking Creek meet A Cording to A pintment aftor worship Sat for buisness first Chose Br Rees Bayles Again for our pastor for the next year 2nd a pointed Br Volintine Nave and Br William Phue to visit Br James PePles and Br Abraham Row to attend and fill up thear Seet nex meeting adgorned in order

Sattorday 14 day of September after worship the Church Sat for buisness nothin WORTH RECORDING ADJorned in order

A Carr C Clark

Sattorday October 19 day 1850

The Baptist Church meet acording to apointment at Sinking Creek aftor worship Sat for buisness first a dor was opened for the recpttion of members by Lettor or Ex Br John Bayles Joined by Lettor 2nd tuck up the refferns from last meeting
Dissmis without any difficulty

Adjourn in order
A Carr C Clark

(P. 188) Sister Elizabeth Wheelor Departed this Life 3rd day of November 1850

-- -- -- --

Sattorday 16 day of November 1850

the Baptist Church of Christ at Sinking Creek meet A Cording to A pointment aftor worship Sat for buisness first Recve Sistor Jule Bang (Rang) By Expearnes and Baptism 2nd tuck up the case of Sister Mary tipton of Coller and was settled Sattisfactory and the Churchs mesengers discharged then adjorned in order

A Carr C Clark

Sunday 17th day of November 1850

Recve Br John Wolf By Exspearens and Baptism adgourned in order
A Carr C Clark

-- -- -- --

Sistor Pheby Hart
Departed this Life November 24 day 1850

-- -- -- --

Sattorday 14 day of December 1850

the Baptist Church at Sinking Creek meet a Cording to Apointment aftor worship the Church sat for buisness nothing Came before the Church
adgorned in order

A Carr C Clark

(P. 189) Sattorday 18 day of January 1851

The Baptist Church at Sinking Creek meet A Cording to A pointment afor worship Sat for buisness no buisness Came before the Church worth recording gournd in order

A Carr C Clark

Sattorday 15 day of february 1851

The Baptis Church at Sinking Creek meet Song and prayed and Cld for buisness nothing worth recording adgornd in order

A Carr C Clark

Sattorday 15 day of March 1851

the Baptist Church at Sinking Creek meet A Cording to A pointment Aftor worship the Church Sat for buisness first the Church withdrew theair fellowship from Br James Peples for Drunkenness and not filling of his seat at Church unanimously with drew the fellow Ship from Br Jefferson Swoner for Drunkenness and not filling his Seat at Church meeting days then adgournd in order

Alfred Carr Church Clark

-- -- -- -- -- -- -- -- --

Sistor Eliza Beth Cashaday Departed this Life April 1 day 1851

-- -- -- -- -- -- -- -- --

(P. 190) Sattorday April 19 day 1851

the Baptist Church at Sinking Creek meet A Cording to A pointment aftor worship Sat for Buisness first our moderator not presant Chos Br William Cate moderator pr tem first Jefferson Swoner Came forward and was Recve Back into fellowship by making Sadisfactory acnolledgement for not attending his Church meetings and Sadisfied the Church that the Charge of drunkeness was not true then adgorned in order

A Carr C Clark

friday May 16 day 1851

the Baptist Church at Sinking Creek meet A Cording to A pointment aftor worship Sat for Buisness nothing worth recording Adgornd in order---

Sattorday May 17 1851

the Baptist Church at Sinking Creek meet acording to A pointment aftor worship Sat for Buisness first tuck up the Case of Sistor Mary tipton of Collar and Apointed Br J H Hyder and William Hatcher to visit her and requist her to fill up her seat next meeting and anser Some Reports aganst her adgornd in order

A Carr C Clark

(P. 191) June 14 day 1851

the Baptist Church at Sinking Creek meet a Cording to A pointment aftor worship Sat for Buisness first tuck up the Case of Sistor Mary tipton of Collar and was refurd untill nex meeting and A pointed Br J H Hyder to see Joaner typton and git in right the fax of the Case
2nd Recve sistor Hettea Orr By Lettor
3rd Apointed H Nave and A Carr Elbert E Range Delligats to the next association
4 the Church apoitted Abraham Jobe and H Nave William hatcher William Pim A Carr to Superenintend recovern the meeting hous adgorned in order

A Carr C Clark

(Note in Pencil) Reference by Henry M. Saylor 1903

Sattorday July 17 day 1851

the Baptist Church at Sinking Creek met a cording to A pointment after worship Sat for Buisness first tuck up the refferens from Last meeting and dismissed it
2nd the Lettor of Adress to the association was red and approve
3rd John Hur Agree with the Committe to Cover the meting hous with 2 foot Bords show 8 inches for 37 dollars and tak the subscription papor and Collect it

A Carr Ch Clark

(P. 192) Sattorday August 16 day 1851

the Baptist Church of Christ at Sinking Creek met aftor worship Sat for Buisness nothing worth recording adgournd in order

A Carr Ch CLark

friday 19 day of September 1851

the Baptist Church at Sinking Creek meet acording to A pointment aftor worship Sat for Buisness first Brother Bayles not present Chose Bro H Nave moderator protem nothing worth recording adJornd in order

A Carr Ch Clark

Sattorday 20 day of September 1851

After worship Sat for buisness our moderator present first Chose Bro Rees Bayles pastor Another Year
2nd the Church unanimously Agreed to Adopt the following Rules for doing buisness to wit
1st Invitation for members
2nd Reffernsces
3rd Letters of dishmision
4th Members Retaining Lettors
5th Disorderly or delinquent members
6th Afflicted or needy members
7th Deaths
8th quarterly Dews
9 Miscellones Buisness
Adjornd in order

A Carr Ch Clark

(P. 193) Brother Joel McFawl Died September 17 day 1851

-- -- -- -- -- -- -- --

Sattorday 18 day of October 1851

the Baptist Church at Sinking Creek met acording to A pointment Aftor worship Sat for buisness first Br Bayles not present Chose Br H Nave moderator protem 2 Sistor Rebecca Martin and Gemyma Martin petishend for Lettors of dishmision and was granted then adgornd in order

A Carr Ch Clark

-- -- -- -- -- -- -- --

Sister Nancy Crowthers Departed this Life November 1851

-- -- -- -- -- -- -- --

November 15th day 1851

Beeing meeting day but Br Bayles was sick and Bad weather there was no meeting

A Carr Ch Clark

Sattorday 20 th day of December 1851

the Baptist Church at Sinking Creek meet A Cording to A pointment Aftor worship Sat for buisness first Chose Br H Nave moderator protem Br Bayles not present nothing worth recording adgornd

A Carr Church Clark

(P. 194) Sattorday January 17 day 1852

the Baptist Church at Sinking Creek meet A Cording to Apointment Aftor worship Sat for buisness first Chose Br H Nave moderator pr tem nothing wortha of recording then adgornd in order

A Carr Church CL

-- -- -- -- -- -- --

Bro Lenord Harte Departed this life January 4 day 1852 A. C. CLark

-- -- -- -- -- -- --

Sattorday 14 day of february 1852

the Baptist Church at Sinking Creek met acording to Apointment Aftor worship Sat for buisness 1st Chose BrO H Nave moderator prtem Bro Bayles not present nothing worth recording adgornd in order

A Carr Ch CLark

Sattorday Match 20 day 1852

the Baptist Church at Sinking Creek meet acording to apointment aftor worship Sat for buisness first Chose Br M V Kitzmiller moderator protem
2nd agreed to eLect a pastor when Rev Wm C Newell was eLected and the CLark ordered to inform him of the same adgornd in order

A Carr Ch CLark

(P. 195) March 21 day 1852 aftor Devine Servis by M V Kitzmiller the church Sat A dore was opend for the recption of members Sistor Debborah Rang Joind by Exsperens and Baptism then adgornd in order

Alfred Carr Ch CLark

April 17 day 1852

the Baptist Church of Christ at Sinking Creek meet aftor worship Sat for buisness first
Chose Br Valentine Bowers moderator protem
Br William C Newell Being present a greed to attend this Church as pastor from August next and that he would attend 1 time a month now if the Church wold altor thar regalar time to the fourth Sunday in plase of the third which was agreed to untill August aftor that to bee on the third Sunday as yousel then adgornd in order

A Carr Ch CLark

Sattorday May 15 day 1852

the Baptist Church at Sinking Creek meet A Cording to A pointment aftor worship Sat for Buisness 1st Chose Br Rees Bayles moderator prtem nothing worth recording adgornd in order

A Carr Church CLark

(P. 196) Sattorday 26th day of June 1852

the Baptist Church at Sinking Creek meet A Cording to apointment aftor worship Sat for buisness first opend a dor for the reception of members by Lettor or Exsperans none came forward 2nd went into the chois of delligats to wit Alfred Carr Elbert Rang Henry Nave and William Phue ther being a ty vote the Church agred to send them both which mad four 3rd Apointed Brother William Phue Jessa Duncan Richard Carr to visit Bro Mikel Smithpeters and wife to and requist them to fill up thear Seet nex meeting day and ansor some Charges against them adgornd in order

A Carr Church CLark

Sattorday 24 day of July 1852

the Baptist Church at Sinking Creek meet A cording to Apointment aftor worship sat for buisness first a dor was opend for members Sistor ~~Mary E Swoner~~ Nancy E Swoner Joind by Lettor 2 tuck up the refferens of Last meeting and Settled Sadisfactory 3rd the Lettor to the association was red and approved 4th the Church younanimously agreed to Lift a Collection Every fawl for forinmishen purposes and Every Spring for home mishen and order to make a record of it

adgornd in order A Carr Church Clerk

Sattorday August 21 day 1852

The Baptist Church at Sinking Creek met A Cording to Apointment after worship sat for buisness 1st Chose Br H Nave moderator protem nothing worth recording adgournd in order

A Carr Church CLark

-- -- -- -- -- -- --

(P. 197) Br David Phue Departed this life August 10 day 1852

-- -- -- -- -- -- --

friday September 17th day 1852

the Baptist Church at Sinking Creek meet aftor worship Sat for buisness nothing worth recording adgornd till Sattorday 18 day 1852 aftor worship sat for business firs opend A dore for members 2nd Rebeca Murry Joind by Lettor and 3rd Sister Mary Seell Joind by Lettor 4th Sister Martha Jane Lisenby applied for a letter of Dishmishion and was granted 5 Sister Hetty Ore was Dismised by Lettor adgornd in order

A Carr Ch CLark

Sattorday 16 day of October 1852

the Baptist Church at Sinking Creek met a cording to A pointment after worship Sat for buisness first Chose Br H Nave moderator promtem 2 Br Jacob Swoner and wife Nancy E Swoner Lettors of Dismishen then adgornd in order

A Carr Ch CLark

Sattorday 20 day of November 1852

The Baptist Church at Sinking Creek meet A cording to A pointment after

worship Sat for buisness nothing worth regarding the meeting was protracted some 9 days and during the meeting the following pursons Joind by ExSpearens and Baptism to wit---
(P. 198) Note in Pencil- Refference by Henry M. Saylor in 1903 C C
Elizabeth Scot John Wolf Martha Saylor Noa Saylor Eliza Yorley Mary Saylor of Isaac Saylor Martha McFawl Mary Saylor of henry Saylor John McFawl ~~James Jeffersen~~ Augusta Hatcher Catharine Hix Minerva Jane Phue Elizabeth Henry then adjornd in all 13

Alfred Carr Ch CLark

Sattorday 18 day of December 1852

the Baptis Church at Sinking Creek met aftor worship sat for buisness first Gorge P Umphris Joind by Ex and Baptism then adjornd in order

A Carr Ch Clark

Sattorday 15 day of January 1853

the Baptist Church at Sinking Creek met A Cording to A pointment after worship sat for Buisness first inventation for members none Came forward 2 Appointed the following Brethren A Carr and Wm Phue to Cite Bro James Cashaday and wife to fill up there seets next meeting and clen up some unfavourable Reports in Circulation about them 3 Sis Susan Nave applid for a Lettor of dismission and was granted 4 Br Wm Nave and wif all so applied for Lettors and was granted then adjorn in order

A Carr Ch CLark

Saturday Nov the 20th 1853 John Woolf Joind the Ch

(P. 199) Sattorday 19 day of february 1853

the Baptis Church at Sinking Creek meet A Cording to A pointment aftor worship Sat for buisness first Chose Br H Nave moderator prtem Bro Newel not present 2nd Cald for the Refferens of Last meeting and was Continued untill next meeting adgourned in order---

A Carr Church CL

Sattorday March 19 day 1853

The Baptist Church at Sinking Creek meet aftor worship proseed to buisness first Cald for Joiners none Came forward
2nd tuck up the Refferns of Last meeting and heard the Report of the Committee wh was dishCharged aftor dew discussion by the Church Bro James Cashaday and wife was Excluded for keeping Bad Compina about his hous and having too much drinkig about his hous then adgornd in order

A Carr Church CL

Sattorday 16 of April 1853

The Baptist Church at Sinking Creek meet acording to A pointment aftor worship proseded to Buisness first a dore was opend for members Sistor Orph Hamer goind by Lettor 2 Sistor Mary Emmet applid for a Lettor of Dismision and was granted
(P. 200) 3rd Resolvd that hearafter we will not be bound to Confine ourselves Exclusively to members of our own Church or of our denomination in

the Examination of testimony in the transaction of Church buisness then adgornd in order

A Carr Church Clark

Sattorday 14 day of May 1853

the Baptist Church at Sinking Creek meet aftor worship Sat for buisness first opend a dore for members 3 goind by Letter to wit Sistor Mary Catharine Rang and Sister Elizabeth Wieth and Sister Charlotte Duffield of Couler adgournd in order --

A Carr Clk

-- -- -- -- -- -- -- --

Sistor Orpha Hamer Died May 13, 1853

-- -- -- -- -- -- -- --

Sattorday 18 day of June 1853

the Baptist Church at Sinking Creek meet A Coring to Apointment aftor worship Sat for buisness first a dore was opend for members Sister Julia Ann Harshbarger Joind by Lettor 2nd Excommunicated Br Wil Maton from the Church for treting the Church with Contempt 3rd went into the Chois of deligats to the association Chois our beloved brethern to wit A Carr and J H Mulkey and E H Rang then adgournd in order

A Carr C Clk

(P. 201) Sattorday July 16 day 1853

the baptist Church at Sinking Creek meet A Cording to Apointment aftor worship Sat for buisness first A dor was oppend for members Sister Rachall McCluer and Elizabeth McCluer and Marguit McCluer Joind by Lettor 2nd the Lettor of address to the association was red and approvd then adgornd in order

A Carr Ch CLark

Satorday 20 day of August 1853

the Baptist Church at Sinking Creek meeting acording to a pointment aftor worship meet for buisness first dismised Washington Arrons and wife in full fellowship 2nd the Church unanimously agreed to adopt theas Loins to wit Resolved that we disapprove of the practice of making Buying Seling and drinking ardent Sperits as a Beverage and that we will use our Inflewance to discountinence the practice beliving that it Leads to drunkenness one of the gratest evils in our Church Country

A Carr Church CLark

Sabeth granted Sistor Elizabeth Henry a Lettor of Dishmision

(P. 202) friday 16th day of September 1853

The Baptist Church at Sinking Creek meet aftor worship meet for buisness first cald for the Refferns of Last meeting and by requist Raist Bro Andrew Kauns name from the Church book 2nd granted Br Robert Cashadays a letter of Dismision

Sattorday 17th day meet aftor worship meet for buisness first went into the Chois of a deacon and Chois Br R H Mulkey and was ordaind prair by ELdor

Pator Khun 2nd Chose Br W O Newell our pastor for a nother year then adgourned

A Carr Church CLark

Sattorday 15 day of October 1853

The Baptist Church at Sinking Creek meet aftor worship sat for buisness nothing worth recording then adgornd

A Carr Church Clerk

Sattorday 19th day of November 1853

The Baptist Church at Sinking Creek meet after worship meet for buisness first Cald for members none Came forward 2nd Dismiss Br R H Mulky and wife by Letter then adgornd in order

A Carr Church CLark

-- -- -- -- -- -- --

Br Joel Coopper Departed this Life December 4 Day 1853

-- -- -- -- -- -- -- --

(P. 203) Satorday 17 day of December 1853

The Baptist Church at Sinking Creek meet A Cording to A pointment after worship met for buis first A gred to go in to the Chois of A Deacon at the next meeting then adgornd in order

A Carr Church CLark

-- -- -- -- -- -- -- --

Sister Julian Bang Died January 17th 1854

-- -- -- -- -- -- -- --

Saturday 14th day of January 1854

the Baptist Church at Sinking Creek meet aftor worship sat for buisness first went into the chois of a deakin ELected E H Rang and was ordaind prair by M V Kitzmiller then adjourned in order

A Carr Ch CLark

Satorday 18th day of February 1854

The Baptist Church at Sinking Creek meet after worship Sat for buisness first granted William Jobe a man of Couler A letter of dismision allso the Liberty to exersise his gift in publick 2nd granted Elizabeth tapp a lettor of dishmision then adgornd in order

A Carr Ch CLark

-- -- -- -- -- -- -- --

february 26th 1854
Br John Roow Died 26th 1854

-- -- -- -- -- -- -- --

(P. 204) Sattorday 17 day of March 1854

the Church at Sinking Creek meet aftor worship meet for buisness nothing worth recording adgournd in order

A C Ch CLark

Sattorday 15 day of April 1854

The Baptis Church at Sinking Creek meet aftor worship meet for buisness

first Cold for Joiners Sistor E A. Combs Joind by Lettor then adgornd
A Carr Ch CLark

friday 19 day of May 1854

The Baptist Church at Sinking Creek meet aftor worship meet for Buisness first granted Br Abram Jobe a Lettor of dishmision then andJornd ----

Sattorday 20 day of may 1854
meet after worship met for buisness nothing worth recording then adJornd
A Carr Ch Clark

Sattorday 17th day of June 1854

The Baptist Church at Sinking Creek meet aftor worship meet for buisness first chose H Nave moderator 2nd Went into the Chois of dellagats to the association Choose Br A Carr and Henry Nave and William hatcher as ther deligats then adgournd
A Carr Ch CLark

(P. 205) Sattorday 15th day of July 1854

The Church at Sinking Creek meet aftor worship meet for buisness first the Lettor to the association was red and approved
2nd receved Rachel Pugh By Exspearens and baptism then gournd in order
A Carr Ch Clark

Sattorday 19 day of August 1854

The Baptist Church at Sinking Creek meet aftor worship meet for buisness first Excluded Vollentine Nave for moving away without Calling for a letor and not paying his pledges to the Church
2nd Excluded Mikel Smithpeters and wife for not attending there meetings adgornd in order

~~Sunday 20 day of August 1854 after worship come forward and mad Sadisfaction to the Church and was Reseved back in the Church again~~
A Carr Ch CLark

~~Sattorday 19th day of January 1856~~
~~The Baptist Church at Sinking Creek met after worship Cold for buisness none was presented then adgornd in order~~
A Carr Ch CLark

(P. 206) friday 15th day of September 1854

The Baptist Church at Sinking Creek meet aftor worship meet for buisness first Cold for Joiners none Came forward 2nd tuck up the Case of Bro Noa Saylor and Laid it over untill to morrow 3rd Chose Br W C Newel our pastor for the next yeair then adgornd in order
A Carr Church Clark

Sattorday 16 day of September 1854

Aftor worship meet for buisness first tuck up the Case of Noa Saylor and Ex-scluded him from the fellowship of the Church for drinking and running after bad wimmen 2nd Bro Newel agreed to A tend the Church anotheryeair on Condishion tha wod giv him a Saport the next yeair and was Left untill nex meeting then adgorn in order

A Carr Church CLark

Sattorday 14th day of October 1854

The Church at Sinking Creek meet aftor worship meet for buisness first Chose J H Hyder moderator prtem first dismiss Br J H Hyder by Lettor 2nd the Church tuck up the Resalution of the association in regard to holding up of Lettors and adopted it in the minit of 1854 that any person ~~obtain~~ giting a Lettor of dismision ~~and not laid in~~ and bin in the Bounds of this association and dont Lay it in in 3 months it is dead and no more a member of the Church (P. 207) and any purson that has got a lettor and dont lay it in in three mounths is nul and void then adgournd in order

A Carr Ch Clark

November 18th day 1854

The Baptist Church at Sinking Creek meet aftor worship meet for buisness nothing worth recording then adgournd

A Carr Ch Clark

December 16th 1854

The Baptist Church at Sinking Creek meet No preacher adjourn and no meeting

A Carr Ch Clark

January the 20th 1855

the Baptist Church of Christ at Sinking Creek met after worship the Door was opend for the reception of members receivd J. M. P. Peoples Buy Letter

A Carr Ch Cl

The Following members Joind at the ministers & Deacons meeting Held at this place on Christmas 1854

Namly- Saphronia Saylor	Hannah Cooper	John Huphres
Lucindy Hicks	Susan Loudermilk	Marthe Loudermilk
Mingumary Saylor	Abaham Saylor	Hanna Saylor
J. William Humphris	Eliza Haner Humphris	Martha Smith

in all 12

(Note in Pencil) Refference by H. M. Saylor C C in the year 1903

(P. 208) Sattorday 17th day of february 1855

the Baptist Church meet aftor worship the Church meet for buisness nothing worth recording then adgornd in order

A Carr Church CL

Sattorday 17 day of March 1855

the Baptist Church at Sinking Creek meet aftor worship meet for buisness nothing worth recording then adgournd in order

A Carr Church CL

Sattorday 14 day of April 1855

the Baptist Church meet aftor worship meet for buisness first Cold for goiners none Came forward 2nd the Church withdrew thr fellowship with sistor Sara Helton for not filling up her Seat at her respectiv meeting allso sistor Hart for the Same Charg then adgournd in order

A Carr Church CL.

friday 18th of May 1855

The Baptist Church at Sinking Creek meet aftor worship meet for buisness Calld for goiners none Came forward then adgourn untill
Sattorday May 19th 1855
Aftor Preaching the Church meet for Buisness first Cawld for joiners none Came foward 2nd the two sistor Nancy Cashadays Cawled for Lettors of dishmision and was granted 3rd Br Pinkney Peoples Cawled for a letter and was granted 3rd the fowling Recpt was Recvd and requisted to be spread on record
(P. 209) (Receipt pasted in book.)

Recd Nashville, April 18, 1855 of Sinking Creek Church and Congregation, pr W. C. Newell, Six 30/100 Dollars, amount of contribution to the Bible Board of So Baptist Convention for Bibles for China $6.30

Charles A Fuller, Treas
Bible Board of So Bap Con.

then agournd in order

A Carr CLark

Sattorday June 16th day 1855

The Baptist Church at Sinking Creek meet aftor worship meet for Buisness first Cawled for goiners none came foward 2nd Elected Delligats to the nex association Chois A Carr E H Range and Richard Y Carr as ther delligats 3 send 6 dollars and 15 cents for home mishion and 1 dollar for printing minets then adgournd in order

A Carr Ch CLark

Sattorday July 14 1855

The Baptist Church at Sinking Creek meet aftor worship meet for buisness first the Lettor of an adress to the association was red and approved 2nd granted Sistor Margurt Coper a lettor of Dismision then adgournd in order

A Carr CLark

(P. 210) Sattorday 18th day of August 55

The Baptist Church at Sinking Creek aftor worship meet for buisness first Cald for Joiners and recived by lettor Wiley Coper and his wife Elender and Patsey Shuffield nothing more worth recording adgournd

A Carr Ch Clark

Sattorday 21st day of Octob 1855

The Baptist Church at Sinking Creek aftor worship meet for buisness first Excluded Sistor Elizabeth Wyat for Joining the Camelites 2nd Dismissed Sistor Elizabeth Combs by Lettor the adgornd in order --

Sattorday 17th day of November 1855

The Baptist Church at Sinking Creek meet aftor worship meet for buisness first chose W. C. Newell Pastor for the nex year then adgorned in order
A Carr Ch CLark

(P. 211) Sattorday 15th day of December 1855

The Baptist Church at Sinking Creek meet aftor worship meet for buisness first Cold for Joiners 2nd granted Br Henry Nave and wife Mary F Nave Lettors of Dishmision then adgourne in order
A Carr Ch Clark

Sattorday 19 day of January 1856

the Baptist Church at Sinking Creek meet aftor worship meet for buisness none worth recording then adgornd
A Carr Ch Clark

Sattorday 16th day of february 1856

The Baptist Church at Sinking Creek meet acording to apointment aftor worship meet for buisness nothing worth recording Then adgournd in order
A Carr C Clark

Sattorday 15 day of March 1856

the Baptist Church at Sinking Creek aftor worship meet for buisness first Cold for goiners none Came fowward
2nd granted the 3 Sistors McClewers Lettors of Dismission to wit Rashel and Marguit and Elizabeth don by order of the Church then adgornd
A. Carr Ch Clark

(P. 212) Sattorday April 19th 1856

The Baptist Church at Sinking Creek meet aftor worship meet for buisness Nothing worth recording
A Carr Ch CLark

friday 16th day of May 1856

The Baptist Church at Sinking Creek meet aftor worship meet for buisness first Cole for goiners None Came fowward then adgournd

Sattorday 17th of May 1856
Aftor worship meet for buisness first Cold for goiners Richard Jefferson Joind By Recentation then adgorned in order
A Carr C Clark

May 18 1856 then tennesee Addames Joind by Lettor
A Carr C C

Sattorday 14th day of June 1856

Aftor worship meet for buisness first Cold for goiners none Came fowred

2nd ECluded sistor Elizabeth Combs for goining the Camelits 3rd Sent Br Jessa Umphris for to demand of her lettor 4th Chose Brethrn A Carr and R Carr William Hatcher Dellegats to the nex association
A Carr C C

(P. 213) Sattorday 19th day of July 1856

The Baptist Church at Sinking Creek meet aftor worship meet for buisness the lettor to the association was red and approved then adjornd
A Carr Ch Clark

Sattorday 16th day of August 1856

The Baptist Church at Sinking Creek meet aftor worship meet for buisness first Cose Brother Hatcher moderator prtem
2nd Cold for goiners none Came fowward
3rd Granted lettors to Br John Mcfawl and wife Sophrony of Dishmision Then adgournd in order
A Carr C Clark

-- -- -- -- -- -- --
Sis Sara Right Departed this Life September 14th 1856
-- -- -- -- -- -- --

friday September 19th 1856

the Baptis Church meet aftor worship meet for buisness first Chose Br William C Newell pastor for the next year then adgornd -
A Carr C Cl

Sattor 20 of September 1856

Aftor worship meet for buisness first Cole for Joiners Sister Elizabeth Wyet Joind by Recantation
A Carr C Clark

(P. 214) October 18 day 1856

The Baptist Church at Sinking Creek meet aftor worship Cold for goiners none Came fowward then adgornd in order
A Carr C C

Sattorday November 15th 1856

The Baptist Church at Sinking Creek meet aftor worship meet for buisness first coled for Joiners Recived Sistor Woolf by Exsperance and baptism 2nd Whear thear is A report a broad in the neighbourhood pregudicial to the Christian Charrstor of Sistor Eliz Gorley appointed Breth William Hatcher and Jessa Humphris to inquir into the foundation threof and report next Church meeting ----

Sattorday 20 day of December 1856

the Church meet aftor worship meet for buisness Cold for goiners none Came fowward 2nd Cold for the reffernces of last meeting the Committee Reported and was discharged and aftor some conversation was agreed to lay it over untill next meeting day and apointed Br William Hatcher and James Taylor to inquir in and find out all the proof tha Can and report next Church meeting 3rd tuck up the Case of Sistor Polley Hoss and was Excluded for wilfull lying and Slandering Br William Hatcher ------

Sattorday 17th day of January 1857

Aftor worship meet for buisness first cold for goiners non Com foward 2nd Cold for the refferens of las meeting the committee reported and was discharged (P. 215) 2nd Aftor herring all of the testimony on both sides desied that said Eliza Gorley is guilty of adultray
3rd Excommunicated her from the fellowship of the Church then adgornd in order

A Carr Ch Clark

february 14th day 1857

the Baptist Church at Sinking Creek meet aftor worship meet for buisness first Cold for Joiners none Came foward nothing more then adgornd in order

A Carr C. C.

March 14th 1857

the Church meet aftor worship meet for buisness first apointed William Hatcher moderator protem Br Newell not present 2nd tuck up the Case of Bro John Wolf and was layed over untill next meeting 3rd adgorned in order

A Carr C C

April 18 day 1857

the Baptist Church meet at Sinking Creek aftor worship meet for buisness first Bro Newell not presant adgournd

A Carr C Clark

May 15th 1857

The Baptist Church at Sinking Creek meet after worship meet four buisness first Cole for the Refferns from last meeting first the Case of sistor Mahala Swooner and Excluded her for not tending her Church meeting and for Bad Conduct with other men 2nd tuck up the Case of Bro John Wolf from last meeting and after some Conversation aquited him of the Charge the charg was this that a mis Sellers sowor (swore) a child to him but the Church aquited him

Sattorday 16th of May after worship meet nothing worth recording adgornd in order

A Carr Ch Clark

(P. 216) Sattorday June 20th 1857

The Baptist Church at Sinking Creek meet aftor worship meet four buisness first Cole for goiners none Came foward firs tuck up the association requist and went against it instructing our dellagats the propriaty of measures to build up and stranthen the weaker Churches of our association ---

2nd Excluded Br Mingumary Saylor for not attending his Church meetings and Joining the Methodis
3rd Dismissed Br Elbert Range and wife Catharine Range by Lettor and Sistor Debora fulkerson by Lettor 4th went into the Chois of Delligats to the association and Choas A Carr Wm Hatcher and Wm Phugh aus our Delagats to the nex association to bee held in Carter County then adgornd in order
A Carr Ch Clark

Sattorday 18th day of July 1857

The Baptist Church at Sinking Creek meet aftor worship meet for buisness the Lettor to the association was red and approved nothing moor worth recording adgorned
A Carr Ch Clark

Sattorday August 22th 1857

the Church at Sinking Creek meet aftor worship meet for buisness nothing worth recording adgournd
A Carr Ch Clark

(P. 217) friddays 18th of September 1857

the Baptist Church at Sinking Creek meet aftor worship meet four buisness first dismised Sistor Martha Mcfawl and Sistor Dianna Mcfawl by Lettor

Sattor 19th of September meet aftor worship firs recieve Bro Will Jobe and wife Vina by Lettor 2nd Exsclude Mingumry Saylor for drunkenness and Swaring 3rd Dismised Sistor hanna Saylor and Mary Dier and Elizabeth Scot by Lettor then adgorned in order
A Carr Ch Clark

Sattorday 18 day of October 1857

the Church meet nothing worth recording ----
A Carr Ch Cl.

Sattorday 15th day of November

the Baptist Church at Sinking Creek meet aftor worship meet nothing worth Recording adgournd in order
A Carr Ch Clark

-- -- -- -- -- -- --

Sistor Rachel Phugh Departed this life November 28th 1857

-- -- -- -- -- -- --

Sattorday 19th day of December 1857

the Baptis Church at Sinking Creek meet aftor worship meet for buisness nothing worth recording then adgornd in order
A Carr Ch Clark

(P. 218) Sattorday 16th of January 1858 the Baptist Church at Sinking Creek meet aftor worship meet for buisness nothing worth recording adgornd in order
A Carr Ch CL

Sattorday february 20th 1858

the Baptist Church at Sinking Creek meet aftor worship meet for buisness Dismised Sistor Shuffield by Lettor then adgorn in order
A Carr Ch Clark

Sattorday 20th of March 1858

the Baptist Church At Sinking Creek meet aftor worship meet four buisness first Cold for Joiners and Recivd Sistor Martha Linvill By Exspearns and Baptism 2nd thee Chur adopted the following Reslutions to bee annext to the Church Covinent
(Inserted in back of book Resolutions Copied on loose paper but filed here)

(P. 219) Sattorday the 17th day of April 1858

the Baptist Church at Sinking Creek meet four buisnesss first Cold for goiners and Recivd Wm Perry by Recantation and then dismissed Br Perry by Lettor 2nd Excluded Wiley Coopper and wife Elender for mooving off in dishorder and for mistreatment to sistor Shuffild adgornd in order
A Carr Ch Clark

Sattorday May 15th 1858

the Baptist Church at Sinking Creek meet aftor worship meet four buisness first Cold for goiners none Came foward 2nd Dismissed Sistor Mary tipton of Collar by lettor 3rd Excluded polla Moor from the fellowship of the Church 4th apointed Br Jessa Duncan to visit Sister Crouthers and request her to fill up her seat 5th apointed Richard Carr to visit tennessee Adames and wife to fill up ther seat then agorned in order
A Carr Ch Cl

Sattorday 19th of June 1858

the Baptis Church at Sinking Creek aftor worship meet for buisness first Restord Sistor Crouthers to fellowship of the Church
2nd Restord Br tennesee Adams and wife to fellowship again 2 Appointed deligats to the association A Carr Richard Carr and Jessa Duncan then adgornd in order
A Carr Ch Clark

— — — — — — —

Sistor Sary Range Departed this life June 8th 1858

— — — — — — —

(P. 220) Sattorday 17th of July 1858

the Church at Sinking Creek aftor worship meet for buisness firs Cold for goiners non Came foward 2nd Excluded Jessa Humphris and George Humphris and William humphris from the fellowship of the Church for drunkenness 3 receve the Lettor to the association the adgorne
A Carr Ch Clark

Sattorday October the 16th 1858

the Baptist Church at Sinking Creek meet aftor worship meet for buisness first Cold for goiners none Came foward 2nd Exsclud Eliza Humphris for sending A insulting lettor to the Church and trying to in Sult the Church then adgournd in order

A Carr C. Cl.

Sattorday November 20th 1858

The Baptist Church at Sinking Creek meet aftor worship Sat for buisness firs Chose Br W Hatcher moderator pr tem 2nd Chois J B Stone pastor of this Church for the next year 3rd Elected Br John Bayles and James taylor deakins 4th Excluded Martha Lowdy from the fellowship of the Church allso Martha Linvill for goine another Church then adjourd in order

A Carr C Clk

(P. 221) Sattorday December 18th 1858

The Baptist Church at Sinking Creek meet aftor worship meet for buisness first Chose J B Stone moderator 2nd Recivd Br/Thomas Hatcher by lettor 3rd Exclued Margurt MCnab for goinen the Metchodis Church then adgornd in order

A Carr Ch Clark

Sattorday January 1859 the Church at Sinking Creek meet aftor worship nothing worth recording then adgournd in order

A Carr Ch Cl.

Sattorday 19th day of february 1859

the Baptist Church at Sinking Creek meet aftor worship meet four buisness firs Cold for goiners and Recive Sistor Rispha M Edwards and Sistor Agness Hatcher by lettor then adgorn in order A Carr Ch Cl.

Sattorday March 19th 1859

the Baptist Church at Sinking Creek meet aftor worship meet four buisness nothing worth recording adgornd in order

A Carr Ch Cl.

Sattorday April 16th 1859

The Baptis Church at Sinking Creek meet aftor worship meet for buisness first ordaind Brother James taylor and John Bayles Deacens in the Sinking Creek Church Prisby Revent Jessa Riggs and James B Stone

A Carr Ch Clark

(P. 222) Sattorday May 14th 1859

The Baptist Church at Sinking Creek aftor worship meet four Buisness first Cald for Joiners none 2 Ex Sis R P Edwards for imprudent Conduct nothing moor adgournd

A Carr Ch Clark

-- -- -- -- -- --

Br John Khun Died January 1859

-- -- -- -- -- --

Sattorday June 11th 1859

The Baptis Church meet and Bro Stone not present nothing warth recording adjournd
A Carr Ch Clark

Sattorday 16th of July 1859

The Baptist Church at Sinking Creek meet aftor worship meet for buisness first Cald for goiners none Came fourward 2nd Went into the Chois of a Degagat to the association and apointed A Carr and Jessa Duncan and William Hatcher and John Humphris our delligats nothing more then adgornd
A Carr C Cl

Sattorday August 1859

the Baptist Church at Sinking Creek meet aftor worship meet for buisness nothing worth recording then adgornd in order
A Carr Ch Clark

Sattorday September 17th 1859

The Baptist Church at Sinking Creek meet aftor worship meet four buisness 1st Cold for goiners none Came fowward 2nd apointed William Hatcher and William Phue with William Wheelor and A Carr trustees of the Sinking Creek meeting house then adgournd
A Carr Ch Clark

(P. 223) Sattorday 15th day of October 1859

the Baptist Church at Sinking Creek meet aftor worship meet for buisness first Cold for goiners James Poples Joind by Recentation 2nd Br J B Stone agreed to attend the Church at Sinking Creek the next year for sixty dollars then adgornd in order
A Carr C Clark

Sattorday 19th day of November 1859

The Baptist Church at Sinking Creek meet aftor worship meet for buisness first Cold for Joiners and Recivd the following members by Expirens and Baptism Elizabeth Carr Susanna ~~Carr~~ Caraline Carr Martha Jane Carr and Susannah Duncan Bro Stone and McGarra protraced the meeting and Recive the following persons by Exspeirens and Baptism to wit Arshabell Colwell and David Hatcher and Martha Hatcher Amandy Oliver and Sara Phugh Elizabeth Gourley and Margurt Woolf 11 in all 11111111111
then adgournd in order
A Carr Ch Clark

Sattorday 16th day of December 1858

The Baptist Church at Sinking Creek meet aftor worship meet four buisness first Cold for goiners Martha Linvill Joind by Recantation Nothing more then adgornd in order
A Carr C Cl

(P. 224) January 14th day 1860

The Baptist Church at Sinking Creek meet aftor worship meet for buisness firs coled for goiners none Came fourward then adgorned
A Carr Ch Clark

february 18th 1860

The Baptist Church at Sinking Creek meet aftor worship meet for buisness first Cold for goiners nothing worth recording adgornd in order
A Carr Ch Clark

March 17th 1860

The Baptist Church at Sinking Creek meet aftor worship meet aftor worship meet for buisness first Cold for Joiners none Came fowward 2nd Exscluded Martha Smith for not filling up her seat at her Church meeting 3rd apointed Br White and William Phue to visit Br William Wheellor ~~to fill up his~~ and requist him to fill up his seat at the next Church meeting 4th Dismissed Brothers and Sistors to wit by Lettor
William Hatcher and Rhubin Hatcher Agness Hatcher and Augusta P Hatcher and Martha E Hatcher and David J Hatcher 6 members then adJornd in order
A Carr Ch Clark

(P. 225) Sattorday 14th day of April 1860

The Baptist Church at Sinking Creek meet after worship prossed to Buisness first Cold for Joiners none Came fowward 2nd Cald for the refferens of last meeting and aquited Br Wheellor A Carr Ch Clark

Sattorday May 19th 1860

The Baptist Church at Sinking Creek meet A Cording to A pointment aftor worship meet for buisness 1st Cold for goiners and Recived Sistor Elizabeth Hice by Exsperence 2nd Excluded Sis Hanner Humphris for using Profain Langua in time of worship to Br J B Stone and was Ex for the same then adgornd in order A Carr C Clark

Sattorday 16th day of June 1860

the Baptist Church at Sinking Creek meet thear pastor not present adgourned without meeting A Carr Ch Clark

Sattorday July 16th 1860

The Baptist Church at Sinking Creek meet Brother Stone not present But proseaded to point dellagates to the association to wit Jessa Duncan James peoples and John Bayles and A Carr then adgornd
A Carr Ch Clark

(P. 226) August the 18th 1860

The Baptist Church at Sinking Creek meet aftor worship meet four buisness Bro Stones time exspiered and the Church maid Chois of Br E Spurgin for the next year then adgornd A Carr Ch Clark

Sattorday September 15th 1860

The Baptist Church at Sinking Creek meet aftor worship meet four buisness first Bro E Spurgin was with ous and Agreed to attend this Church twelve menthes from this time 2Nd Agreed to have our Communicun Season on the 2nd Sabbeth in October in plase of the 3rd then adgourned
A Carr Ch Clark

Sattorday October 21st 1860

The Baptist Church at Sinking Creek meet aftor worship meet four buisness Bro Spurgin not present then adgornd in order

A Carr Ch Clark

Sattorday November 24th 1860

The Baptist Church at Sinking Creek meet aftor worship meet for buisness first Cold for Joiners none Came fowward
2nd Dismissed Sistor Catharine Loudy by Lettor then adgornd

A Carr Ch Clark

December 1860
No meeting in this month A Carr

(P. 227) January Sattorday 19th 1861

The Baptist Church at Sinking Creek meet aftor worship meet for buisness nothing worth recording then adgornd in order

A Carr C Clark

february no Meeting

Sattorday March 17th 1861

the Baptist Church at Sinking Creek meet aftor worship Sat for buisness 1st Chose J H Hyder moderator 2 restord Sara Helton to fellowship with this Church again 3rd Dismissed her by Lettor then adgournd

A Carr C Cl

Sattorday April 13 1861

The Baptist Church at Sinking Creek meet A Cording to A pointment first Chose Br J. H. Hyder moderator protem 2nd Recivd Brother Washington Arriens and his wife Nancy Arriens by Lettor
then adgornd in order A Carr Ch Clark

May 11th 1861

Meet agreeable to apointment no preacher adgornd with out meeting

A Carr Ch Clark

June 8th 1861

The Baptist Church at Sinking Creek met aftor worship meet four buisness Chose James taylor Archabel Colwell A Carr our deligats to the association then adgornd in order A Carr Ch Clark

July 13th 1861

The Baptist Church at Sinking Creek meet aftor worship meet for buisness the Lettor to the association was red and approved nothing more adgornd in order A Carr C Clark

(P. 228) August meeting was the time of the association and was no meeting

Sattorday September 8th 1861

the Baptist Church at Sinking Creek meet aftor worship meet for buisness nothing worth recording adgornd in order A Carr Ch Clark

Sattorday October 12th 1861

the Baptist Church at Sinking Creek meet nothing worth recording then adgornd
A Carr Ch Clark

Sattorday 9th day of November 1861 the Church meet Bro Hyder not present adgornd
A Carr Church Clark

December 7th 1861

the Baptist Church at Sinking Creek meet nothing worth recording adgorn
A Carr Ch CL

January 12th 1862

the Baptist Church at Sinking Creek meet aftor worship meet for buisness nothing worth recording A Carr Ch Cl

february 8th 1862

The Baptist Church at Sinking Creek meet aftor worship meet for buisness nothing worth recording adgornd in order A Carr Church Clark

— — — — —

Old Sistor Swinney Departed this life february 1862

— — — — —

March 8th 1862

The Baptist Church meet aftor worship Cold for buisness nothing worth recording and Jornd A Carr Ch Clark

— — — — —

Sistor Elizabeth Lowdymilk Departed this Life allso Sistor Susanna Willims Departed this life february 1862

— — — — —

(P. 229) April 1862

the Baptist Church at Sinking Creek meet aftor worship meet for buisness nothing worth record Sister Lucy Loudymilk died April 1862 then adgornd A Carr Ch Clark

May the 10th 1862

The Baptist Church at Sinking Creek meet aftor worship met for buisness nothing worth record adgornd in order A Carr Ch Clark

Sattorday May 1862

The Baptist Church at Sinking Creek meet after worship meet for buisness and Choase A Carr and J. W. taylor as our messengers to the association nothing worth recording adgornd A Carr Ch Clark

July 12th 1862

the Baptist Church at Sinking Creek meet aftor worship meet for buisness first the lettor to the association was read and recivd then adgornd
A Carr C. Clark

August 9th 1862

No meeting on account of the Association at the same time

Satterday 13 day of September 1862

the Baptist Church meet aftor worship meet for buisness nothing worth recording and Jorned in order A Carr Ch Clark

October 11th 1862

the Baptist Church meet and no preacher Br Hyder not present

-- -- -- -- -- --

(P. 230) feather Rees Bayles Departed this life November 1864

-- -- -- -- -- --

Brother Richard Y Carr Departed this life June 22nd 1865

-- -- -- -- -- --

Washington Arrons Died 1865

-- -- -- -- -- --

August the 19th 1865

the Baptist Church at Sinking Creek meet aftor worship meet for buisness 1st agreed to meak a new record of the members of this Church

(Left side of page 230)

(William Pugh Joind	1833	James Peoples	1852
William Wheellor	1833	John Humphrs	1855
Jessa Duncan X	1844	Lucindy Hicks	1856
Catharine Barns)	1836	teenesee Addims X	1856
Deceased Apr 25th 1871)		Elizabeth Wiyet	1856
A Carr	1843	Elizabeth Carr X	1859
Nancy Jefferson X	1834	Susan Caroline Carr X	1859
Sary Carr X	1845	Martha Jane Carr X	1859
Will Jobe of Coller X	1846	John Bayles	1857
Nancy Hicks X	1846	(Right side of page 230)	
Richard Jefferson X	1847	Archable Colwell X	1859
Marier Umphris of Couler	1847	Sarah Phugh	1859
Mary Wolf	1850	Margurt Wolf	1859
Rebeca Murray	1852	Maryann Taylor	1859
Susanna Saylor	1850	Rachel Row	1860
Martha Barns	1848	Haner Cooper)	1854
Mary Lyle	1850	Deceased Nov 25th 1871)	
James taylor	1850	Rachel Phugh X	1854
John Wolf	1852	Jane Addoms	1854
Mary Saylor	1852	Martha Jane Linvill	1850
Mamurva Phugh	1852	Pernecy Wolf	1849

Sharlot Duffield of Coller X	1840	Henry Pris, Ex.	1866
Richard N Stanly X	1866	N W taylor Deceast Sept	1866
Edmon Phillips of Coullor X	1866	Margret taylor	1866
Landon Duffield X	1866	~~Martha Sayl~~	1866
Olema Jane Taylor	1866	Martha Orina X	1866
Columbus Shipley watch ker X	1866	Martha Jane Loudy	1866
Jessa Humprhis recantation	1866	~~Elizabeth Grant----------1866~~	
Eliza umphris Recantation	1866	Gorge W Carr X	1866

(P. 231) 2nd Apointed James Taylor and James Peoples and William Phugh with the former trustees to wit A Carr and William Whellor trustees for Sinking Creek Church 3rd agreed for A Carr to have new dors and window shettors put to this Church as soon as convent the adgornd in order
A Carr C Clark

Sattorday 16th of September 1865

The Baptist Church at Sinking Creek meet aftor worship meet for buisness first Cold for goiners none Came foourward 2 Cld on Br J H Hyder to Serve this Church as pastor the next year and Br Hyder agreed to do so if the Church on thar part wood agree to pay him A Reasonable pric for his Scerveses and Jornd in order A Carr Ch Clark

November 1865
Br Richard Jefferson Died

Recevd by Lettor
A and A E Vines

June 20 1865
Richard Y Carr Departed this life

William Daniels By Exp.

(P. 232) Sattorday May 19th 1866

the Baptist Church at Sinking Creek meet aftor worship Cold for any unsettled buisness first Cold for goiners and Recived Edmon Phillips a man of Coullor under the watch ker of this Church
2 Recivd Richard N Stanley by Exsperns
3rd Dissmiss Sistor Elizabeth Devenport by Lettor 4th this Church agrees to adopt the resalutions of the Holston Conventin Held at Cherokee December 1865 5 Brother James P taylor presented a Lettor to this Church Requting to do away with all Church Covinents that is not according to scriptor------

John S Humphry ~~1111~~ 1111
Wm Whellor 1

James S Taylor ~~10~~
Wm Whellor 10
J Humphrys- 10

(P. 233) June the 14th 1866

the Baptist Church at Sinking Creek meet aftor worship meet for buisness first Cold for goiners Landon Duffield Joind by Ex and baptism
2 Recivd Sistors Celma Jane Taylor by Lettor 3rd Dissmis Br Jobe of Coller and wife by Lettor 4th Apointed deligats to the association to wit A Carr Gorge Humphris James P Taylor and James Poples as our deligats 5 this Church sends up a request for the next association to bee held with the Sinking Creek Church as she clames it A Carr Ch Clark

Sattorday 14th day of July 1866

the Baptist Church at Sinking Creek meet aftor worship meet for buisness 1st Cold for goiners none Came fowward

2nd the Lettor to the association was red and recevd nothing moor then adgornd A Carr Ch Clark

August 18th 1866

the Baptist Church at Sinking Creek meet aftor worship meet for buisness nothing worth recording Br Noffsinger and J H Hyder agreed to hold a protraced meeting and the following persons goind to wit jessa Humphris and wife Eliza Humphris by recantation Henry Pris Ex and baptism Gorge W Carr Ex N W Taylor Ex Marguit taylor Ex Martha Orines Ex Martha Jane Taylor Ex ~~Elizabeth Grant Ex~~ Columbus Shipley under the watch ker of the Church adgornd in order A Carr Ch Clark

September 15th 1866

the Baptist Church at Sinking Creek meet and no preacher adgornd
A Carr C Clark

(P. 234) Sattorday October 20 1866

the Baptist Church at Sinking Creek meet aftor worship meet for buisness Recivd Br John Bayles into fellowship with this Church
2nd Recive Sistor Rispa M Smith formerly Rispa Edweards by Recantation and dismiss her by Lettor then adgorn in order A Carr C Clark

November 17th 1866

the Baptist Church at Sinking Creek meet aftor worship sat for buisness nothing worth recording adgornd in order A Carr C Clark

December 1866

Church meeting day no meeting no precher

Sattorday January 19 1867 the Baptist Church at Sinking Creek meet aftor worship sat for buisness first A pointed J P Taylor clerk protem 2nd Recivd A and A E Vines by Lettor 3rd Exscluded Nancy Jefferson for goining the Camilit Church 4 Resolved that the Church invite all Delinquent members to fill up ther seets or tha will bee delt with by order of the Church
J H Hyder modtor
P J talor Clerk protem

february 16th 1867 the Baptist Church at Sinking Creek meet aftor worship meet for buisness firs Cold Br J H Hyder to attend us a nother year which he agreed to do on condishions if the Church would pay him 25 or 30 dollars then adgornd in order A Carr Church Clark

(P. 235) Sattorday 20th 1867 April

The Baptist Church at Sinking Creek meet A Cording to A pointment aftor worship meet for buisness first dismiss Br Jessa Duncan and J W Carr and Sara Carr Martha Carr then adgorn in order A Carr Ch CL

Sattorday May 18th 1867

the Baptist Church at Sinking Creek meet acording to apointment aftor worship

meet for buisness first Exscluded tennesee Addams for not filling up his seat at his Church meeting days 2nd appointed Sister Orrins and Sister Woolf to visit her and report nex meeting day in Cors 3rd Exscluded Richard Sttanley for not attending his Church meeting 4 Exscluded Archable Colwell for not filling up his seet at Church meeting days
adgornd in order A Carr Ch Cl

June 15th 1867

the bapist Church meet at Sinking Creek after worship Cold for refferences of last meeting and was discharged 2nd granted Lettors to Br Landon Duffield Edmon Phillips of Coullor Sharlot Duffiel 3rd apointed dellegats to the association to wit A Carr James P Taylor and James Peoples as our delagats then adgornd A Carr Ch CL

July 20 the baptis Church at Sinking Creek meet A Cording to Apointment after worship prosseded to buisness firs Cold for Joiners George Hail Joind by Recantation 2 Dismiss Br Hail by Lettor 3rd the lettor to the association was red and approvd and Jornd in order A Carr Church Clark

August 17th 1867

the Baptist Church at Sinking Creek meet aftor worship Cold for buisness nothing worth recording and Journd A Carr Ch CLark

September 21th 1867

the baptis Church at Sinking Creek meet aftor worship Cold for buisness nothing worth recording A Carr C Clark

(P. 236) Sattorday 19th October 1867

the Baptist Church at Sinking Creek meet aftor worship Cold for buisness nothing worth recording A Earr Ch CLar

November 16th 1867

the Baptist Church at Sinking Creek aftor worship meet for buisness 1st Chose William Hatcher moerator prtem Br Hyder not present 2nd Cold for buisness Sistor Juley Harchbarger did November 1867
Nothing moor adgornd A Carr C CLark

December 14th 1867

the Baptist Church at Sinking Creek meet aftor worship meet for buisness 1st ~~Chois Br William Hatcher mederater pretem~~ nothing mor
Sistor Juley Harchbarger Departed this Life in this mounth nothing more than adgornd A Carr C CLark

Sattorday January the 18th 1868

the Baptist Church at Sinking Creek meet aftor worship Cold for buisness Dismiss Archable Colwell by Lettor
adgornd in order A Carr Ch CLark

Sattorday february 15th 1868

the baptist Church at Sinking Creek meet aftor worship meet for buisness 1st Chose Br James taylor moderator py tem 2nd Dismissed Sister Elizabeth Hise by Lettor 3rd Excluded sister Nancy Arrins from the fellowship of the Chrc for bad conduct
adgornd in order A Carr C CLark

(P. 237) Sattorday March 14th 1868

the baptist Church at Sinking Creek meet aftor worship met for buisness first Cold Joiners non Came fowward and 2 ~~Dismissed Sister GG by Lettor~~
nothing more adgornd in order A Carr Ch CLark

April 18th 1868

the Baptist Church at Sinking Creek meet aftor worship meet for buisness nothing worth recording adgornd in order A Carr Ch CLark

May 16th 1868

The Baptist Church at Sinking Creek meet aftor worship prosed to buisness first granted Brother John Bayles a lettor of Dishmision
2nd Excluded Nancy Orins for living disorderly 3 Excluded Amanday Oliver for not filling her seet on Church meeting days and Joinging a nother Church 4 William danils Came fourward and Joind by Exsperns and Baptism
5 Sary Kinnick and Evaline taylor by Exsperens and baptism
then adgornd in order A Carr Ch CLark

June 19 the baptist Church at Sinking Creek meet aftor worship meet for buisness first Cold for goiners 2nd Balitd for deligats to the association A Carr and ~~James taylor~~ John Humfors then adgornd in order
A Carr Ch CLark

Sattorday July 18th 1868

Met aftor worship met for buisness first Cold for goiners none Came fourward 2nd the Church resolvd to petishen the Holston Association to dishmishen her to Join in new association organation
then adgornd in order A Carr Church CL

(P. 238) August 15th 1868

No meeting it being the time of the association thare was no meeting

September 19th 1868

the Baptist Church at Sinking Creek no meeting it was the time of the convention for the new association

Octo 17th 1868

the Baptist Church meet aftor worship meet for buisness first Cold for goiners none Came fowward then adgornd A Carr Ch CL

Nov 14th 1868

the baptist Church at Sinking Crek meet aftor worship meet for buisness nothing worth recording adgornd in order A Carr Ch CLark

December Sattorday 19th 1868

the baptis Church at Sinking Ceek meet aftor worship meet for buisness 1 Cold for goiners by lettor or Expers none Came fourward 2nd unanimously agreed that members that miss over two meetings in sucksesion wood render ther reasons for not filling up the seet at Church meetings and that tha wood Cole the rol and mark the absentees 3rd Br A Carr maid a move that he be releast from acting as Clark for this Church Whitch was granted and Br John S Humphris Apointed to akt in his plais
adgornd in order A Carr Ch Clar

(P. 239) State of Tenn Carter County January 16th 1869 John S Humphreys January the 16th 1869 We the Baptist Church at Sinking Creek meet according to appointment & after worship Called for Joiners by letter or expirence none Came forWeird- than Called over the role of the members & marked those absent
Jo. S. Humphreys, Ch Clk
J. H. Hyder., Mod.,

Saturday Feb the 20 1869 We, the Baptist Church of Christ at Sinking Creek meet according to appointment..and after worship..Set for buisness-First Called for Joiners by letter or expirence none came forward Called the role-Seckon Excluded Sister Jane Adams for delinquency- and also dismiss Br Henry Prise & wife & also Sister Susan Dunkin by letter..
(J. S. Humphreys..Ch..Clk..)
(J. H. Hyder Mod..)

Saturday March The 20th 1869

There was no meeting John, S. Humphreys Ch Clk

(P. 240) April 17th 1869 We the Baptist Church of Christ at Sinking Creek meet according to appoint and after worship we proceded to buisness as follows Viz. first Called for Joiners no Came forward Secon Called the role of the members marked those abscent.. J. S. Humphreys Ch..Clk..
J. H. Hyder..Mod--

Carter County Tenn May 15th 1869
We, the Baptist Church of Christ at Sinking Creek meet according to appointment..And after worship by J..H..Hyder a proceeded to buisness as follows..to (viz) 1 Called for Joiners none Came forward S2 Called the role of the Church members & marked the abscentees, "3 artical" and then by order of the Church that the mimmit of the last meeting be read & Corrected at the meeting following-, It being prior to any other buisness. J. S. Humphreys, Ch..Clk..
J. H. Hyder Mod..

Carter County Tenn June 19th 1869

We the Baptist Church of Christ at Sinking Creek meet according to appointment and after (P. 241) worship by J. H. Hyder The Church Sat for buisness and proceed as follows first read and Corrected the mimits of the last meeting Second Called for Joiners and none Came forward Third Called the role of the Church members and marked the abscentees, Fourth then by a re-

quest of Bro Alferd Carr That he Should have a letter of dismission which was granted unto him done by order of the Church Now in Session
J. H. Hyder Mod
John S. Humphreys C H Clk

Carter County Tennessee July the 17th 1869

We the Baptist Church of Christ at Sinking Creek Meet according to appointment..and after worship by Ed..A.J.F.Jyder- the Church Sat for buisness.. and proceeded to buisness as follows first read & Corrected the minute of the last meeting..Second Called for Joiners eaither by letter or exspirence none Came forward..Third Called the role of the Church members and marked the abscenttees Fourth then by motion and Second of the Church elected our repescentatives to the Watauga association which resulted in the election B. John S. Humphreys (P. 242) Bro James P..Taylor & Bro Wm Pugh..Fifth then by motion and Second of the Church that it Sendes up one dollar for the printing of the miniutes..& Sixth then by motion & second of the Church that a letter be written and read at our next meeting for to be Scent to the Association by our repscentatives done by order of the Church now in Session..-
A.J.F.Hyder (Mod) protem.. & John Humphreys Ch Clk

Carter County Tenn August the 14 1869
We the Baptist Church of Christ at Sinking Creek di not meet according to our last appointment & therefore no buisness was transacted..
Sister Rachel Row
Departed this life the 10th day of August 1869
John S. Humphreys Ch Clk.

Carter County Tenn September the 12 1869
We the Baptist Church of Christ at Sinking Creek did not meet according to our last appointment and therefore there was no buisness to transact..
Johns. Humphreys: Ch: Clk:

October Saturday the 16th 1869 Wee the Baptis Church at Sinking Crick met in regular cession after worship organised for Buisness First appointed Brother W Pugh moderator protem Second Elected Brother J. P. Taylor regular Clerk 3rd granted Cister Sarah Kinch a letter of Dismission October the 16 1869
(P. 243) Done By Order of the Church W. Pugh moderator Protem
J. P. Taylor Ch Clerk
November term the Church failed to Set

March the 19th 1870 Wee the Baptist Church at Sinking Crick met according to previous appointment after worship sat for buisness nothing Came up werth recording Adjourned in order
J. H. Hyder M. D.
J. P. Taylor Ch Clk.

April the 16th 1870 The Baptist Church of Christ at Sinking Crick Met and after worship Set for Buisness First Recinded an act adopting a rule to Call the role of the Church members and mark the absentees
Nothing more presenting itself adgournd in order
J. H. Hyder md
J. P. Taylor Clk

May the 14th 1870 The Baptist Church of Christ at Sinking Creek met and

after worship organize for Buisness Nothing worthy of Consideration Came Forward AdJournd in order
J. H. Hyder Md
J. P. Taylor Clk

August the 20th 1870 Wee the Baptist Church of Christ at Sinking Crick met in regular Cession organized for Buisness First Elected Deligates to the Association as follows (William Pugh J. P. Taylor A. S. Vines) Second Elected A. J. F. Hyder Pastor of the Church By order of the Church
William Pugh MD protem
J. P. Taylor

Nov the 12th 1870 Wee the Baptist Church of Christ at Sinking Crick after worship Sat for Buisness first Elder A. J. F. Hyder agrees to take the Charge of the Church as pastor one year
Nothing more to record only the Death of Sister Ann Vine Deceased this life September the 29, 1870
A. J. F. Hyder Md J. P. Taylor Clk

(P. 244) December the 10th 1870 Wee the Baptist Church of Christ at Sinking Crick met and after worship organized for Buisness Nothing Presenting itself Adjournd in order
A. J. F. Hyder M D J. P. Taylor Clk

January the 7th 1871 The Baptist Church of Christ at Sinking Crick assembled after worship Called to Buisness Nothing presented for record Adjournd in order
A. J. F. Hyder M D J. P. Taylor Clk

February the 11th 1871 the Baptist Church of Christ at Sinking Creek met according to adjournment after worship Called to order nothing worth Bringing to record Adjournd in order
A. J. F. Hyder M D J. P. Taylor

March the 17th day the Baptist Church met according to Adjournment after worship Called to order Nothin Presented to Bring to record adjournd in order
J. P. Taylor Ch. Clk.

Aprile 1871 the Church met and after worship adjournd

May the 20th the Church at Sinking Crick met on the above date nothing worth recording only Sister Catherine Barns Deseased on the 25 April 1871 Adjournd in order

July the 8th 1871 Wee the baptist Church of Christ at Sinking Creek met according to adjournment and after worship Called to order first appointed delegates to the association to wit
Abner S Vines & James Peoples Second granted Brother James Peoples liberty to Exercise his gift in public don by order of the Church
A. J. F. Hyder J. P. Taylor Clk

(P. 245) August the 12th 1871 We the Baptist Church of Christ at Sinking Crick met accoding to appoint and after worship Called to order first opened the door for the reception of members none came forward Second Red and ratifyed the letter to the asso thence adjournd in order done by order of the Church A. J. F. Hyder Md J. P. Taylor Clk

Nov 10th 1871 The Baptist Church of Christ at Sinking Crick after worship organized for Buisness nothing to Reduke to record adjourned in order
A. J. F. Hyder mo J. P. Taylor Clk

December the 23d 1871 The Baptist Church of Christ at Sinking Creek after worship Called to order opened the door for the reception of members none came forward then Reduced the death od Sister Hannah Cooper to Record as follows
Sister Hannah Cooper deceased this life on the 25 day of November 1871
Done by order of the Church
A. J. F. Hyder M D J. P. Taylor Clk

February the 10th 1872
The Baptist Church of Christ at Sinking Crick met according to apointment and after worship organized for buisness first opened the door of the Church for members and two Came forward with letters from Zion Church and was recieved To wit Martin N Taylor and Mary E Taylor
Nothing more came forward Adjourned in order Done by order of the Church
J. P. Taylor Clk.

March the 9th 1872 The baptist Church at Sinking Crick after worship organized for buisness first Dismised By letters 2 towit John S Humphreys & Nancy Jane Taylor then adJournd in order
A. J. Hyder, Md, J P Taylor Clk

Aprile No Church Meeting)

May the 2 ond Saturday 1872 the Baptist Church of Christ at Sinking Crick met according to appointment after Worship Called to order first Choose Br Hall M D protem nothing to record adJournd in order
Wm Hall M D J. P. Taylor Clk

(P. 246) July 13th 1872 The Baptist Church of Christ at Sinking Creek met in regular Cession & after worship organized for bisness first Chose brother James Dunkeon MD. protem Second Elected Brothers as follows to the association nothing more to record adJournd in order James Dunkeon Md
James P. Taylor Clk

} Jessy Humphreys
} J. P. Taylor
} A. S. Vines & M N Taylor

August the 10Th 1872 The Baptist Church of Christ at Sinking Creek Met in Cession and after worship Organized for Buisness first Reviewd and Approved the Report to the Association, Second unanimously Elected Brother J. H. Dunkin pastor of the Church
Done by order of the Church J. P. Taylor Clk.

October the 12.. 1872 The Baptist Church of Christ at Sinking Creek met in Regular Cession & after worship organized for Buisness first granted Cister Mathia Jane Jefferson a letter of Dismission in full faith with us, Second agreed that next meeting bee our Comunion that wee invite our Cister Churches to attend with us on that occasion Done by order of the Church &c
J. H. Dunkin M D
J. P. Taylor Clk

November the 8th 1872

The Church at Sinking Creek in regular Cession after worship Called to order nothing presenting itself worthy of Consideration adJournd in order

DC the 7th 1872 the Baptist Church of Christ at Sinking Creek met in regular Cession after worship Called to order nothing to attend to on this the above date but agreed to Baptism on tomorrow Baptised Marthea loudermilk on the 8th no more

(P. 247) Feb the 8th The Baptist Church at Sinking Creek met according to regular Cession aftor worship Called to order nothing appearing to record adJournd in order
J. H. Dunkeon, Md, J P Taylor Clk

March the 8th 1873 Wee, the Baptist Church of Christ at Sinking Creek met in regular Cession and after Worship Called to order first Opened the dore for the reception of members & 4 came forward and united with the Church as by letter from disoluted Churches To wit
Elbert H Range & Catherine Range also Jessy Dunkeon & Sarah C Dunkeon
Nothing more appearing adJournd in order J. H. Dunkeon Md
J. P. Taylor Clk

May the 10th 1873
The Baptist Church of Christ at Sinking Creek according to regular Cession met and after worship Called to order opend the dore of the Church for the reception of members none Came forward 2 agreed to hold Communion on tomorrow nothing more adJournd in order J. H. Dunkeon M D
J. P. Taylor Clk

June the 7th 1873 the Baptist Church at Sinking Creek Relected J H Dunkeon MD ADJournd in order J P Taylor Clk.

July the 12 the Church met in regular Cession no Buisness to attend to Dismist

August the 9th 1873 The Baptist Church at Sinking Creek met in regular Cession after worship proceeded to Buisness first opend the door for members Brother James H Dunkeon Regular ordained minister Came in By letter 2 Appointed our Representative to the Assosiation to wit, J. H. Dunkeon W Pugh and James Peoples adJournd in order

(P. 248) September the 20-1873 The Baptist Church of Christ at Sinking Creek in regular Cession after worship Called to order
first agreed to Change the time of our Meetings to Embrace the third Sabbeth in Each month, further agreed that our next Meeting be a Communion meeting Nothing more appearing AdJournd in order
J. H. Dunkeon M D
J. P. Taylor Clk

October the 18th 1873 the Baptist Church of Christ in regular Cession after worship organized for Buisness first opened the door one Came forward By letter to wit Cister Catherine Taylor Nothing more adjournd in order
J H Dunkeon M D J P Taylor Clk

December the 20th 1873 The Baptist Church of Christ at Sinking Creek in regular Cession after worship Called to order first Reduced to record the

Death of Brother William Danielson the first day of Dc. 1873 Second Excluded Marthia Loudermilk for Disorder and wee are to bee Chargeable no more for her Conduct No more at present to Record AdJournd in order
By order of the Church J. H. Dunkeon MD
J. P. Taylor Clk

Jan the 17th the Church of Christ at Sinking Creek after wor organized for Buisness nothing appearing AdJournd in order
Jessy Humphreys Clk protem

Feb the 14th 1874 the Church organized for Buisness nothing appearing AdJournd in order J. P. Taylor Clk

(P. 249) March the 17th The Baptist Church of Christe at Sinking Creek met in regular Cession after worship called to order nothing appearing ADJournd in order

Aprile the 18th 1874 the Baptist Church of Christ at Sinking Creek met in regular Cession after worship Called to order first Elected Br A J F Hyder moderator and Pastor of this Church Second made a matter of reffer© ence untill our next meeting to raise remunerations for his Services nothing more at preasant Adjournd in order

May the 16th 1874 The Baptist Church of Christ in Regular Conference after Worship Called to order nothing to record adjournd in order
A. J. F. Hyder J. P. Taylor Clk

June the 21st 1874 The Baptist Church at Sinking Creek in regular Cession after worship Called to order first recinded an act or resolution to exclude all members that fail to fill their Seats 3 times at their respective Church meetings in Concideration of this repeal Wee invite Sister Jane Adoms back to full fellowship with this Church Done by order of the Church on Sunday the 17th the Church to order granted Br John Woolf letter of dismission A. J. F. Hyder Md J. P. Taylor Clk

July the 16th 1874 The Baptist Church at Sinking Creek in regular Conference after worship Called to order First Elected Brs. Jessy Humphrey James Peoples & E H Range Representatives to the Assosiation no more AdJournd in order

August Cession First Read the letter to the assosiation & Adopted the Same No more to record Adjournd in order

September the Assosiation in Cession

Oct. No Buisness

Nov. No Buisness

DC the 19th 1874 in Regular Cession Dismist E. H. Range & Wife No more adjournd in order

January the 17th 1875 the Church in Cession Recd Eld E. D. Silver AdJournd in order

Feb No Meeting.

March No Church Meeting

(P. 250) Aprile the 17th 1875 The Baptist Church of Christ at Sinking Creek in regular Cession after worship Called to order first Chose Eld E D Silver Md protam Nothing Came up for consideration adjournd in order

May the 15 1875 the baptist Church at Sinking After Worship Called to order first Choosed Eld E. d. Silver Md. 2ond Agreed at the nexte meeting to Elect a deacon no more Adjourned in order J P. Taylor Clk

June the 19th 1875 the Baptist Church of Christ after Worship Called to order first Elected & Sat a part Br Jessy Dukeon for ordination to the office of Deacon Secondly apointed Jessy Humphrey trustee to the Sinking Creek Church property in the room an Stead of Br James Peoples Dest nothing more appearing then Adjournd in order Done By order of the Church
J. P. Taylor Cl.

July the 17th 1875
The Baptist Church of Christ at Sinking Creek in regular Cession after worship Called to order 1st Red publickly the title to the Church property 2nd Red the Covenant 3 & last apointed Representatives to the Association to wit Jessy Humphriys Jessy Dunkeon & J P Taylor Done by order of the Church A. J. F. Hyder Md J. P. Taylor Clk.

August No Church Buisness

September No Church Buisness

October the 15th 1875 Recevd 2 by letter Mary E Bunton & Neoma E Vines Dismist Abner S Vines by letter

(P. 251) November No Buisness Done

Dc the 18th the Church in Conferance first Excluded Cister Elizabeth Wyet for Herisy nothing more adjournd

January the 15th 1876 The Baptist Church of Christ in Regular Cession after Worship Called to order first opened the dore for the reception of members one Came forward by letter to wit Cister Eliza Kayes from Watauga Church Second Resolved unanimously that thare Shal not be any mor Schools taught in the Church house done by oder of the Church &c
J. P. Taylor Ch Clk A. J. F. Hyder Md.

Feb No Church Buisness.

March No Church Buisness

Aprile No buisness

May Sacrimental Season Dismist in order

June no Buisness

July Ditto

August in order apointed Rep to Association

September the 15th 1877 the Church met in ragular Conference after preseeded to Bisness as follows first Br A. J. F. Hyder ast the Church to discharge him from the pastoral ship which was Cordially granted Second agree to procure a new Ch Book as this is filled and to notify the Delinquent to Come up for new enrolement or they will be lefte out in adj in order

J P Taylor Clk

(P. 252)

Alfred Carr	1	James taylor	22	
Richard Carr	2	Joel Cooper	23	
Sary Carr	3	Nancy Jefferson	24	
Robert Cashaday	4	Jane Ore	25	
James Cashaday	5	John Woolf	26	
Rebeca Cashaday	6	Polla an Woolf	27	
Jessa Duncan	7	Polla Moor	28	
Iba Duncan	8	Susana Saylor	29	
Abraham Jobe	9	Catharine Barns	30	Departed
Will Jobe	10	Sara Bang	31	this life
William Hatcher	11	Elbert H Rang	32	
Henry Nave	12	Juley Rang	33	
Cary Nave	13	Debory Rang	34	
Martha Jane Lisenbay	14	J H Mulkey	35	
William Wheeler	15	Liza Mulkey	36	
Sary Right	16	Susan Cross	37	
William Fhue	17	J H Hyder	38	
Volentine Nave	18	Elizabeth Lowdy	39	
Jessa Umphris	19	Mary tipton	40	
Liza Umphris	20	John Khun	41	
Diana MCfawl	21 Dced	Mary Ann Taylor	42	

(At right hand side of Page under 42)
At a protracted Meeting held By David Kitzmiller Davidson & Faw Commenced the last Sunday in Nov 1878 & held two weeks following names Joind this Church

A D Taylor	All By
J L Taylor	Experience
Wm Keyes	& By Letter
H Lawson	Elizabeth Humphreys
J Estepp	
Jack Colwell	Ex Louisa E Range
Nanny A Taylor	Ex Liza F Range
Martha A Estepp	

(P. 253) The Names of the Church Members

Males		and Females	
1	A Carr Dissmiss by letter	1	Ann E Vines Decesed
2	Henry Prise Dismises	2	Elizabeth Weyet Excluded
3	James P Taylor 1	3	Cathern Barnes 1 Decesed
4	James Peoples Died	4	Clemma Jane Taylor
5	John Woolf 1	5	Eliza Humphrey life
6	John S Humphreys Dismist	6	Evaline Cooppper Deceast this
7	Jessee Humphreys	7	Hannah Coopper Deceast
8	Abner Vines Dismist Letter	8	Jane Adams Excluded X
9	William Wheller Dc Feb 22	9	Mary Woolf 1
10	~~William Pugh Dec~~	10	Mary Lyle Decesed
11	William Daniels Decest	11	Mary Saylor Excluded

Jr Dismist	
12 John S Woolf by letter	12 Mary Ann Taylor
13 Martin N Taylor	13 Marthy Barnes
14 E H Rang Dismist	14 Manervia Price 1
15 Jessey Dunkson Dismist Ordained minister	15 Nancy Jane Taylor Dismist Jefferson
16 James H Dunkson X	16 Marthy Jane ~~Linvill~~ Dismist
17 E D Silver Dismist	17 Margret Taylor
18 Alford D Taylor	18 Margret ~~Woolf~~ Lawson Excluded
19 James L Taylor	19 Marier Humphreys Decest
William Keyes	20 Perney Woolf Excluded
Henry Lawson	21 Rebecca Murry Dismist
20 John Estepp-Excluded	22 Rachel Row Deceased
Jackson Colwell	23 Susan Saylor Deces Mar 6 1879
21 Taylor Colwell X	~~Susan Saylor Jr~~

(P. 254) 1820 members that have deceased this year in Sinking Creek
Sarrah Boring Deceased November
Sisters Names Continued
Mary E Bunton
Neoma E Vines
on right side of page
24 Susanna Jr Saylor Decest Feb the 26, 1875
25 Susann Carline Prise Dismissed by letter
Sary Pugh Treadaway 1
27 Sary Kinnick Dismist
28 Susan Duncan Dismised by letter

March the 15th 1879	Mary E Taylor total 28
The Church met after worship Called	~~Marthia Loudymilk~~ Exclu
to order first recorded the Death	Catherine Range Dismissed
of Bro Wm Wheler feb 22 1879	Jarah C Dunkin Dismissed
Sister Susan Saylor deceased	Catherine Taylor 25
March 6th 1879	Nancy Ann Taylor 24
2 ordered that Broth James H	Elizabeth Humphreys

Dunkson appear and make Satisfaction (?) 3 Excluded Sister Margaret Lauson for Joining the Methodist Church
April the Br Dunkeone Case lade over Br Estep sited to trial Receivd 2 sister ranges daters.

AdJournd in order
~~Sinking Creek~~

January the 18 1879 the Church in Cession motion Second unanimously to hold prair meting Every Sabbath at Candle lighting Adjournd in order

G Faw Md
J P Taylor Clk

(P. 255) March 18th 1820 Reced the Churches fund

	S - d
Solomon Hendrix	1 - 6
Samuel Tipton	1 - 6
Elijah Buck	1 - $1\frac{1}{2}$
John Dunlap	1 - $1\frac{1}{2}$
Joshua Edward	1 - 6
Richard Carr	1 - 3
Joel Cooper	1 - 6

(Rest of page cut off)

(P. 256) Mary Lyle Decest January 1875
Susan Saylor Decest Feb the 26 1875
James Peoples Decest March 25 1875
(Rest of Page Cut Off) (End of Book)

The Following Pages are loose records concerning the book.
(P. 256) Pasted on inside of front cover.
We the Baptist Church of --------Elizabethton Tannessee dism------Elbert Range, and our Sister ------in good order; as deacon & deaconess when united w---------Church of the Same Faith a ------ by oder of the Church this 26 --------1873
J. H. H-----
Thos. C.

(Pasted on Board of Book)
Jo Taylor Ch Clk Trustee Deacon of Sinking Creek
1876
1742
134
Baptist Church of Christ at
Cister Mary W Taylor
in full faith and good
and Consider her dismissed
when Joind to a Cister Church
faith and order
der of the Church fel
M N Taylor Clk Protem

The Baptist Church of Christ at
union Certifies that
ine Tailor is a member in full
th is at this time and is dismissed
watch care when Joind to another
the same faith and order
Done in Conferance Oct 11 1873
by order of the Church
Peoples Clk A Routh Moderator

Washington County Johnson City
this Church now in Seshion
Jessa Dunken and wife
fellowship with us untill
some other Church of the

Sinking Creek Baptist Church (Copy of Deed to Sinking Creek Church property Records of Carter County Tennessee) Register's Office- Deed Book C, page 393 (Spoken of on Page 58 also filed at same)
(P. 258) This Indenture made this 18th day of July one thousand Eight Hundred and Eighteen between Joel Cooper, Senr. of Carter County and State of Tennessee on the one part and David Pew and Joseph Renfro trustees of the Baptist Church at Sinking Creek of the other part.

WITNESSETH that the said Joel Cooper for and in consideration of Five Hundred Dollars to him in hand paid, the receipt whereof the said Joel Cooper doth hereby acknowledge and hath hereby bargained and sold unto the said trustees forever one acre of land where the meeting house now stands and bounded as follows, Viz, Beginning on a Sourwood dogwood and linn on the

South bank of Sinking Creek, thence South Forty Five° E. Five poles and fourteen Links to a blackgum, thence North 48 d. E. Twenty four poles to a Stake thence North 31 d. West. 11 poles ten links to a beach on the bank of the Creek, thence up the Creek to the beginning One Acre, be the same more or less.

For the sole use of the Baptist Church and their successors and the said Trustees and their successors to have and to hold said acre of land with all and singular the appertanances hereunto belonging forever I the said Joel Cooper, for himself and his heirs will forever warrant and defend the title & right of said acre of land from him and his heirs and all and every person or persons, whatsoever will warrant and forever defend by these presents in witness whereof the said Joel Cooper hath hereunto set his hand and seal the day and date above written.

Signed Sealed and acknowledged
in presence of
Attest:
Daniel Stover
Samuel Tipton, Junior
George Lacy, Junior
E R Berry
Frank Hinkle
John Hinkle

Joel Cooper (Seal)
his X mark

Filed in Book No. 3, Page 58.

(P. 259) State of Tennessee) May Session One Thousand and Eight Hundred
Carter County) and nineteen the within deed was exhibited and proved in open Court by Samuel Tipton and George Lacy and admitted to record Let it be Registered Given under my hand and the Seal of my office this 12th day of May in the year of our Lord 1819.

Test. Geo. Williams, Clerk

State of Tennessee) The within Deed with the Certificate was duly registered
Carter County) in the Register,s office of Said County this 3rd day of July 1821

A. B. Brewen
Depty

Godfrey Carriger
Register

State of Tennessee) I, D. K. Lovelace, Register for said County do hereby
Carter County) Certify that the foregoing is a full true and Complete Copy of the Deed from Joel Cooper to David Pew and Joseph Renfro, Trustees of the Baptist Church of Sinking Creek as the same appears of record in my office in Deed Book C Page 393

D. K. Lovelace
Register

This March 24th day, 1903
(Recopyed by H. M. Saylor this the 15th day of May 1905)
Copy of Deed to Sinking Creek Church Property.
(Filed in Church Book No. 3 page 58

(P. 260) Temperance Resolutions filed in Book 3 page 218
(Loose sheet found in Sinking Creek Baptist Church Minute Book)

Whereas, Intemperance is manifestly increasing in our Community and County, the efforts of the various temperance societies having failed to reform Stay the evil and our state Legislature having withdrawn restraints heretofore imposed on the liquor buisness; we deem it of increased importance that the Church of Christ raise her voice against it, and use her influence

to stay its progress, and, inasmuch as Consistency in so doing, requires her to withdraw her own patronage from it. Therefore, Resolved,
1. That we, as such, will not use intoxicating liquor as a beverage, being Satisfied that such practice induces habits of intemperance or drunkenness.
2. Resolved that, we will neither buy, sell, manufacture, nor furnish intoxicating liquor to be used by others as a beverage.
3. Resolved that, we will not furnish fruit or grain for the manufacture of the article to be so used
4. Resolved that, as we consider a violation of any of the above resolutions a violation of the Scripture law of temperance, which law we consider of binding authority upon every one, and of vital importance to the spiritual prosperity of Christians and of the Christian Church therefore we will not hold in our fellowship any one who will not conform thereunto.
(P. 2) Resolved further, that there is also another evil in our times, calculated to lead astray Church members, especially the young & inexperienced, which we Consider it our duty to notice, Viz: those gatherings Called Balls; and also all dancing & frolicking parties and the like, all of which we consider of pernicious influence and inconsistent with Christian profession, therefore we will not patronize nor encourage them nor hold in fellowship those who do.

3

Furthermore resolved, that we will drop from our fellowship those of our members whom we find to be habitually and unnecessarily delinquent in their attendance upon their Church meetings and in the discharge of other duties binding upon them by our Church Covenant.

Resolved that the above resolutions be appended to our Church Covenant and made binding as a part of the same.

(P. 261) (Loose paper in back of book)
Sinking Creek Baptist Church Chose Alfred Carr Cleark on Aprile 15, 1848 and he Served the Church as Cleark till Dec 19th 1868 making a Periodd of 20 years & 8 months

H. M. Saylor
Cleark of Church this Feb. 2nd 1905.

www.ingramcontent.com/pod-product-compliance
Lightning Source LLC
Chambersburg PA
CBHW080420270326
41929CB00018B/3096
* 9 7 8 0 7 8 8 4 8 9 9 1 4 *